A Mountain Village
Under the Spell of South Italy

Michele Antonio DiMarco, MA

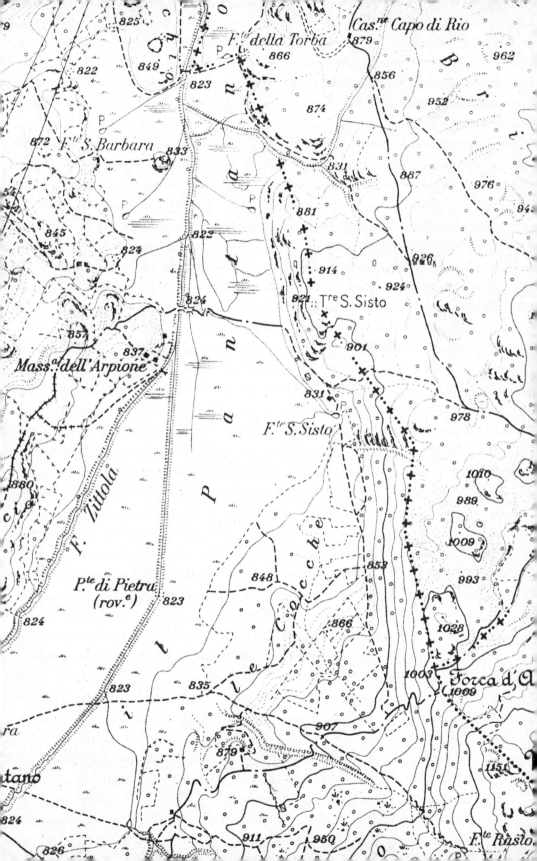

Dedication

To my grandparents,
Michele DiMarco & Lucia Caserta,
and those with roots in
a small village like Montenero,
regardless of geographic location.

contents

foreword

"What did my ancestors do in the village for work? What was their daily life like from morning 'til night over the seasons? What would they think of Montenero today?"

These are the questions Michele DiMarco had been asking himself for a long time, wondering about his origins and about the distant land where his grandparents were born. The author's grandfather, Michele DiMarco Sr., left Naples at the age of twenty-seven and arrived at Ellis Island on 25 August 1920 to join his many fellow citizens who were already living in Erie, Pennsylvania. Michele was originally from Montenero Val Cocchiara [Mundunur], a village in southern Italy that had just over 1,600 inhabitants when he left. Today Montenero has a population of just over five hundred.

Montenero's history is similar to that of many other small towns in Molise, a region located in the inner Apennine area. The inhabitants of this mountainous terrain had long been tied to an agropastoral economy. Therefore Michele DiMarco's story is common to many other Molisans and Italians who, between the last decades of the nineteenth century and the first decades of the twentieth century, participated in the great migratory wave that led from the Mediterranean ports to America.

It can also be said that the author's inquisitiveness regarding his ancestry is common to many other descendants of emigrants. However, it requires a strong personal drive to reconstruct a family's genealogy and to learn about the land of ancestral origins.

Inspired by the lives of his family members, our author inevitably researched the history of that small, distant village in Molise where his grandparents were born. At an early age, Michele collected photos, postcards, letters, and village stories from his grandparents and other Montenerese. This led to his conducting in-depth research utilizing articles, books, and numerous archival documents to learn about the *Mountain Village Under the Spell of South Italy*. As a result, this book starts with an autobiographical account in which the author shares a touching emotional journey about his early contacts with Montenerese in Erie and Italy. He also shares first-person recollections of several trips to the village.

Michele's academic voyage finds parallel in physical travels as well. He went to Italy for the first time in 1979, returning several times since. During recent years, he noted many changes in Montenero's daily life and, above all, observed the unfortunate changes in the attitudes of the local people who have now become more wary of the past. Despite the veiled disappointment that seems to emerge from Michele's writings, it did not extinguish his interest in delivering a treatise valuable for future generations who too often forget or show total disregard for their origins.

The present volume, therefore, responds very well to this last objective. Drawing on a rich bibliography, even a specialized one, and from numerous sources of civil and ecclesiastical archives, local and otherwise, Michele reconstructs the history of Montenero from its origins to the present day. Michele's work fills a void in local historiography, given the absence so far of a historical monograph entirely dedicated to this community of Molise.

The volume unfolds in sixteen chapters. In the first three, the author illustrates the history of his family and the link with Montenero and then reviews all the historical periods from antiquity to the present. He always pays attention to provide the historical context of reference, taking care to explain to a readership—which may not be very familiar with Italian history—the dynamics and historical processes that affected the history of southern Italy in past centuries.

At the end of the volume there is a rich and interesting appendix containing the names of the mayors of Montenero from 1809 to 2015 and of the archpriests of Montenero from 1600 to 2018. These lists, taken from the documents of the municipal and parish archives of Montenero, will allow people with roots in the village who read this book to recognize their ancestors and begin a personal journey in their own family history.

Whoever reads this book will have no difficulty in understanding every aspect of the history of this territory. While *Mundunur: A Mountain Village Under the Spell of South Italy* presents the fascinating history of a small village, in reality, the book is an interesting starting point for learning about the centuries of Molise history and its interrelationship with south Italy. Its richness in detail distinguishes this substantial work of Michele DiMarco.

Dr. Valeria Cocozza

Dr. Valeria Cocozza
Doctorate in History
University of Molise

introduction

In 2014, just after I returned from a summer trip to Italy, I visited a relative, Vincent Caserta, who told me: "You should write a book about Montenero." Besides founding my own publishing company in 1999, he knew I authored over one hundred articles, have an academic background, and love the village. That gave me some qualifications; however, I certainly was no authority on Montenero. But I always wanted to know even the tiniest details about the mountain village where my grandparents were born. Realistically, writing about a relatively unknown village by itself seemed of little value. Not many would be interested. But a detailed study of Montenero and its relationship to south Italy would be a worthwhile venture. Only in this way can a full picture of the village be presented. Plus, I felt that how people lived over the centuries in Montenero was not unlike many other villages in the world.

"OK, Vince," I said. "I'll do it!"

Aware of my own shortcomings—I wasn't born in Montenero and have a limited grasp of Italian—I dove into research anyway. There is little information in English about Montenero or Abruzzo and Molise, the two regions the village borders. Over the past decades I collected what books and articles I could find that had any relation to the village. In recent years I asked others if they could help by making suggestions and sending any information if possible. What I received was negligible. I was on my own.

In both English and Italian, I started to search for all articles, books, and videos with any mention of Montenero. The internet facilitated research, allowing me to borrow rare books through interlibrary loan, plus download excellent articles and books from websites designed for academic researchers. Montenero's vice mayor, Carmen Marotta, was extremely helpful. Without her, there would have been serious gaps in covering Montenero's history. From France with Montenero heritage, Sandra (Di Fiore) Caserta gave me a vision of Montenero, impossible to get without her guidance through the village streets and buildings, and sharing tales as passed down over generations from the elders.

Chapter 1 tells the story of a young lad growing up in Erie, Pennsylvania—a second-generation Italian-American surrounded by immigrants from Montenero and south Italy. That pipsqueak was me. I often listened to the elders sitting around the dinner table, talking about Mundunur, which is how Montenero is pronounced in the village dialect. I used this spelling for the book's title because its resonance reaches to the depths of the hearts of all native speakers. By the time I was college age and filled with tales of Montenero and pasta fazool, I decided to make my first trip to Italy. Chapter 2 recounts a few of those visits.

In the following chapters, you will experience a discovery of Montenero, an uncovering of its many layers from its origins to the present. The full story begins with a look at the movement of tectonic plates about thirty million years ago and the gradual formation of Italy. This study of land formation shows us the foundation, the terra firma, upon which Montenero would later be founded. We then move to the flora and fauna that bring life to the land. These determined how people could live in the mountainous regions of Molise, providing the materials required to build homes and tools, what animals were near to hunt, and which plants could be found or grown to eat.

After the overview of the land, plants, and animals, we can envision a virgin environment ready to be occupied. The very first inhabitants on the Italian peninsula showed up over seven hundred thousand years ago at a site only about twenty miles from present-day Montenero. Since Paleolithic times, many other groups influenced the land and people in Abruzzo-Molise, including the Samnites, Romans, Lombards, and Arabs. Then, in the late tenth century, a few families chose to settle near the marsh (*pantano*) below where Montenero sits today. Perhaps today's Montenerese have genetic inheritance from these first homesteaders?

Much changed in Molise when the Normans arrived from France and molded south Italy into a kingdom, instilling feudalism that played such a great part in coloring peasant life in all the small villages. The impact can still be seen today in the land, buildings, and personalities in south Italy. Other foreign conquerors followed, including the French and Spanish. Through these periods, Montenero grew slowly as a medieval agricultural village, owned by a number of nobles. Hence, we find familiar landmarks in the village as the Palazzo De Arcangelis del Forno and the Baronial Palace. Eventually came the "Unification" of 1871, which was a conquering of the south by north Italy. So brutal was this forced union that millions of Italians immigrated.

Montenero men were sent to fight in World War I, removing husbands and sons from their field work and families. World War II added to the misery, especially because German troops occupied Montenero. Some of the atrocities committed during this time will never be told. Italy is still rebuilding, hampered by the recent decades of arriving migrants during a period of intense political and economic hardship. Living with crises has become the norm. Of course, the centuries of foreign domination and the recent predicaments bear heavily on all Italians.

In large part, this book starts out as a quest to discover how Montenero influenced the personalities of my grandparents, close relatives, and friends. What was the special connection between them and the ancestral village? Culture influences how populations think and behave in society. The people of south Italy are different from the Northerners, and those born in Montenero are, we can safely say, special. They are unique. Since this is Italy we're discussing, let's use pizza for an analogy. An acquaintance in the produce business once told me that you cannot eat a Neapolitan pizza except in Naples. Why? Because the olive oil, tomatoes, cheese, and other ingredients are unique to the area. Not one of the ingredients is exactly the same when grown in any other region, and the resulting flavor cannot be the same. Montenerese are homegrown! Let us say that they have their own distinct character.

If we look at the social elements that forged the south Italian spirit, this book highlights some of the major factors that appear during specific periods. In addition to the numerous invasions and resulting foreign domination came recurring bouts with epidemics, earthquakes, bandits, and rebels. Following Turkish and Arab raids, thousands of captured southern Italians were sold into slavery and shipped to places such as North Africa. This social insecurity fostered the growth of the Mafia, which today may be the best-run business in Italy.

When we focus our attention on Montenero, archeological artifacts and early written records let us see the birth of the village and its evolution through today. Chapters 4 through 14 give a historical overview of south Italy and Montenero's place in the timeline. The village inherited a number of important elements from early times. Of course the village is famous for the special breed of Pentro horses that have been grazing in the marsh since the Samnite times, over 2,500 years ago. The origins of wide trails for the seasonal movement of sheep can be credited to the Samnites too, trails often used today for hiking.

In the handwritten Latin script in the *Chronicon Volturnensis* dating 1100, a monk records the first settlement called *Mons Nigro*. Under the direction of the Spanish, a 1447 census reveals for the first time the surnames of those living in Montenero. An assessment made in 1685 registers details regarding all property, the value of lands, homes, churches, and chapels. Plus, this document gives many details about the people and living conditions, and it even clearly marks the extent of Montenero's borders with its neighbors. The 701-page tax registry from 1753 can be seen as an update, providing even more details about individual families.

The body of Saint Clemente arrived in 1776 to bring spiritual protection to the residents. His relics brought some strength and encouragement for facing the future. By the time Joachim Murat arrived from France to become the king of Naples, there was a threat of Austrian troops invading from the north. Murat and his Neapolitan army went north to face the challenge. In 1815 his army was scurrying south, away from the Austrian troops. Murat's soldiers were overwhelmed in the Battle of Castel di Sangro, which actually took place in the fields near the Montenero train station. The tussle over land continues.

During the late nineteenth century, North Italy became interested in uniting all regions on the peninsula and Sicily into one country. The population of Montenero was split over political objectives. In 1860 a dozen village men were arrested for political subversion, and murder and thievery occurred among the townspeople. Deaths also resulted from an 1865 epidemic and a famine following in 1869. Closer to the end of that century, sixteen men from Montenero went south with flocks of sheep during the winter season for grazing. All died during an earthquake that happened near Foggia in 1879. From such happenings, we see that life in Montenero during the latter part of the nineteenth century was filled with strife.

World War I affected Montenero greatly, as we can guess. Details in chapter 11 mention the men who died or were wounded and provide some oral histories. One war-related incident is the Peat Revolt. Montenero's marsh contains tons of peat. Some entrepreneurs wanted to take the land from Montenero in order to extract the peat as a product useful for military and business purposes. In protest, villagers attacked members of the municipal council on 22 July 1917. Some injuries occurred, and people were jailed. In the following year an actual rebellion led to deaths, and 123 people were arrested, including my great-grandparents. Peat was also used as a fuel for the famous brewery Birre d'Abruzzo, founded in 1921 and built near the Montenero train station. Despite its great success, the brewery mysteriously dissolved in 1936.

The difficulties present in south Italy at this time pressured more to immigrate. Because Italy was also a major battleground during World War II, all residents suffered greatly. Chapter 13 includes much on the German occupation of Montenero, especially information gleaned from Polish, Scottish, and Irish war diaries, among other military records. Montenero was not alone in these times of strife; it shared much with other cities and villages of the south.

Throughout Montenero's history there have been special ties with other towns large and small. There has long been a connection to San Vincenzo al Volturno and its abbey, and to Trivento as the seat of the diocese. In nearly every chapter in this book you can find special relationships with Alfedena, Rionero Sannitico, Castel di Sangro, Agnone,

Isernia, and Naples. Montenero's aristocratic families usually had a role in the interconnections.

Up to the most recent time, Montenero has been an agricultural community. All aspects of life in the village have revolved around farming and animal husbandry. But this has been changing with the start of an elementary school and the growth of a variety of businesses. Early in the twenty-first century, foreigners began moving into the village as well as others from different parts of Italy. Chapter 15, devoted to the future of Molise and Montenero, discusses these changing demographics. Since the region has been drastically losing population due to lack of jobs, how can residents create a new future? There is much discussion about this now, and it seems the biggest obstacle is the apathetic state of residents that brings all to an impasse. Even the mayor shows little interest in the future of Montenero. All the experts on developing rural areas in Molise stress the importance of promotional materials, such as flyers, books, and websites. Despite this fact, the mayor and others in Montenero never took a minute to discuss this book project. Probably they cannot see the great potential the village holds, or they simply do not want to make the effort to discuss its future. In my youth, I was too naïve to recognize that indifference is an art form in the village.

Others, usually not born in Montenero, love the area and have been inspired to invest time and money into improving the village. If others do this, Montenero can transform from the struggling agricultural village it is into a modern town with a high standard of living and rewarding work for all. No doubt there will be more foreigners contributing to the process. The European Union is helping with funding for rebuilding and the creation of new jobs. It will take some more years to see if Montenero will recreate itself—or suffer abandonment like many other small Italian villages.

Chapter 16 will take you on an imaginary three-day tour of Montenero. Get on the bus! Through the narrative, you will see the village with the aid of the material covered in previous chapters. History comes to life as you walk through the alleys and main piazza to the churches, chapels, bars, and restaurants. At the same time, you will get to know some of the people living here, visit businesses, go horseback riding in the valley, and feel the excitement of the special festivals as organized for Saint Clement, the patron of the village.

Like many others, I often thought of the beauty of Montenero and how wonderful it would be to live in such an idyllic location. After the recent visits and five years of research, it is easy to see how the beauty of the land is marred by an ingrained negative attitude. Bill Emmott, the author of Good Italy, Bad Italy, published by Yale University Press, concludes that Italy needs another major crisis to force Italians to cooperate and work toward improving the future.

I hope it will not take a catastrophe to force Italians to learn how to be more patiently cordial and cooperative in order to solve their problems. They are not alone. Cultures around the world have pushed individuals to become more self-centered and hostile toward others. Is everyone in competition? I think so. This stems from our Paleolithic ancestors' quest for survival. Shouldn't we acknowledge this tendency but make a greater effort to educate ourselves to be more thoughtful of others in order to live with greater harmony and for mutual benefit? I fear if we don't, disaster is imminent. Perhaps we have not reached the stage in human evolution where this is possible.

Montenero is but a microcosm of our world, and its inhabitants possess the same human defects as elsewhere. We are all impatient, but southern Italians seem to have a shorter fuse. Centuries of invasion, foreign dominance, and crises no doubt contribute to this sense of urgency. We are all shortsighted. We are born to see the world only through our own eyes. We are the center of the universe—or so we think. It takes work to sense and understand how we are all interconnected, to see how each of us is a drop of water in this vast ocean.

The afterword in this book is about Montenero's Grand Relationship —how we can find in a small, remote mountain village all of what is most important in life. There are people, businesses, pastimes, and relationships that reflect all aspects of life found in any social environment. There are the differences in wealth, education, dress, and character. One thing you may find in an ancient farming village is a wise old peasant who can see things clearly without the bias that formal education can unwittingly foster. Truly admirable!

A variety of topics and ideas punctuate the pages of this book. I hope readers will ponder over the underlying significance for themselves and their own situations. There are many lessons that can be learned through the case of Montenero. It is often easier to understand our blessings and curses by looking at a simplified example, rather than wrestling with the complex. In the long run, perhaps others will contribute by helping places like Montenero to overcome fear with courage, impatience with calmness, and apathy with enthusiasm. Perhaps by cultivating empathy, the finest of human qualities will emerge. It's been a long time coming.

Michele Di Marco

Michele DiMarco, MA

Onward

Wedding of the author's grandparents, Michele DiMarco and Lucia Caserta.
Married at St. Paul's Church, Erie, Pennsylvania, 17 September 1925.

chapter 1

Table Talk: Legends of the Old Country

It was a blessing to sit at my grandparents' kitchen table. As a child, of course, I had no idea of just how the cumulated hours spent in that room would come to affect my life. Over the mounting years, the significance became more and more apparent. I've had the fortune to be able to live, study, and work in two dozen countries—experiencing their histories and cultures—but no travels or schooling provided more to enrich life than the time spent at my grandparents' kitchen table.

We may think of a kitchen simply as a place to satisfy our hunger, like a gas station where we fill up and go. Grandma Lucia (Caserta) DiMarco had a simple kitchen, equipped with the common appliances, food and drink, albeit with an Italian flair. There was a hand-painted ceramic on the wall with a household prayer in Italian. Grandma used only one brand of olive oil, a special ingredient for the taste buds that no other oil seemed to satisfy. Blocks of cheese were always graded by hand. Coffee beans came to life in the air, drawing one to the table to share both drink and conversation.

▲ Grandma Lucia gabbing with a friend.

From the stove top, oven, or broiler, whatever Gram made burst with flavors I rarely tasted elsewhere. Quality food was the priority for family and friends. All the grocery shopping was done at the Brown Avenue Food Market, run by Danny Savocchio and Frank Leone, who had family origins in the village of Rocca Pia, not far from the village where my grandparents were born: Montenero Val Cocchiara.

If you know little or no Italian, you may ask, "Monte what?" There are a few places in Italy called Montenero, which means "Black Mountain." This one, located about eighty miles east of Rome, is about three thousand feet in altitude, but surrounded by mountains reaching higher than seven thousand feet. The additional "Val Cocchiara" is a mouthful, so to speak, but it helps distinguish this village from other Monteneros in Italy. Val Cocchiara directly translates as "valley spoon," or valley shaped like a spoon, since the village homes face southward toward a huge flat marsh having an expansive oval-shaped area at one end that quickly tapers to an elongated "handle" between the hills. Hundreds of wild horses freely roam this lush area.

Italian is a foreign language to me. Since my mother, Janet Balchunas, was of Slovak-Lithuanian descent, and we lived in Erie, Pennsylvania, English was our only common language. My father's two siblings, Philip and Dino, married young ladies of German and Polish descent. All ethnic groups felt a need to become "American." Unfortunately, some of the old-world traditions, including the language, were amputated to assimilate to the New World.

I didn't understand conversations between my grandparents when they spoke to each other in their dialect or when they spoke with Italian friends. If I tried to pronounce words like Val Cocchiara, they would be garbled as if I were trying to speak with a mouth full of stones. Impossible! Even one-syllable words were difficult to pronounce correctly, like *zia* (aunt). The tongue and lip placements for the phonetics just don't exist in English. At least I could pronounce *pizza* perfectly! Of course, Gram and Gramp could talk in coded dialect whenever they wished to keep us kids from understanding their secrets.

Although both were from Montenero, my grandparents were married in Erie. Upon arrival, other relatives and Montenerese helped them settle by offering food, room, and clothing. The story was the same for all the immigrating Montis. ("Monti" is a short form for "Montenerese" that Americans used when referring to those with roots in Montenero.) Many settled Montis would assist Monti immigrants in whatever ways they could, such as introducing language teachers and potential employers. Any labor to be done was met with willing volunteers. Men cooperated to construct buildings, barns, and fences. Women did loads of laundry together, or took turns stirring boiling pots of cornmeal (*polenta*).

Grandpa Michele "Mike" DiMarco worked as a bricklayer and, because he had a truck, he did some odd jobs, such as delivering coal to homes. Once an acquaintance asked him to make a delivery at night. He returned at dawn, looking pale and anxious. We're not sure what he was asked to deliver, but he never said what happened or spoke of that night afterward.

Following the American dream, Gramp saved and finally opened his own bakery. It was during Prohibition (1922–1933), when it was illegal to make, transport, or sell alcoholic beverages in the United States. The bakery used much gas during the long nights of bread making. Brewing ingredients to make alcohol also requires a lot of gas, a fact well known by the local Mafia. Nobody would suspect the gas used to make liquor would be abnormal usage for a bakery. So, it seems men in pinstriped suits came to make my grandfather an offer: work with them or go out of business. He chose the latter. He worked as a custodian at a large company (Kaiser Aluminum and Chemical Corporation) until retirement. His hard work and sweat provided a comfortable home for his family.

My grandparents' home was actually a duplex. My parents Ralph and Janet, sister Sandy, and I lived on the second floor. There were no distinguishable physical or psychological barriers between the living spaces. As a result, my sister and I were often on the first floor. When not eating, we played hide-and-seek, ran around the basement, watched TV, and generally tested our grandparents' patience. Or we'd play outside with other children in our spacious backyard. Originally my grandfather had planted the entire area with vegetable plants and some herbs. A peach tree was in front of the kitchen window. But after my parents married, half of the yard was seeded for lawn to form our playground.

When Uncle Phil got married, my parents purchased their own home so the newlyweds could move into the cozy second-floor apartment above my grandparents. More grandchildren started to arrive nine months later. After a few years, they purchased their own home, and so another pair of newlyweds moved in: cousin Vincent Caserta and his wife Carmela (Freda). Later various grandchildren took over the apartment.

This was our home at 949 West 20th Street in Erie, Pennsylvania. No need to describe every room or inch of ground. Clearly, the most important room was the kitchen. Two key factors make this proclamation easy to state without hesitation. The first involves food, the sustenance of life. It is not just the food but how the ingredients were selected and prepared for each meal. It is no joke to say that love is the secret ingredient. An old proverb sums it up: "If you want to know how much an Italian loves you, ask them to cook you dinner."

The second factor is that the kitchen table was the meeting place for relatives and friends who shared their thoughts and feelings. How about that? People actually cared enough to make the time to be together, to talk, and know each other intimately.

It was a daily occurrence that some guest or guests would arrive, knock at the door, and meet a warm welcome. "Come in! Sit!" Then would come the questions: "You want something to drink? Are you hungry?" If you said, "No, thank you," coffee would still be made. Cookies would come out of the pantry, probably Stella D'oro. Depending on the time of day, other food would mysteriously appear. When did the sandwiches, cheeses, meats, and pasta arrive? Who brought those out? Sleight-of-hand master magician Houdini?

What better way to show you care for someone than to give the best quality foods possible, nourishing and health sustaining? The kitchen was no drive-thru. Any who cared enough to visit got the best of food and drink. That was good for the body. What was even more important was the food for the soul—the conversations between family and friends.

Whoever was living on the second floor would certainly visit Gram in the kitchen on a daily basis. Other relatives came regularly, some on a weekly basis, some monthly, some yearly. The stronger the personal bonds, the more visits. When an uncle would visit, usually the upstairs people would join at the table too. Often couples or families would come: Uncle Dino and his wife Mary Ellen and son Danny; Uncle Phil, Aunt Carol, and their five children. Great-Uncle Pat (Pasquale) DiMarco. Grandma's twin sister Jenny (Genneve) and her daughters Gloria and Viola. And on holidays and special occasions, all relatives came.

When my great-uncle Oreste Caserta, his wife Elia (Miraldi), and their five children emigrated from Italy in the 1960s, there was a big welcoming dinner at the DiMarcos'. All the women labored in the kitchen to prepare a sumptuous feast. I remember cousin Enio with a big smile outlined with sauce. All were family. You were always welcome.

One Christmas morning, my sister Sandy found a gift from Santa Claus that ignited her creative talents. After opening the box, she worked continuously until finishing a highly colorful Paint By Numbers oil painting of roses. The fresh pigments glistened with brilliant hues of pinks, reds, and whites on the canvas. That evening, following the holiday dinner, the living room filled wall to wall with relatives. Sandy found it an opportune time to show off her masterpiece. After all politely praised her work, she left the painting on a small footstool, which everyone soon forgot about. As a group returned to their adult discussions, my grandfather sat down to share in the conversation, but soon got up to get a drink from the kitchen. While he was walking toward the kitchen, everyone noticed how realistic my sister's Paint By Numbers flowers looked—clearly transferred upon the backside of my grandfather's new dress pants. Embarrassment was trumped as usual by a dose of humor.

From such regular visits came many stories of present-day life, as well as memories of life in Italy. Gradually, I learned what some Italian words meant, like paisano (a countryman), *comadre* and *compadre* (reflecting the most intimate of friends). Usually adults didn't exclude youngsters from being around, so I often just sat at the kitchen table, listening to their discussions. Over time, I learned a little about Italy, but more about Montenero. Table talk painted an Impressionistic image of the home village that captured the place as it was at the turn of the twentieth century.

Gram's kitchen was often visited by DiMarco and Caserta relatives, and also by numerous Montenerese with surnames including Bonaminio, Calvano, Cacchione, Danese, DiFilippo, DiNicola, Donatucci, Gonnella, Iacobozzi, Mannarelli, Narducci, Orlando, Pallotto, Pede, Scalzitti, Torn-incasa, Zero, Ziroli . . .

Montis patronized other Montis' businesses: Aqualino Orlando's grocery store carried our favorite foods; Richard Donatucci Lopez provided produce to local businesses; Rose Donatucci Gamble made a number of restaurants famous for her home-style cooking; father-son Antonio and Arturo DiFilippo provided nostalgic Italian themes in their music; Elmer Yacobozzi gave guitar lessons; Nello (Bonaminio) Fiorenzo sold and delivered laundry bleach to homes; the Narducci brothers tended to our dental and general health; Vincent Caserta held Italian-language classes; Ziroli brothers built and maintained our homes; realtor Rocco Orlando sold our homes; and John Orlando Funeral Home put us to rest.

A few times per week, my grandmother would ask my sister or me to go to the Brown Avenue Market to buy something. We didn't understand dialect, but we understood broken English. She'd ask for a "box of blue," which we knew meant Woolite fabric softener, or a packet of "raisin blades," which were razor blades. We only learned years later what some of the specialized vocabulary really meant.

At least once every two weeks, Gram Lucy would also order "a pound of bullaham." So, we'd walk to the store, be greeted by Esther Savocchio, and go to the butcher counter at the back. Usually other Italians were there waiting for their orders.

"Hey, you a Mike DiMarco's grandson, eh?" Anyone waiting for an order would pass the time by talking with others.

My turn to order: "Hi, Mr. Savocchio. Can I have one pound of bullaham?" He'd give it to me with no questions asked. Same order for years. About thirty years later we found out that "bullaham" wasn't an Italian specialty meat. It was simply boiled ham.

Many items would come from my grandfather's well-tended garden. Sometimes he'd pack a large brown bag full of vegetables and walk to his brother Pat's with thoughts for his eleven-member family. He'd then walk home, repeat the packing process, and walk to a son's, then another son's . . . . He grew so many vegetables that he sold some items to the Brown Avenue Market to resell. Everyone was surprised by his potent and unusually large garlic. He said he got them to grow this way by tying the green tops in knots so more energy would go to the bulbs. Apparently it works.

When no Monti could provide a product or service, we'd look to fellow Molisani and Abruzzese. Montenero is situated on the north border of Molise, and Abruzzo was over the bordering hill. Actually, my grandparents called themselves Abruzzese because Molise didn't formally become a region until 1970.

It was natural that some people with roots from near Montenero were in the close social mix. Giuseppe "Joe" Montagna and brothers (Pratola Peligna) built homes for Montis. Brothers Patrick and Italo Cappabianca (in-laws in Rocca Pia) were political representatives. A good number of immigrants came from Alfedena, Rocca Pia, Pratola Peligna, and Montenero. Couples were married at St. Paul's Catholic Church, and their children went to Columbus Elementary School, both located in the heart of Little Italy.

▲ Grandpa Mike DiMarco holding his namesake and future author, cir. 1955.
A peach tree and his garden in the background.

Erie's Little Italy area was primarily populated by other southern Italians, so Montis also mingled with many Calabrese and Sicilians. We went to barber Carmen Panetta, to Raymond Ferritto to bet on sports teams, Father Marino for masses and church funeral services, Pedano's florist, and Gannon College President Scottino for academic advice.

I am aware that Montenero had mirror images in other cities besides Erie, such as in Lorain, Ohio; Chicago, Illinois; Toronto, Canada; and Mulhouse, France. The first-generation immigrants must have had similar experiences in transplanting into their new cultural settings. They naturally felt closer to their countrymen and village brethren than to other ethnic groups.

Besides the moral support of Italian kin, other sources of comfort were the social clubs based on regional locations, such as the Montenero Men's Club, the Ladies Montenero Society, the Pratola Peligna "P.P." Club, the Calabrese Club, and La Nuova Aurora Club. Social clubs further developed into business organizations such as the Wolves Club, which helped incubate local businesses and offered educational grants to promising Italian-American students.

As immigrants became settled, they soon branched out to have a profound effect in local politics and business, first with the city, then the state or further. In Erie, the Italian community came to be the dominating ethnic group in any area and activity—be it sports, construction, education, religion, entertainment, or the arts. Perhaps this can be best reflected in the political reigns of city mayors. There was Louis J. Tullio (1966–1989), who became the first Italian-American elected to this position. He was the son of an Italian immigrant who couldn't read or write. Next was Joyce Savocchio (1991–2000), the first female mayor of Erie. Then there was Richard E. Filippi (2001–2005), whose father at age fourteen arrived in the United States from Italy after World War II.

Cradled within this Italian-American community, elbow to elbow with first- and second-generation Montenerese, I inherited ways of thinking and acting from "the Old Country." That's what culture provides. For any self-aware person, what we do with that culture is up to us as we mature into adulthood. Some ignored their ancestral background just because they were born in America. One had to fit in. Of course by the third generation, many were now living in homes away from Little Italy, had less contact with Italian-Americans, and were heavily influenced by American culture. Many were truly "Made in the USA," with all their senses being washed by mass media and elements that included music, television, movies, fast food, pulp fiction, clothing fashions . . . and growing individualism.

7

Anyone who lives in one country and has remaining ties to his or her nation of origin is constantly pulled between two cultures. It's a polarizing experience, much like biparty politics. And, not unlike politics, we are fortunate to have the options to study, experience, and learn from more than one culture or political group. My youth was touched by many cultures, primarily the Italian, but also by other ethnic groups that were going through the same adaptation to American society. It is a melting pot in which we get the choice to brew our own broth.

During my high school days, I made an even greater variety of social contacts, and I became more conscious of this cultural diversity. In retrospect, this probably aroused a curiosity to learn more and more about my Monti roots. I collected any information I could about Montenero and Abruzzo-Molise in particular. It wasn't easy to find. There was no internet, and you certainly couldn't find "Montenero Val Cocchiara" on any library catalog card. The main source remained the ol' timers, the hard-drive memory banks of elderly relatives and their friends wired around the kitchen table.

Over my youthful and impressionable years, I learned something about Montenero by osmosis. Of course, from kindergarten through high school, I was surrounded by kids steeped in American culture, and all of us received the same homogenous education. The first- and second-generation Montenerese added a special color to our life that I always felt fortunate to have experienced. They were foreign and somewhat mysterious

to the native-born American. Their presence gave me a glimpse into an Italian personality that was uniquely Montenerese.

    While others drank their coffee, I sipped a latte macchiato (hot milk with a dash of coffee), which was more suitable for a child—and I listened. "What do you remember about Montenero, Grandma?" She searched her memories. She remembered sitting on a chair on her balcony during the fresh winter months, crocheting sweaters. The balcony faced the scenic mountain valley and the midday sun, which kept her comfortably warm.

▼ National Mutual Aid Society, Montenero Val Cocchiara Branch of Erie, Pennsylvania, 16 October 1927.

Row I, left to right: E. Macerata, Carmen Montevecchio, Giuseppe Scalzitti, Carmen Fabrizio, Tommasso Presogna. **Row 2:** Vincenzo Orlando, Sylvester Pallotta, Barone Cacchione, Felice Scalzitti, Nunzio Cacchione, Niccolo DiMarco, Pasquale Pallotta, Tommasso Miraldi, (?) Cappabianca, Emideo DiFilippo, Filippo DiNicola, Giovanni Presogna, Carlo Orlando, Mario Caserta, Guglielmo Pallotta. **Row 3:** Raymondo DiNicola, Raffaele Presogna, Niccolo DiNicola, Gilbert Presogna, Alberto Totleben, Pietro Pallotta, Tommasso Orlando, Clemente Orlando, Franco Mannerelli, Clemente Fabrizio, Pasquale DiMarco, Julio DiMarco, Alfonso Pallotta. **Row 4:** Giuseppe Calvano, Casimo Surace, Mariotene Ricciuti, Vittorio Bamberga, Domenico Tetuan, Tommasso Pallotta, Tony Iacabozzi, Beniamino Di Nicola, Daniele Ziroli, Salvatore Torincasa, Tommasso Iacabozzi, Marco Colonna, Amico Fabrizio. **Flag sponsors, left:** Ermida Orlando, Filippo Scalzitti, Anna Marie Scalzitti (child). **Flag sponsors, right:** Alberto DiNicola, Elsie DiNicola, Theresa Miraldi. *Photo courtesy of John Fiorenzo.*

"Why do you wear the ACE bandages around your leg, Grandpa?" He told me a little about his days in World War I, when the Italian Army fought Austria-Hungary for years at a stalemate on the battlefront in northeast Italy. Over a half million died by bullet, shrapnel, and rock fragments thrown by exploding shells. Some succumbed to illness. Others froze to death. Still others were shot by their fellow soldiers under orders by their own field marshal, Luigi Cadorna. This practice of decimation, as done during Roman times, coerces soldiers toward the option of charging uphill, toward the enemy and their repressive force of lethal weapons.

"Were you shot, Grandpa?" He pointed at scattered spots on his legs, then to other areas. All in his troop were killed except two. Gramp and another soldier were wounded, captured, and eventually moved north to various labor camps, such as in Zossen, less than thirty miles south of Berlin, through the Carpathian Mountains, somewhere near the Russian border. He was held in a makeshift prison cave and ate grass to stay alive. Somehow he escaped and walked southward, across Hungary, Romania, and Bulgaria. He found refuge and help from priests along the way. Eventually he got to Thessaloniki, Greece, and took a boat back to Italy. All in Montenero thought Gramp was dead. He returned home to loved ones, homegrown food, and homemade wine.

My grandparents saved every postcard and letter received from Montenero. Classic photographs of the village in black and white. Some were colored by hand. A photograph of Great-Uncle Berardino Di Marco in military uniform. He served in the Second Italo-Ethiopian War from 1935 to 1936. Great-Uncle Clemente Di Marco wrote the most. As a child he fell off a chair and broke his back, so he never grew much taller. As a tailor, he made clothes for many in the village. My grandfather's two other brothers, Carmine and Filippo, immigrated to Argentina and were never heard from again. Trying to find them through the Red Cross and other means all failed.

I couldn't read the newsletters, but they seemed to give some summary of what was going on with Montis in the village. Because Saint Clemente was the patron of the village, there were postcards showing his statue, and church bulletins featured the saint.

We were fortunate to have a few photos of my great-grandparents, who were born around the mid-1800s. I don't know much about their lives, but I imagine they were generally like others in the village who worked their farms and tended livestock. I heard more about the most recent generation, like my dad's, who served in World War II.

The men of that age group sometimes told tales of their wartime experiences. The Italian theatre was well represented in television shows, documentaries, and movies. Adults who knew of Montenero were certainly aware of the war's timeline and realized how the village was being affected.

The Germans were retreating from Africa to Sicily, then up the boot. Hitler drew a line just south of Rome with the demand to hold it at all costs. The Winter Line, or Gustav Line, as it was also called, went right through Montenero. What happened during this occupation? I heard enough to get an idea.

As I reached college age, I still had only a rough sketch of the reality of life in Montenero. Italy was over three thousand miles away. What I knew for certain about the Montenerese was through those who were close at hand, the closest being my grandparents and other relatives.

▲ Men at work in Erie, Pennsylvania . . . and proud to get it done.
Michele DiMarco is sitting in the middle and on his left is Anthony Orlando.

11

What stands out is how devoted my grandparents were to each other and to the family. Family was their breath. It inspired them to rise early in the morning. Gram cleaned and cooked for her husband, children, and grandchildren. Gramp worked long hours, even when retired, as he tended his garden. They sacrificed more than just their time for family.

Rather than spend money on themselves, my grandparents gave to others. Gramp saved all shapes of wood, lengths of wire, and pieces of pipe, knowing they may prove useful later. Gram kept pieces of thread and rubber bands in abundance. Heck, she even saved the keys that came with coffee cans, even though every new can came with a key attached.

"A penny saved is a penny earned," as the proverb states. Grandma Lucy saved. Then she could leave a dime on the window sill for my sister Sandy, who'd retrieve it when she passed by on the way to school in the morning. Sandy could then buy some candy and my mother wouldn't know.

During grade school, I walked to Gram's for lunch every weekday. Both my parents worked, so Gram provided. Sometimes my father would meet me there. Sometimes I'd take a friend or my father's friends would show up. All knew they would eat well. As Gram washed the dishes, she was planning on what to cook the next day.

All the grandparents did for us were expressions of love. Those who were aware of this couldn't help but to return the love. On Mother's Day, Gram would get a nice bouquet of flowers. "Why you give me these?" she would say. "I can't eat them!" We always thought such a comment odd, but we understood she would rather give than receive. The living room's threadbare carpet bore testament to that.

The value of family and friends stood supreme over the superficiality of material things. If I would miss a day visit to my Grandmother's, she'd telephone to ask, "Do you feel OK?" She wanted to be sure I was well, but also her question was an indirect way to invite me to visit.

• • •

Visiting grandparents. Seeing relatives. Meeting others around the kitchen table, where every conversation seemed to involve Montenero. Story after story of life in the old village, recollections of good and bad times, all colored in layers of Montenerese folklore. Even when talks were not in English, the Monti dialect filled the room with its own sweet melodies that penetrated one's core with emotions. In dialect, syllables were just musical notes of subliminal communication.

There were some common threads embroidered through these kitchen conversations, such as the value of a strong work ethic, being frugal, practical, cooperative, and keeping a sense of humor, even during strenuous times. Many had multiple talents, probably because they always tried to be self-sufficient. My father, for example, was a superb handyman, but also a fine leader in the business world. His elegant signature was seen on every other office desk in the company where he worked. He literally left his mark on all he touched.

Over the years, these stories inspired me to try to emulate the best qualities I saw in relatives and friends. Of course, not all could live up to the exemplar of the most stellar personalities, but there was a good number that made for wonderful relatives and the best of friends. The positive qualities they possessed made me wonder if living in Montenero molded such characteristics. After graduating from college, I decided to go directly to the source. I booked my flight.

Montenero Parentage

Often youth do not see
the older generation
standing behind them . . .

Cir. 1956 photograph courtesy of Sandrino Fontanella.

chapter 2

A Foreigner Discovers the Ancestral Village

"One-way ticket to Monte nero, Val Coc chiara, Povincia Campo basso," I said to the clerk at the Rome railway station. He chuckled, but not at my pronunciation.

"Your grandfather must have told you that," he said. "Now the village is in the province of Isernia."

Gramp emigrated in 1920, and it wasn't until 1970 that Isernia became the provincial capital and took over administrative jurisdiction of fifty-plus municipalities, including Montenero. It was the summer of 1976. This was my first time in Italy, and I didn't know much about its history and politics.

Heading east from Rome by train into mountainous Abruzzo, it takes over three hours to get to the city of Sulmona, where I had to change lines. The local line presented a different cast of characters from those riding the main line . . . a few porting live chickens. Nearing an hour in the antiquated train car, I asked a conductor, "Montenero?" He pointed at a small station we had just passed! The next city was Castel di Sangro, where I got off and found Hotel Bellavista. For about $8 US per night with breakfast, it would be my base for visits to Montenero.

Early the next morning, I decided to make a leisurely walk to Montenero, which is just over five miles away. It would be a way to experience the countryside. Stunning scenery surrounds quaint Castel di Sangro, one of the larger towns with its six-thousand-plus population. It didn't take long to get into farming areas with a landscape of varied green shades, each hue subtly illustrating the wide variety of agricultural and natural vegetation.

About midway, I reached a fork where State Roads 17 and 83 meet. A smaller road branching toward Montenero from there is clearly marked. A few hundred feet along the road, I passed the Montenero train station sitting mutely to the side. A couple of young men, just old enough to drive legally, saw me and pulled over. This road had one main destination. They knew I must have been going to the village, so they offered me a ride. They guessed I was a foreigner by my clothes and knew for sure when our two mother tongues proved mutually incomprehensible. I mentioned names of a few people from Erie whom I knew were already in Montenero.

"Vincenzo or Carmela Caserta?" I said. They didn't recognize the names. "Pasquale Pede?"

"Sì, sì!"

Off we went to find Pasquale.

Their car was an old Italian model with its share of dents and rust. I got in and immediately thought I might be better off to continue by foot. In the middle of the front seat was a bucket filled with gasoline and a rubber hose running to the engine. Not a Lamborghini, but the car did run, and we got to the village without a problem. We found the home of Pasquale Pede and knocked. A bearded Pasquale opened the door, but I didn't recognize him.

"This guy is a local, and I'm looking for a Pasquale from Erie," I thought. But the two were related, and soon I was under the wings of English-speaking guides.

The next days were devoted to meeting relatives. How anxious can one get when encountering the siblings of grandparents for the first time? Vince and Carmela Caserta took me to my great-uncle's home. Berardino Di Marco, his wife Diana (Santilli), and son Carmine were anxiously waiting. Another great-uncle, Clemente, was there too. We gathered around the kitchen table, questions and answers streaming through the conduit of Vincent Caserta. Luckily he was fluent in a number of languages, being a teacher of Italian, French, and English in Erie. A knock on the door and Edilio Di Marco, a distant cousin, entered. He had worked on cruise ships for years and also spoke a few languages. His superb skills took a portion of the load off Vincent.

When my grandfather left Italy for the final time, he was twenty-seven years old. His brothers always thought he'd return. At the time of this trip, I was twenty-four, had a physical resemblance to him, and carried the same name. Through me, Berardino and Clement could see something of their older brother. Of all things we discussed, the main concern was that relatives were healthy and happy—my grandfather Mike, his siblings, their children and grandchildren—all were fine, and those in Montenero certainly looked robust and happy.

We located the site where my grandfather Mike once lived. Only portions of three sides of the stone home were visible. It had been destroyed by bombs during World War II. I could make out a fireplace on the second level amid rubble and cobwebs. The roofless structure was well camouflaged amid bushes and trees.

The house where my grandmother Lucia lived was kept up by her brother Oreste and family. Even after they moved to Erie in the 1960s, they maintained the home and lived in it during their regular summer visits. Now I stood on the balcony where my grandmother used to crochet as a young lady and viewed the same mountain scenery.

On a following evening, we gathered at the home of my grandmother's sister, Ernesta Caserta. Her husband Luigi Mazzocco and son Filippo were there to greet our entourage, including the two trusty interpreters. Great-Aunt Ernesta spoke dramatically as her hands seemed to be conducting each orchestrated syllable. What a vibrant character! We met briefly with Ernesta's daughter Domenica while her young children, Gianna and Oliviero, were busy playing outside. Aunt Ernesta's other son, Mario, was living in France, so we never had the opportunity to meet.

◀ With Great-Uncle Berardino DiMarco in 1979.

▼ Berardino's wife Diana Santilli with her brother Eldo.

17

▲ Great-Aunt Ernesta Caserta and her son Filippo Mazzocco in 1979.

These were the initial meetings with relatives that inspired me to make future trips to Italy. In 1979, I studied Italian for a few months at the University for Foreigners in the city of Perugia, which so happened to be where my grandfather did his military training many years prior. After the language course, I headed for Montenero. As a passenger, I neared the village in a car and the driver spotted my uncle Berardino walking in a meadow. With an umbrella over his shoulder and his flat cap partially shading his eyes, he was tending to cows in the fields. I got out of the car to greet him in traditional manner, with a double kiss-hug, and we walked the remaining way to his home.

During this visit, I stayed in my uncle Berardino's home. The language studies helped some with communication, mainly sharpening my listening skills. Speaking was still very difficult. Berardino asked about my uncle Phil in Erie: "*Che fa tuo zio Filippo?*"

I translated word by word in my head. *Fa*, from the verb *fare*, meaning to do or to make. Uncle Phil, what does he *do* or *make*? Rather than pursue the most common interpretation, I eventually replied: "*Lui fa i bambini*"—meaning he's making babies. Uncle Berardino smiled, knowing Uncle Phil had his hands full with five young bambini.

I was surprised to learn how much my relatives in Montenero knew about relatives in Erie. So many they had never even met, yet they knew about their work and family lives. Regardless of the distance and years of separation, they followed the lives of extended family. This mirrored the thoughts and feelings of my grandparents and other Montis I knew in Erie who always kept Montenero and family in their minds and hearts. We were fortunate to have intermediaries who traveled each year between the countries to share news and enforce the familial bonds.

It is always interesting to see visitors from the United States in the old village setting. I didn't know Rinaldo Freda well because he lived in Lorain, Ohio. Now we met and had time to walk around the village together. I listened to his memories and thoughts of life in the Old Country. I heard his history and could see it on his face. Montenero had sculpted his character.

On the other hand, Phyllis (Bamberga) Pulinski was uprooted early in her life and taken to Erie as a baby. She was visiting Montenero in the company of her husband Edward and daughter Judy. Mr. Pulinski enjoyed joking about "backward Montenero." Rather than praise the spoon-shaped valley where wild horses roamed, he talked of the flies and poop. He certainly didn't romanticize Montenero! Others jest about it too, and the smack of reality is always a good reminder to keep a balanced perspective.

Another great joy is spontaneously meeting the locals. To get an encompassing picture of the village, I chose to walk as many of the meandering lanes as possible. Up and down, down and up through the village, saying *ciao* to friendly faces, observing their daily lives, and being amazed at the antiquity of the buildings. Some were puzzled at the new face in town.

I heard one man wondering aloud to himself in a whispering dialect: *"Chi è stu gauglion?"* Who is this young man?

I greeted him with a smile, a *"Buon giorno,"* and a short list of my relatives' names. He knowingly nodded and I continued my stroll.

"Vieni qui!" came an invitation to lunch in a home. Although not related, the family asked about family and me. They shared their time, food, and drink. An hour later I was walking the path again for a short distance. Another invitation for a drink and conversation.

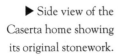

▶ Side view of the Caserta home showing its original stonework.

The invitations happened again and again on a daily basis. I never did get to see every street and alley in Montenero.

The majestic setting of the village lures one to the countryside, especially toward the valley. In addition to the hundreds of horses, cows roam the area, as dairy farming is vital for the milk, cheese production, and meat. Private vegetable gardens checker the distance between the village and the valley floor. As I descended toward the valley, I encountered an elderly couple walking with a burro.

"*Buon giorno!*" they said. Their smiles rose, as did their questions. I learned they were Giuseppe Cacchione and his wife, Dea. He was the brother of Maria Colonna, my grandmother's best friend in Erie

We reached the valley floor, where high grasses were cut to dry in the sun. The donkey had been carrying two wooden poles connected by eight to ten feet of net. Giuseppe removed this and laid it on the ground, using a pitchfork to pile hay on top of it. The poles were pulled together to bundle the hay, which was placed securely on the donkey's back. We were sweating under the midday sun, and it felt good. Although the work had been done in that manner for centuries in that very field, it was a once-in-a-lifetime experience for me.

I can remember all the close relatives I met during the trips to Montenero, and also some semirelated, like Diana Santilli's brothers and sisters. Some lived in Castel di Sangro, where we visited the spotless home and fine carpentry shop of Dianna's sister and brother-in-law, Maria and Umberto Marotta. My cousin Carmine sometimes helped with the work, mainly producing custom-made windows and doors to be installed in many locations in Abruzzo-Molise.

Many others I met at the churches, bocci courts, bars, in the fields, and at the grade school. Even brief meetings offered views into daily village life. We talked with ladies who were washing clothes by hand outside. They were near the large spring-fed fountain built in 1821, just to the southwest side of the village. This was very important before plumbing brought water to individual homes.

Meeting the oldest living person in Montenero was memorable. She had experienced one-hundred-plus years. Wrinkles in her face resembled the deep valleys of the High Molise, but she sat erect, dressed neatly, and her glistening eyes disclosed a total inner serenity. I saw many elderly ladies in their long black dresses, moving like shadows across most of the lanes.

This was Montenero as I found it in the late 1970s to the late 1980s. Everything reinforced the impressions I received from my grandparents and other Montenerese in Erie about the ancestral village. The buildings changed some for sure, with modern colored cement facing of outside walls and the growing use of modern appliances such as washing machines. The splendor of the mountain scenery remained unchanged, except for the addition of some electric power lines. My grandparents never saw a light bulb in the village. Above all, the character traits of Montenerese in Erie and Italy were the same. It felt like home.

I hoped to study Italian again to gain fluency and to return to Montenero. It was one of my big dreams. However, real life and other interests came to the forefront. I pursued a master's degree in Asian studies. Balancing the academic work, I chose tai chi as a physical discipline and moved to Taiwan to study it. In time I started my own business, a publishing company. I was locked to my profession for nearly twenty-five years. My interest in Montenero was sidelined, but it always lingered close enough to pull at the root of my being. A sixth sense told me that I had to return to it someday, somehow.

Each year I hoped it would be possible to return to Italy, and each year something got in the way. Maybe I can go next year? I thought this way for two and a half decades. Having the dream doesn't make it happen. I was tied to the publishing business I founded in 1991. It was a difficult business to start, and it only became marginally successful after eight years of working nonstop. Then came the global economic crisis of 2008, on top of drastic changes that affected publishing: the dynamic growth of the internet and digital publications. Traditional publishing died. During the period while I was desperately trying to adapt my business model, my parents and sister became seriously ill. Within a few years, they died, as did an uncle, an aunt, and a couple of my dearest friends. Without close family around, I decided to go to Italy to commune with the ancestral spirit in Montenero.

I contemplated staying indefinitely in Italy. I wanted to soak in the culture of Montenero while becoming fluent in the language. It would take time. Through the grace of my great-uncle Vincent Caserta, I was offered the home where my grandmother was born. I prepared speedily, renewing my passport, selling my car plus some household and personal items, arranging for my apartment to be rented, and buying airplane tickets.

To stay longer than three months requires a visa. I filled out papers, sent them to the Italian Embassy in Los Angeles, and waited. I heard nothing. I sent e-mails. Heard nothing. Made phone calls. Still no reply. Finally, I received a call. In a trite lecture, the representative told me not to try to get a visa. She urged me not to plan on staying long in Italy. She was rude, saying it is "like the Chinese and Mexicans coming into the USA."

► 1979: The author drinks fresh spring water from the fountain built in 1821.

What? Did that have anything to do with my applying for a visa? I have Italian blood, an ancestral home, financial security—I just could not understand how the embassy representatives could be so discourteous and so useless as a source of information. I figured I could apply for a visa while in Italy, perhaps even registering at a language school to get a student visa if necessary.

My flight for Rome departed 18 August 2014. After landing in the morning at the Leonardo da Vinci International Airport in Fiumicino, I boarded a train for Rome, then another train to Sulmona, then a bus to Castel di Sangro. Although it was less than 150 total miles to travel, because of the connections, I couldn't get to Montenero in a single day. It was a long day after the transatlantic flight.

The next morning I shouldered my backpack and pulled my suitcase by its broken handle. I left the hotel for the bus stop and was soon en route. Thirty minutes later I was dropped off at the base of Montenero. I struggled upward, porting heavy luggage, zigzagging unmarked lanes toward the central piazza. It's up there . . . somewhere. I felt like one of the poor souls in Dante's *Purgatorio* as I climbed up from one level to another. Where is the guide Virgil when you need him?

Finally the incline tapered, and I could lift my eyes and see Roxy Bar. At 8:00 a.m. the thought of java drew me to the tables. Only one customer present. She sat at a table on the patio, absorbing the view of the tranquil valley below as it unveiled the morning glimmer under the rising sun. Her name was Paola D'Avella. She was from Rome, and she had a second home in Montenero. She was an Italian who taught French and was very fluent in English. Courteous, intelligent, friendly, and elegant. How lucky was I to start my time in Montenero with this fine lady? I greatly enjoyed our introductory conversation and knew we would talk again soon. For now, I needed to call Carmelina Pede, who had the key to the Caserta home.

Carmelina came to the Roxy Bar and together we went to the house. It had been empty for five years, but it looked fine. She had cleaned it some in preparation. It had all the basic amenities for the kitchen, bath, and bedroom. I could continue my publishing work on my laptop and keep in contact with friends, relatives, and business contacts in the United States via the internet.

Beside my full-time publishing work in the United States, I also taught tai chi. As a Chinese martial art, it is primarily studied as a system of exercise. I thought it would benefit and be a fun activity for those relatively secluded in the mountains of Molise. Was it possible to start a class? Who would be interested?

I felt teaching locals would be a way to return something of value to my grandparents' homeland. I asked a few people for ideas of where I could teach, but the words dispersed in the wind. Who made the biggest effort to help me was Paola D'Avella. She invited a number of people to her home for a pleasant gathering, which enabled introductions to a few who could help organize a tai chi class . . . if they cared to do so. One present was Carmen Marotta. She is a major force for Montenero's Pro Loco, an organization with a focus on promoting the village. It turned out I had visited Carmen's parents' home about twenty-five years prior. She arranged for me to give a presentation at the municipal hall, and we raised enough interest to start a weekly class.

What is the art of tai chi? What is the value of its practice? Some Montis incorrectly called it yoga because that was a catchall word for any odd Asian exercise. Although we had a nice small introductory class, it can take months before a student begins to comprehend the basics of this system. Of course, some were too impatient to stick with this discipline. Others couldn't make it each week to class because they lived in Naples most of the time, while others had to attend church functions, or perhaps they needed to digest a hearty lunch. As the trial of initial classes continued, life continued in Montenero, which I was learning had been greatly recast by a quarter century of sociopolitical change.

My grandmother's nephew, Filippo Mazzocco, was the only close relative living in the village. Others had since passed on or moved away. My grandfather's nephew, Carmine Di Marco, resettled in Macerata city with his mother, wife, and son some years prior. His home in Montenero, where I stayed years earlier when his parents were alive, was now rundown through neglect. A family from Naples moved in and was repairing the home in lieu of paying rent.

It was apparent that a large number of people born in Montenero have moved away, some to other countries. Like my great-uncle's home, the village was in need of a face-lift. It was also obvious that nonnative Montenerese have moved in, and some had brought noticeable improvements. Everywhere I went I heard Italian with a Romanian accent. A street hawker from North Africa made his rounds, trying to sell cheap clothing items. I soon found out that Italy was experiencing a crisis with the whole of the country in economic chaos, layered by an invasion of political refugees arriving by land and sea from countries such as Romania, Libya, Pakistan, Somalia, and Nigeria. A very long list of people from other foreign countries continued to move to Italy, including many from China and India. In all, applicants numbered in the hundreds of thousands. The instability was seen and felt in every area of the country. Even tiny remote villages were affected.

Once upon a time, someone from a nearby village would have been considered an outsider. Now there were relatively large numbers of people from cities like Naples and Rome who had purchased second homes in Montenero. Of course, if they had the money to do this, they were able to improve the old homes they purchased, build additions, and make other improvements. For example, Lamberto Lamberti and Laura Piccialli created the cozy five-star Pachamama Bed and Breakfast. To see the reconstruction of an old mill turned into a museum, Il Mulino Museo, is an amazing step in recognizing a vital part of Montenero's culture. These "outsiders" appreciate the peace and beauty of the village and surroundings, which contrast greatly to life in the bustling metropolises. Their well-kept habitats add to the natural scenery, and their personalities foster an open-minded worldview in their amicable social interactions.

I met many of the non-Italians and non-Molisani who were now living in the village. I had the blessing to be invited into the homes of people from Naples and Rome for tasty dinners and conversations. Some also expanded my horizon by taking me on day trips outside Montenero. Their kindness and hospitality I will never forget, as with the amiable Montenerese I met during my visits in prior years.

In contrast, the homegrown residents were not so congenial, showing a profound change from the social characters of earlier years. Some opened their doors once to me—perhaps out of a sense of duty to ancestors—only to slam the doors shut. Many were just not happy individuals. They emitted a sense of frustration and irritability, and I wondered why.

The coldness I felt from the Montenerese was not directed solely toward me, but sadly it was evident among themselves too. Relationships between family members and nonrelated neighbors were strained. Local tensions were part of the larger picture, reflected in the crisis shaking Italy like a nationwide earthquake. Broken friendships and growing divorce rates are indicative of the present day struggles. Things have changed.

What was once an agricultural field has been turned into a sports field, where youths noisily play under lights until late at night. On the paths where donkeys quietly transported hay a decade ago, motorcycles now scream for recognition. And the Rodeo Pentro—the longstanding yearly festival exhibiting the rare Pentro breed of horse that largely made Montenero famous—is now defunct. Rumor has it greed killed this golden goose. If you want to make a wish by throwing a coin in the village's old water fountain today, you will have no luck. A modern municipal water system was built, choking the natural spring-fed source. The structure still stands, not only in disrepair, but it bears evidence of vandalism.

As for myself, I didn't attempt to get a visa in Rome. All seemed too chaotic and dysfunctional to waste time trying. I did contact a few language schools. The administrators knew well in advance that I was considering enrolling in classes. They had the authority to apply for visas for students. They contacted the Italian offices to secure a visa for me but failed. I could not apply while on Italian soil, but would need to return to the United States to apply.

For centuries, a Montenerese was someone who was conceived in the village and was surrounded by others born and bred there. The homogenous culture in which that person was nurtured does not exist any longer. The place we call Montenero and the people we call Montenerese have constantly changed, usually at a snail's pace, but quite rapidly in the recent decade. To come to a better understanding of just how and why Montenero has changed and continues to do so, it seems necessary that I try to look at what set it all in motion. A prerequisite is understanding the land and history of the region.

The following chapter is an attempt to gain a view of the geographic setting in which the village took root, since this is what determined the lifestyle most suitable in this high mountain area of Molise. What Montenerese would eat depended upon what crops could be grown and what animals could be raised. Weather and altitude affect home design and clothing. The land presents dangers as well. For anyone who wishes to understand life in Montenero, especially for one like myself not born in Italy, we look first to the land and then to the plants and animals that inhabit the area.

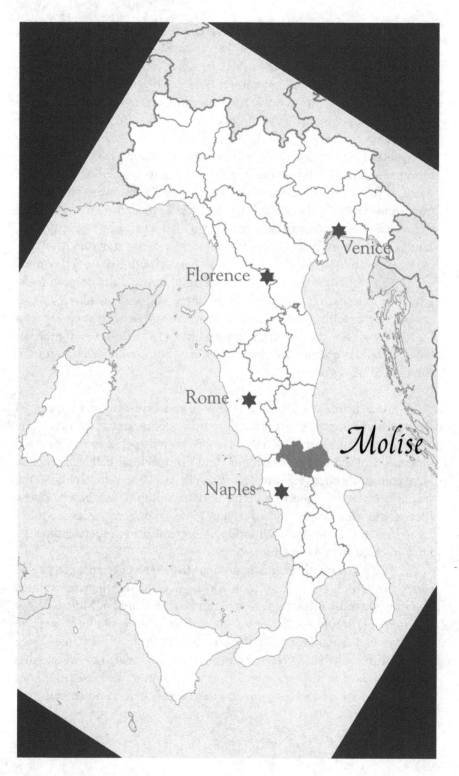

Florence

Venice

Rome

Molise

Naples

chapter 3

Setting the Stage Between Land and Sky

Rome. Florence. Venice. In their itineraries, all big tour companies highlight the Italian cities, which are famed for their rich history and art treasures. Everyone knows where Italy and its famous cities are located on a world map, but where is Montenero? And what will you discover when you get there? It took some years to gather information and form a general picture of the village's geographic setting.

Montenero seems to be an Italian Shangri-la, a remote village tucked away in obscurity, nestled in the central Apennines mountains in Molise, one of the twenty administrative regions in Italy. Molise, about midway between the toe and thigh of the Italian boot, is one of the least known of all the regions. After being formally separated from Abruzzi e Molise in 1970, Molise became the second-smallest region. It is the newest region . . . with a very long history.

What did my ancestors do in the village for work? What was their daily life like from morning 'til night over the seasons? What would they think of Montenero today? If we look closely at the geographic setting, along with the plants and animal life that populate the area, we can gain an understanding of how it cradled the village since its earliest days.

Italy's spectacular mountain ranges and coastline make it a dreamland destination for any tourist. Viewing the breathtaking scenery around Montenero made me wonder how such beauty came to be. I found answers, not in tourist books, but in geography books.

It took millions of years in forming, mostly due to twisting and turning tectonic plates. A large landmass connected to France broke off about thirty million years ago and has been moving eastward ever since. Previously united with Sardinia, Calabria broke away and eventually snuggled into Apulia. Apulia and Sicily are actually parts of the African Plate. The sliding of tectonic plates—grinding over and under one another—occurred underwater until the resulting merge slowly forced the landmass upward to form the Italian peninsula five to ten million years ago. The plates are still moving, and Italy continues to gain altitude. No need to go to the shore to collect seashells. You can find them in the Apennines.

Tectonic activity brought about the geographic grandeur of the Italian peninsula—at a cost. Numerous faults permeate the peninsula, making it susceptible to earthquakes and volcanic activity. "Seismic activity is common along the entire length of the chain (including Sicily), with more than 40,000 recorded events since [CE] 1000."[1] Montenero, like other mountain villages in Molise, is in a vulnerable earthquake zone.

The Molise area is diverse, including a short coastline on the Adriatic, climbing to mountain areas peaking with Mount Meta at 7,352 feet—less than ten miles away from Montenero for a bird, or fifty-five miles by car on switchback roads. The mountain ranges shape the land, which smooths out to low-lying hills and plains. The coastal area is referred to as the Low Molise and the mountainous area around Montenero as the High Molise. The region is divided into two provinces, named after their respective capitals, Campobasso and Isernia. Montenero is in the northwest High Molise in the province of Isernia, where ancestors breathed pure, rarified air over the centuries. To be more precise, the village is in the High Volturno, named after the longest river in south Italy. It begins its course about twelve miles from Montenero in the high mountains.

From Montenero it is easy to see Mount Meta,
7,169 feet, the highest point of Molise.

Molise's mountainous terrain fosters a number of rivers, waterfalls, lakes, and brooks. With its source in the Matese slopes, the Biferno is the principle river of Molise, but other rivers are closer to Montenero, such as the Trigno, Volturno, and the Sangro.

The Trigno, the second longest river in the region, originates in the province of Isernia and is the most important in the High Molise. It forms the border between Molise and Abruzzo from the high mountains to the Adriatic Sea. The Volturno River originates near Castel San Vincenzo, where it contributes to a scenic artificial lake. It is the main river in the province of Isernia, flowing southeast toward Venafro, and it eventually enters the Tyrrhenian Sea just northwest of Naples.

North of Montenero, the Sangro River rises in the middle of the rugged National Park of Abruzzo, Lazio, and Molise. It flows southeast toward Villetta Barrea and floods the three artificial lakes along its course to the Adriatic. Monterese have dipped their toes in the river where it passes by Alfedena and Castel di Sangro, since these two cities are in such close proximity.

There are other rivers and tributaries, such as the Sente to the east, San Bartolomeo near Venafro, and Carpino and Sordo Rivers, which flank the provincial capital. However, a flowing gift to Montenero is the Zittola, a tributary of the Sangro. It passes through the valley and contributes to the scenic marshland, which is walking distance from the village.

Although the highly complex subterranean makeup of the Italian peninsula is a fascinating geographic wonder, the spectacular surface features are what leave us mesmerized. The terra firma one steps on in the High Molise is largely limestone, which tends to be soluble when it meets water and acidic solutions, eroding it over the centuries. The resulting landscapes are called karst formations, which are also characterized by underground drainage systems that include sinkholes, dolines (funnel-shaped depressions), and caves. Clays of varied colors have filled lower-lying areas. Their hues, ranging from brownish terracotta to white porcelain, result from the differing amounts of iron oxide in their composition. In contrast to the rugged limestone surfaces, clay appears to the eye as a softer ground texture.

The geodiversity of the High Molise is matched by its biodiversity nurtured by a warm temperate climate. The four seasons give a regular cycle to life in the High Molise, with the warmth of summers fading to cool by mid-September. Snow often blankets the hills by November, bringing a cold winter. Details regarding Montenero's climate are provided in the following chart.

CLIMATIC TABLE

	January	February	March	April	May	June	July	August	September	October	November	December
Median temperature (°C/F)	2 35.6	2.7 36.9	4.8 40.6	7.9 46.2	12.5 54.5	16.3 61.3	19.3 66.74	19.4 66.9	16.1 61	11.3 52.3	7 44.6	3.4 38.1
Minimum temperature (°C/F)	-0.7 30.7	-0.3 31.5	1.4 34.5	4.1 39.4	8.2 46.8	11.7 53.	14.2 57.6	14.4 57.9	11.6 52.9	7.6 45.7	4.1 39.4	0.7 33.26
Maximum temperature (°C/F)	4.7 40.5	5.8 42.4	8.2 46.8	11.8 53.2	16.9 62.4	20.9 69.6	24.4 75.9	24.5 76.1	20.6 69.1	15.1 59.2	9.9 49.8	6.1 43.0
Rainfall (mm)	67 2.6	63 2.5	61 2.4	63 2.5	58 2.3	48 1.9	39 1.5	49 1.9	64 2.5	85 3.4	102 4.0	86 3.4

Climatic details—including temperature, cloud cover,
precipitation, rain, snow, sunshine, humidity, and wind—
can be found on this website:
https://it.weatherspark.com

The pristine High Molise landscape is embellished with a diverse palette of flora, home to over two thousand types of plants and trees. Oak and silver fir are always in view, and at altitudes above 3,600 feet, beech trees dominate. The forests include the chestnut tree, which provides nuts used in a number of the region's dishes. Although in lower numbers, flowering ash, black pine, silver birch, maple, sycamore, and hornbeam add variety to the land. Rare white fir trees can be spotted, as they stand out for their height and width. Other rare specimens include the sorbo, yew, and wild cherry.

Montenero sits at the southern border of the National Park of Abruzzo, Lazio, and Molise. The park is adorned through the seasons by a spectrum of morphing colors from 2,841 species of flora populating the high mountains, low valleys, grasslands, swamps, and river basins. A few species unique to this area are the Martian iris and the carnivorous Pinguicula. You can easily stumble upon the common meadow Turk's cap and fire lily. If you are lucky enough, you will also encounter rare species, such as the holly, edelweiss, yellow and black orchids, and the well-known but elusive lady's slipper. Some are protected species, including the kingcup (marsh marigold) and the early marsh-orchid, which is a perennial herb. In addition to the flowers, there is a lengthy list of lichens, algae, and mushrooms.

Of particular interest are the plants used for medicinal purposes for both human and animal. One study shows the results of 128 interviews with people living in the High Molise in which seventy different medical uses were presented as well as their methods of preparation. Another study collected data on eighty species, which included sixty-one used in herbal remedies and twenty-three that were utilized in cooking. Numerous other edible plants grow in Isernia province, such as truffles and wild berries. In particular, the white truffle is highly prized. Molise is the second-largest producer of truffles in Italy.

Lady Orchid.
Courtesy of
Ginevera D'Angelo
© 2019.

Mouse-ear chickweed.

Snowdrop.

Liverleaf.

Flowering apple.

Flowers on rock.

Primrose.

Photography by Ginevera D'Angelo © 2019, taken in Montenero Val Cocchiara.

32

Silver-washed fritillary.

Clouded yellow.

Southern white admiral.

Lesser spotted fritillary.

Silver-studded blue.

Large wall brown.

Photography by Ginevera D'Angelo © 2019, taken in Montenero Val Cocchiara.

The temperate climate and lush and varied vegetation favor an equally magnificent population of wildlife. The Marsican brown bear has been a longstanding symbol of the national park and the people who live in the area. Recent decades brought an unfortunate decline in the bear population. The number is now only thirty to forty, due to poaching and land development. Other animals are experiencing growth in population, such as the Italian wolf. It remains one of the more common animals you are likely to see.

Hikers often see red foxes, weasels, moles, hedgehogs, red squirrels and other rodents, porcupines, wildcats, deer, and large mountain hares. Echoes of the Eurasian lynx are sometimes heard, but the animals usually elude sight. The thick forest was once a famous hunting area for wild boar, driven to near extinction, but now prospering due to its reintroduction to the national park. Other reclusive inhabitants of the forest include the polecat, the badger, and the otter.

▲ Apennine chamois. *Courtesy of polifoto © 123RF.com*

Above the forest in high mountain spaces, Apennine chamois nimbly make their way across the rocky terrain. They live alone or in small groups. This spectacular animal has often been photographed in the national park, but the population has decreased by 30 percent in the past decade. Recent accounts estimate the total population of chamois at about 1,700, with about four hundred of those living inside the national park. On the other hand, the red deer numbered only eighty-one individuals in the park previous to a reintroduction in the 1970s, which led to a great increase. The individual number reached 2,500 by 2010. A study shows that the nutritious plants eaten by both the chamois and the red deer overlap, and the red deer are cutting into the chamois' food supply, leading to their starvation. On top of this, some chamois actually get killed by lightning strikes at the high elevations. The crisis regarding the overlapping food sources between the deer and chamois is a good example of the biodiversity in the High Molise, where the plants, land, and animals live in a fragile balance.

The province of Isernia provides hunting guidelines for a variety of animals, announces the dates for the hunting seasons, and posts rules and regulations, such as those regarding the use of dogs, vaccinations, testing captured game, and removal of carcasses.

The Marsican brown bear, which is only found in Italy's Central Apennines, is considered critically endangered, and as such it is a protected species. Today the main dangers for them come from poaching and collisions with cars. However, a lengthy list of animals indicates the scope of possibilities for hunters in the High Molise. Hunting is permitted for the following species:

blackbird	cesena	coot	deer
early bird	fallow deer	fox	gadwall
hare	hooded crow	jay	lapwing
magpie	mallard	moorhen	pheasant
pigeon	pintail	pochard	quail
red deer	redwing	shoveler	snipe
song thrush	taupe	teal	turtledove
water rail	whisk	wigeon	wild boar
woodcock			

One majestic bird that can be seen soaring in the High Molise altitude is the golden eagle. Others often seen in the wild are sparrow hawks, falcons, buzzards, martens, and owls. Depending on the elevation and surrounding vegetation, different birds populate the area. The High Molise attracts migratory birds such as woodpeckers, choughs, rock partridges, pheasants, snow finches, jays, and others. Frequenting areas around water are gray herons, dippers, and wagtails.

The colors and calls of the bird population add much to the scenery of the High Molise. In addition, ninety-five of the 115 species of butterfly in Molise are found in the mountainous area. Unfortunately, these winged creatures are being reduced by the encroachment of modern lifestyles, including sport rock climbing, ATVs, and the crisscrossing of electrical power lines.

▲ Aspis viper in camouflage.
Courtesy of Guillermo.
Avello © 123RF.com

Regarding fish, there are many types that can be caught on the coast of Molise. Within the region itself, twenty species have been recorded. The most common of the freshwater species are the brown trout, the chub, the south European roach, and the Italian barbel. Such populations keep people fishing for pleasure as well as providing the catch of the day for the dinner table. For the less adventurous, some salmon are bred in tanks near Rocchetta al Volturno and can be picked up for a pocket of euros. Many customers get hooked by this convenience.

If you grew up in an area devoid of snakes and scorpions, you may want to become familiar with what creeps and crawls around Montenero. In all of Italy there are four poisonous snakes. In the High Molise there are two: the common asp and the less common Orsini viper, also known as the field adder. Compared with other viper species, their venom toxicity is relatively low. The bite of the Orsini viper carries roughly the toxicity of a few bee stings, meaning they are relatively harmless to a human. They have, however, claimed their casualties. Most of those came from heart attacks brought on by sheer fear—or, ironically, severe allergies to the antivenin. Visual differences exist between these snakes and their nonpoisonous counterparts. The poisonous species have larger, triangular heads; are not as lengthy; and have fatter bodies and short tails.

Just an hour's drive north of Montenero is the commune of Cocullo, where the people hold a yearly procession for their patron saint, Dominico di Sora. A statue of the saint, draped in snakes, is ported through the streets, and brave locals carry snakes in their bare hands and over their shoulders. This appears quite scary, but the snakes are not venomous.

The region is also home to a variety of nonpoisonous snakes, each species with its individual characteristics. The four-lined rat snake (cervone) and the red-eyed Aesculapian can be six or more feet in length. The quick-moving semiaquatic grass snake plays dead if irritated. The green whip snake is even swifter (moving up to 6.8 miles per hour) and can also swim. If you plan to hike in the High Molise, get a good herpetological treatise to identify and memorize what serpents are present there.

▲ Italian scorpion.
Courtesy of buffy1982 © 123RF.com

A fear factor also comes into play when viewing scorpions. There are seven species in Italy, and you'll find the *Euscorpius italicus* visiting Montenero homes. Like the poisonous snakes, the scorpion's sting is painful, said to be equivalent to a few bee stings, but not fatal. Check shoes before putting them on and bed covers before tucking in for the night. In contrast, other reptiles you may find adorable, such as lizards and tortoises. Many amphibians are quite beautiful in coloration, like the fire salamander, tree frog, and newt.

Emerging from the encounter of tectonic plates, the pristine high lands of Molise became a natural habitat thriving with plant and animal life. From brown ants to brown bears, from giant firs to dainty lilies, the area around Montenero was wisely chosen to be part of the National Park of Abruzzo, Lazio, and Molise. The natural phenomena to be discovered there are a pleasure for all the senses, enticing not just for their beauty, but for nurturing the spirits of those who have made this land their home.

The Capestrano Warrior

Statue of a warrior, dated to around the sixth century BCE, found in Capestrano, Abruzzo, about fifty-four miles from Montenero. He wears a wide-brim hat, a wide belt, necklace, armlets, and a disk-type armor protecting his chest and back. He holds a short sword across his chest, knife, and an axe.

Courtesy of Museo Archeologico Nazionale Chieti.
Photograph by Elisa Triolo.

chapter 4

Footprints in Isernia Leading to Romanization

Planted on a hill in the High Molise, Montenero Val Cocchiara is in a stunning mountain setting alive with a large variety of plants and animals. But who originally settled this area, built the first homes, planted crops, and raised animals? Although the first document to reference the village dates to the late tenth century, there's evidence showing that people walked on this land long before.

Archaeologists dug up traces of the first inhabitants of the Italian peninsula that date to more than 850,000 years ago. More pertinent for Montenero are the finds at Isernia La Pineta, roughly twenty miles away. It is there that in 1979 the oldest and most extensive Paleolithic settlement in Europe was found. The site has been hailed as the most important paleoanthropological discovery in Europe. The artifacts show that *Homo Aeserniensis* living here used fire and limestone tools. Their diet included elk, bear, wild boar, birds, and fish, which are found on the Montenerese table today. But other animals—such as bison, rhino, elephant, and hippopotamus—have long since disappeared from the area. Artifacts from the Paleolithic and Neolithic ages provide no insight into how Montenero came to be, but at least we know that some small groups of people lived off the land in the general area for thousands of years.

During a legendary period from about 1200 BCE to 500 BCE, a number of peoples from the Western Steppe brought Indo-European-based languages into Europe. Some came through the eastern Alpine passes to settle in the Po River plain, while other groups moved farther south. A number of tribes shared Italic characteristics in their language because of their common origins. Others, such as the Etruscans, did not. There is still much mystery about the various early tribes that started to populate the Italian peninsula, but they made their presence and had an influence on the future of Italy.

The Oscans were one Italic group that moved into southern Italy, mainly into the regions of Latium and Campagna. Their language and culture no doubt influenced early settlers in the Montenero area. Edward Salmon writes, "[I]n antiquity the 'Oscans' enjoyed a reputation for grossness and obscenity, but this was simply due to a crude piece of popular etymology: obscenus from *Obscus* (*Oscus*)."[1] Did this trait have a lasting impact on future generations?

We really don't know much about these tribes, but we have some linguistic reference. About an hour's drive from Montenero, a bronze plaque dating from the third century BCE was found near Agnone. The inscription on the tablet is in the Oscan alphabet and represents one of the most important records of this long-extinct language.

ARRIVAL OF THE SAMNITES

Another wave of immigrants came to central Italy, gradually replacing the Oscans. These were the mighty Samnites who, with their warlike mentality, settled in Molise and Campagna. They were rugged peasants and herdsmen, and they used their strength to protect and cultivate their lands and raise sheep. They utilized communal grazing land and grew crops for food. Plus, they had a thriving metal industry, although there is not much to show for a higher culture, which would reflect lifestyles of an elite class. These were hardworking people who toiled close to the land.

The Samnites actually consisted of five tribes, a confederation of the Caraceni, the Frentani, Caudini, Pentri, and the Hirpini. The Caraceni, the least populous of the five tribes, made their presence in the Montenero area, since their principle town was just over the hill in Alfedena, which they controlled between 700 BCE and 600 BCE. Their presence formed the north boundary of Samnium along the Sangro River. They lived in the Sangro River Valley as well as in the mountains overlooking the lush valley. During the next four centuries, the Pentri highlanders intermingled with the Caraceni and gradually assimilated them. Excavations at Pietrabbondante and Alfedena are famous sites for the territory of the Pentri.

If we research the name "Pentri," we first notice the word derives from *pen*, meaning "summit," and hints that their rustic habitats were located in the highlands. Sheep herding provided them with wool for making warm clothing for the harsh winters, as evidenced from gravesite excavations in Alfedena. The burials there show that the population lived at subsistence level. There was a high birth rate but a short life expectancy. Any so-called aristocrat in this society was basically a well-to-do peasant. The day-by-day thoughts for survival led many to raid neighboring areas to plunder goods. The Pentri earned a reputation for their aggressiveness over the centuries.

Although much of the land was unsuitable for cultivation, the chief crops for the Pentri were cereals. "In some districts," in the High Molise, "it was stock-raising rather than agriculture or forestry that was of chief importance. This is especially true of the country of the Caraceni and Pentri, much of which is unsuitable for cultivation. Cattle-raising has been practised there from prehistoric times and was certainly of great importance in the economy."[2]

TRANSHUMANCE

As populations grew, so did stockbreeding. Other animals the Samnites bred were horses, donkeys, mules, goats, pigs, and a variety of poultry. However, they were famously known for the sheep they bred. They benefited also from the sheep by-products of milk and wool. This valuable life-sustaining food source required its own feeding, but the winter months proved difficult to keep the animals supplied with food. Thus began a regular seasonal routine of moving livestock from the high grazing grounds to lowlands in winter and back to the highlands in summer. This seasonal migration, known as *transhumance*, accounts for a network of drover roads (*tratturi*) established through systematic use by herdsmen.

The drover roads are found in southern Italy, with the best known found in the regions of Apulia, Molise, and Abruzzo. They touch all areas of Molise. The longest drover road runs between L'Aquila and Foggia for a total distance of 151.6 miles. Significant for Montenero is the drover road between Pescasseroli and Candela. This is the third-longest drover road in southern Italy, running the distance of 131 miles via Barrea and Alfedena before traversing the Zittola Bridge toward Rionero Sanitico and Isernia. Plus, there is another major branch from the Zittola Bridge, known as the Castel di Sangro–Lucera Drover Road. From Lucera there is a route leading to Foggia, which was a hub for the whole drover road system for southern Italy.

The crossroads where the Pescasseroli–Candela and Castel di Sangro–Lucera Drover Roads meet must have been fortuitous for the nearby population. At an unknown date, locals took advantage of this location to construct some sort of tavern. "Here was the 'Taverna della Zittola', an important stopping place for transhumant shepherds and to spend a night and perhaps exchange products. In fact, the taverna was located exactly at the point where the Royal Pescasseroli–Candela intersects the Castel di Sangro–Lucera."[3]

The Samnites had formed not only a fine road network for the seasonal migrations for animals, but these drover roads also served as conduits for trading goods and lines of communication. Beside the work involved with animal husbandry and the use of drover roads, what else do we know about Samnite life? They were not people known for commerce but plain peasants focused on working directly with their land.

In the highlands, very small settlements seemed to randomly appear. In the centuries BCE, most homes were made of wood and had only one room. Absolutely no luxuries! "It seems probable that many Samnite houses were of a temporary, makeshift character suited to the needs of herdsmen who moved their quarters along with their flocks."[4] Most villages only had a simple organization. They did not make ceramics, nor did they mint any of their own coins. They simply bartered for any goods they needed.

RELIGIOUS THOUGHT

We learn about everyday Samnite life primarily through archeological studies as well as some early literary references. As with any culture, religion is woven through the thoughts and actions of the people. Among the Samnites, people believed as they wished. There is no evidence that a priestly caste existed. Some forms of worship are evident, including those taking place in natural surroundings, such as forest groves. In Alfedena "an open-air sanctuary surrounded by a simple portice was found, with a shrine at its centre . . . a kind of half-way house from open grove to roofed temple."[5] Nature was filled with the supernatural, and magic was believed to influence the future for the people's benefit. Thus, offerings of pigs, sheep, and oxen were made to the gods to procure their good graces. Plus, amulets were made to protect their owners from harm. Such amulets were also found in Alfedena. Ancient forms of paganism continued to influence people's beliefs through the following centuries and haven't yet fully disappeared.

In the face of chronic tribal warfare, natural disasters, and other trials, the populace relied on divine intervention to help them through any trouble. They supported their ancient pagan beliefs by adding Greek and Italic gods to their pantheon. Divinities were adopted and worshiped to bring prosperity to the land and health to the people. Regarding natural disasters, for example, coins found in Isernia show that Vulcan was worshipped for his association with earthquakes. Apollo was the dispenser of agricultural wealth. A gold ring excavated in Isernia shows Angitia, a goddess of healing and security. Goddess Diana was prayed to for a successful hunt. For the formidable Samnites, Mars—the god of war—was ever present. In fact, the most common bronze idols are small warrior figures like those found in Barrea and Alfedena. On a larger scale is the symbol of Abruzzo, the Warrior of Capestrano. Dating to the sixth century BCE, this Samnite statue is now in the Louvre Museum in Paris.

Warrior traditions are also evident in construction projects. Of course the common domestic buildings were quite rustic. The modest shepherd's hut didn't win praise for any architectural achievement and didn't survive more than a few decades. In a number of locations in Molise, we find stone structures made specifically for protection from invaders. "Built to guard against invasion, the polygonal fortifications on the mountain heights of Samnium are its earliest considerable monuments. . . . Unquarried, or at best roughly quarried, limestone boulders of moderate size were placed one on top of the other without cement and kept in place by their own weight."[6]

Early migrations, Aesernia Man, the Oscans, and later the varied Samnite tribes came into the lands we now call Molise. Each left its marks as settlements were made in places like Isernia and Alfedena. The land around Montenero was attracting settlers. The rustic huts provided basic shelter for those starting to farm the land and raise animals. The agricultural setting in the High Molise was difficult enough, even without the threats of marauding neighbors. Pagan religion soothed the souls, and simple works of art pleased the aesthetic tastes. The hard life must have been conducive for a warrior mentality. Samnites are most noted for their staunch independence, aggressiveness, and fighting skills. They relied on such strengths as more migrations arrived to put pressure on Samnium.

Migrations and Warfare

As the numerous tribal groups on the Italian peninsula gradually developed, their populations grew, bringing need for more agricultural land and mineral sources. The same process was occurring to the far north, beyond the Alps. Germanic tribes were moving into neighboring lands as they searched for greener pastures. As part of this process, they elbowed the Gallic Celts out of the Danube regions, where they were living. The Celts moved over the Alps into Italy. Conflicts predictably arose as they sought out new territory in northern Italy. Eventually, the Celts pushed farther south and sacked Rome in 387 BCE. It is probable that the shock of the incident led to a treaty between Rome and the Samnite League in 354 BCE with hopes that a united front would prevent a return of the Celts.

In peninsular Italy, the Samnites dominated more territory than any other group—about six thousand square miles—and it seems they had the largest population too. The Samnite League was a loosely structured alliance—the major players being the Caraceni, Pentri, Caudini, and Hirpini—that came together whenever necessary to squelch any belligerent actions from neighboring tribes. The Samnites had a longstanding reputation for their own aggressive actions. They possessed superior fighting skills and often utilized the mountain fastness to cloak their movements.

During the fifth and fourth centuries BCE, population growth forced the Samnites to push south and southwest in search of grazing lands. Some of the encountered tribes cooperated with the Samnites; some didn't. The aggressive mountain people moved south through the river valley routes to gain control of new areas into Apulia. Predictably, a main area of contention was at the border, where the Liri River flows into Roman-dominated Latium. The Volsci populated this area, where both the Romans and Samnites coveted the copper and iron deposits—vital, of course, for making weapons. Another main route into Samnium was through the Volturno Valley to the stronghold of Isernia. Isernia was a logistic key to northern Samnium, although the main city for the Samnites became Benevento

First Samnite War (343–341 BCE)

The inevitable happened. There came a butting of heads among those trying to settle in the adjacent lands under Samnite and Roman influence. Small disputes ignited into larger confrontations as these two powers were destined to compete for supremacy of the peninsula. To say the least, the following three hundred years were not good for Samnium, for there were few days without horrific violence.

Conflicts first started between weaker, smaller tribes in the Liri Valley. When faced against the odds, the smaller powers asked for aid from either Samnites or Romans. What followed was a long series of threats, invasions, retreats, short periods of peace, changing alliances, and more fighting. The major events are referred to as the three Samnite Wars and the Social War—the latter often known as the fourth Samnite War.

During the First Samnite War, there were two major engagements. In 342 BCE, the Romans routed the Samnites at the Battle of Mount Gaurus. When the Romans tried to invade Samnite territory, they were ambushed but eventually defeated the Samnites anyway. In the following year, the Romans threatened again to invade Samnium. The Samnites sent envoys rather than warriors to meet the invaders, and, with some conciliatory arrangements, secured a peace treaty. The First Samnite War caused major destruction, and it also set the Romans in a better strategic position. For example, the Romans expanded their territory by taking over smaller tribes on the Samnium border.

Smaller groups touching the Samnite and Roman borders were resistant and resentful of their powerful neighbors. Many protested in defiance. One result was the Latin War (340–338 BCE), in which Samnite and Roman troops worked together to quell the disruptors into submission. Roman troops, for example, traveled over a route from Isernia and Alfedena on way to subdue the Marsi and Peligni in today's Abruzzo region. As the dust from these battles of pacification settled, the Romans placed a colony at Fregellae, on the bank of the Liri River, which the Samnites greatly resented for being too threatening and too close to their own territory. This irritation led to another outburst of war.

The Romans expanded their territories, made alliances, and consolidated their power. At the same time, the Samnites tried to make alliances, but historians failed to accurately record their degree of success. It has been theorized that, because of their unsavory reputation, the Samnites failed in this important aspect of diplomacy. As Salmon writes, "Perhaps their reputation as barbarous, unscrupulous and rapacious neighbors worked to their disadvantage."[7]

SECOND SAMNITE WAR WITH ROME (326–304 BCE)

The newer acquisitions of lands in Campagna gave Rome a tremendous boost in power and prestige. Their presence alerted the Samnites, who feared losing a pro-Samnite faction in Naples. The Samnites sent an army of about six thousand men to Naples as a show of force, and the Romans responded en masse to bring Naples into their sphere. The Second Samnite War thus began in 326 BCE with numerous border conflicts between the two superpowers continuing for years.

Tired of stagnation with the border skirmishes, the Romans decided to attack into Samnium in 321 BCE. Two Roman legions of eighteen thousand men departed from Campagna toward their enemy's heartland. The Samnites, under a brilliant generalissimo, Gavius Pontius, ambushed the Roman army using guerilla warfare tactics. This ignominy at Caudine Forks remained an embarrassment during the centuries of Roman rule. A peace agreement was made and fighting ceased, at least for a while.

For a couple of years, both the Romans and the Samnites worked diplomatically to strengthen their individual situations in their strategic positioning. By gaining allies far and wide, their efforts changed the pieces on the political game board. Such maneuvering brought tensions to the pawns in this game. In 316 BCE the Romans had to deal with rebellions by small tribes in the Liri Valley, where their growing presence became unbearable for the original inhabitants. Most were pro-Samnite, and soon

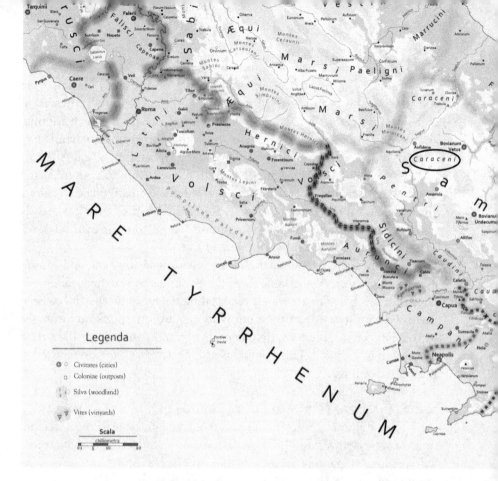

the Samnites went to their aid, renewing confrontations with the Romans.

Roman leaders decided to attack the Samnites in Apulia and in the Liri Valley. The Samnites, on the other hand, charged toward their enemy's center, straight toward Latium. They reached just south of Rome, which drew all available Roman warriors together in defense. This made it easier for the other Samnite units to take lands east of Rome, such as Sora and other lands in the Liri Valley. Despite the great Samnite victories, the Romans regrouped and retook much of the areas. Their advances struck fear into the Etruscans and other tribes, who soon raised their weapons. Conflicts erupted. In 311 and 310 BCE, the Romans held off the Etruscans and by 308 brought them to heel.

Border raids were conducted regularly between the Romans and Samnites, with some noted bursts of more formidable aggressions. While the Romans were settling matters with the Etruscans, Samnite armies headed south, making way into Apulia. This gave the Romans an opportunity. In 310 they decided to attack western Samnium in the Matese mountain areas. The Samnite armies not only held but also made headway

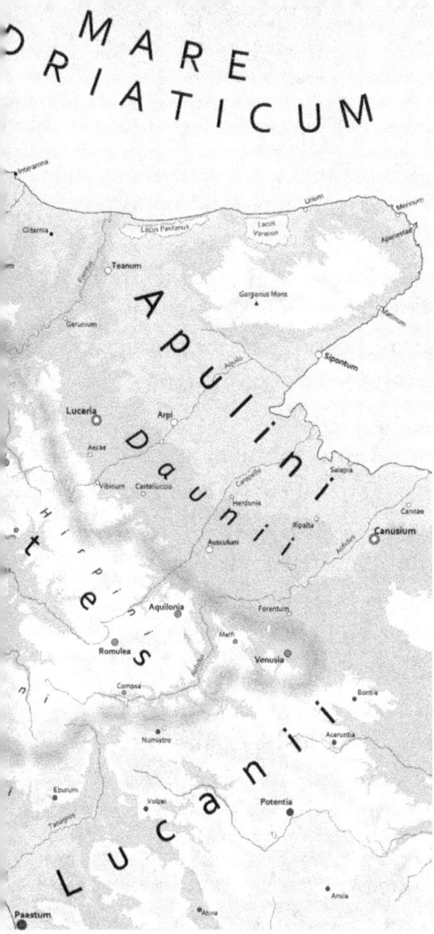

MARE ADRIATICUM

Apulia

Daunii

Hirpini

Lucania

(map labels: Larinum, Gargānus Mons, Sipontum, Luceria, Arpi, Teanum, Lacus Pantanus, Lacus Varanus, Geruncum, Aecae, Vibinum, Castelluccio, Herdonia, Salapia, Ripalta, Ausculum, Canusium, Cannae, Aquilonia, Forentum, Melfi, Romulea, Venusia, Compsa, Bovita, Numistro, Acaruntia, Eburum, Volcei, Potentia, Tanagrum, Atina, Paestum)

Second Samnite War

in Apulia and struck into central Campania. Newly elected leaders directed Roman armies to the heart of Samnium in 305 BCE, eventually conquering its capital, Bovianum. Thus ended the Second Samnite War with peace agreements made in 304 BCE. Additionally, the Romans made alliances with a number of smaller tribes.

The Roman army was exerting greater control over central Italy. It built military highways, such as the Via Minucia, that lead from the Castel di Sangro–Alfedena junction to follow the old Pescasseroli–Candela sheep track (today's State Highway 17). There the new military roads encouraged growth in the urban settlements in Boiano, Sepino, and Isernia.

Third Samnite War (298–290 BCE)

Like an aftershock from two previously strong earthquakes, the Third Samnite War broke out in 298 BCE. It was predictable that some discontented tribes would try to wiggle their way out of the tightening Roman or Samnite grip. For example, the Lucani called for Roman help when they supposedly were facing a Samnite invasion. Although the exact predicament is unclear, the situation did bring a renewed confrontation between the old enemies. The Romans were also fighting the Celts again in the north, diverting some of their forces, which resulted in their bringing smaller armies against the Samnites.

It seems the Romans were busy attacking numerous Samnite cities, including Alfedena and Bovianum. However, a major tactic they used was to destroy the Samnite agricultural base and disrupt their seasonal herding

47

on drover trails. Hard pressed, the Samnites managed to unite forces with the Etruscans, even though the Romans had previously been successful in keeping these two anti-Roman forces apart. About one hundred thousand warriors were called upon to turn the tables for the Romans. The decisive engagement was the Battle of Sentinum—one of the most crucial in Roman history—which took place in 295 BCE in the modern-day region of Marche. It was reported that over one hundred thousand Samnites perished, and most of the remnants returned to their mountain homes. More were killed as they passed through the Paeligni territory.

As the Romans were beating smaller tribes into submission and forming treaties, the Samnites mustered all they could to bear against the Romans. Their forces ranged from the youngest boys who could carry weapons to the famed *Linen Legion*, an elite unit of masterful warriors.

In 293 BCE, engagements were made in the northwestern border region, where the Caraceni and Pentri lived in proximity. The Samnites were overpowered and their best agricultural lands confiscated. The Roman troops slit throats, raped, and pillaged across much of modern-day northwestern Molise, from Alfedena to Isernia. By 290 BCE, the last flickers of Samnite resistance were seemingly extinguished. With the former superpower crushed, the pathway for Roman subjugation of the entire peninsula was now the objective.

There's an interesting story told of a Caraceni who was taken to Rome as a hostage. In 269 BCE, he somehow escaped and returned to his mountain home. The exact location is not clear, but no doubt it was close to today's Abruzzo-Molise border. Once home, he stirred up anti-Roman sentiments to carry on guerrilla warfare when possible. Although the Romans took Alfedena in the same year and the Caraceni had evaporated as a separate tribe, this sole revolutionary continued to fight for freedom. Perhaps he lived to raise a family who later had descendants living on the hill that today we call Montenero.

PYRRHIC WAR (280–275 BCE)

Rome continued to pacify various tribes in the north and south. Of course the southern area known as Magna Grecia had been under the Greek sphere. It seemed evident that the Romans would eventually attempt to dominate these southern neighbors to secure the peninsula. General Pyrrhus, from the Greek state of Epirus, came to protect Magna Grecia. The inevitable conflict became known as the Pyrrhic War, or often as the Fourth Samnite War. The Samnites, siding with the Greeks, took the opportunity to rebel, as Rome was fighting on two fronts, in the north and south.

The Romans suffered what was perhaps their greatest defeat during their entire rule in the north, close to Arezzo in Tuscany. Despite the defeat, Rome eventually came out as victors over the Etruscans and the Gauls. The Samnites fought on for about twelve years. It seems that Castel di Sangro became a stronghold where even a remnant of the Caraceni contributed. The Samnites caused damage by using their guerrilla-warfare tactics. However, in the end, many of the rebels were executed or sold into slavery. The number of remaining Caraceni was made inconsequential.

Pyrrhus's last engagement was at the Battle of Beneventum in Molise. As this Samnite stronghold fell, Pyrrhus was departing for Greece with much of the booty for his efforts, leaving Samnium and the south to fall to the Romans. One by one, many Samnite tribes were subdued. For roughly a hundred years, between 200 and 100 BCE, ravaged Samnium was tranquil. No doubt the inhabitants became focused on rebuilding their homes and farms.

ROMAN WARS WITH CARTHAGE (264–146 BCE)

Rome, on the other hand, grew more and more prosperous while still dealing with bellicose neighbors. When fighting broke out between the Romans and the Gauls in the north, the Samnites didn't submit to their usual inclination to join in rebellion. The burgeoning of Rome also caught the attention of the powerful Carthaginians, whose empire stretched across the North African coast into lands that include what we know now as Spain, Sicily, Sardinia, and Corsica. Three attempts were made to curb the upstart Roman Republic in the Punic Wars in which the Carthaginians set forces against Rome. Because Carthage was the major sea power in the western Mediterranean, this threat prompted Rome to build its own powerful navy. Rome emerged victorious in the First Punic War and a treaty was signed, but only to buy time for the Carthaginians to return in force. Because their navy was largely destroyed, the Second Punic War was conducted by land.

Known to the Romans as the War Against Hannibal (218–201 BCE), the Second Punic War involved the invasion directed by General Hannibal Baraca—noted among scholars as one of the greatest military commanders who ever lived. He certainly left a lasting mark not only on Rome but also in the lands of modern-day Abruzzo-Molise.

From his base in Cartagena, Spain, Hannibal led his army, including thirty-seven elephants, overland toward the Alps. Along the way, he either forced or negotiated with local tribes to assist him with the invasion.

▲ *Hannibal Crossing the Alps*. A detail from a fresco by Jacopo Ripanda, ca 1510, Capitoline Museum, Rome. © *José Luiz Bernardes Ribeiro* / *CC BY-SA 4.0*

The Romans had already sent forces to Spain and North Africa, where they were successful in hindering the supply lines and potential military personnel from reaching Hannibal. Gallic tribes in northern Italy were quick to rise up with the Carthaginians against Rome. Their united forces defeated the Roman armies in the north, and Hannibal was able to proceed toward central Italy.

The tactical genius of Hannibal led to a major victory over the Romans along the north shore of Lake Trasimeno in 207 BCE. Part of his strategy was to persuade Rome's allies to break off their support by either claiming neutrality or joining the Carthaginians. Being cautious, none of the Samnites were yet persuaded. The General's method of inducement became more brutal. For example, areas around the Samnite stronghold of Benevento were devastated while Hannibal moved his troops toward Campobasso. He continued to destroy the farms and lands in his path while stocking up on provisions and capturing prisoners. This did not deter the Samnites. They not only remained loyal to Rome but today are credited for battling the Carthaginians to their first military defeat near modern-day Casacalenda, Molise.

As the Carthaginians moved closer to Rome, some Italian and Samnite tribes began to renounce their allegiance to Rome. Of the

Samnites, only the Pentri remained loyal. It was with added vengeance that Hannibal torched territory as his armies passed through Pentri lands on the way to Rome. He did so later too, as he retreated. In 203 BCE, Hannibal was recalled from Italy to defend Carthage against another military genius, Scipio Africanus, who brought the threat to the Carthaginian core and eventual defeat of Hannibal at the Battle of Zama.

The peace settlement between Rome and Carthage proved a great burden on the Carthaginians. Growing Roman demands were unbearable, and the Carthaginians rebelled to start the Third Punic War (149–146 BCE). The Roman armies tightened the noose until the Carthaginian capital was largely starved out under years of siege. The city was eventually ravished and burned for seventeen days, and most of its population was sold into slavery.

SOCIAL WAR (91–88 BCE)

Part of Rome's plan to control the Italian peninsula was to further weaken the tribes that collaborated with Hannibal. Lands and goods were taken from them. Sulla, a very powerful Roman general, led his army to the mountains east of Rome with the task of destruction and massacre. Most lost any autonomy when Rome turned their lands into prefectures. Roman colonies were established across the land, and their power came to affect the lives of everyone. Place-names became Romanized, signifying the reach of political power on the peninsula. Roman allies were required to regularly pay tribute money and meet a quota of soldiers for military service. Stripped of power to make their own political decisions, the allies also had no say in foreign policy or even their mutual interactions. Booty from Roman wars went only to Rome.

Although the Samnites formed the bulk of Rome's army, contributing greatly to its military successes, they were not rewarded. If anything, the recruits often used their military service to immigrate to more prosperous areas, even to the foreign lands were they served.

As noted earlier, the Pentri was the only Samnite tribe that remained loyal to Rome during Hannibal's invasion, and the tribe seems to have received some leeway to develop on its own initiative. According to Dench, by the late second century BCE, "they were building a monumental theatre-temple complex at Pietrabbondante, which was clearly a new and improved central sanctuary and meeting point for all the second century."[8] Nevertheless, Rome did not feel morally responsible for the Samnite peasants. As Salmon adds, "Ultimately it was Roman unconcern for Allied economic welfare that was chiefly responsible for bringing Roman-Italian relations to the breaking point."[9]

51

Rome was growing more and more corrupt and rich, and Romans thought only of themselves, importing grain and metals from the conquered provinces. This stifled the production by allies on the peninsula. The enormous financial strain united the oppressed toward action. When rebellion broke out in 91 BCE, all the non-Roman tribes joined to fight for equality. The Pentri were one of the stronger powers that stood for the rights of the non-Roman peasant. The Roman stronghold of Isernia was of major importance as the passage leading to Rome and the Naples area. At the outset of the rebellion, it was the primary focus of Pentri forces. They successfully captured Isernia and turned it into a strategic stronghold throughout the war.

Anti-Roman sentiment was so pervasive that Rome had to take heed. The Samnites demanded the following:

1) Roman citizenship,
2) the right to retain any booty taken in wars, and
3) the return of all captives and deserters.

Thus the Romans offered "citizenship to any Latin or Italian people that was not actually in arms or that laid down its arms promptly."[10] Of course, any non-Roman serving in the Roman military received citizenship. The new bill registered all new Roman citizens, legally ending the previously discriminatory practices.

MAKING THE ROMAN REPUBLIC GREAT

The Rome victors cooked the books regarding their history, aggrandizing their own accomplishments while belittling the Samnites. As a result, many are not aware that Rome's eventual rise to greatness was in large part due to cultural elements it adopted from the Samnites. After conquering lands, Romans had to keep control of the conquered peoples. Thus, perhaps the most important elements adapted from the Samnites were related to the military, including cavalry tactics and weaponry such as the pilum-type javelin and the scutum-style shield. Gladiatorial combat was copied as a form of entertainment and as a superb way for training and cultivating a martial spirit.

Potential enemies surrounded Rome. For their own security, it was logical to create military roads to reach areas where uprisings may occur. Some of these main arteries were developed upon Samnite drover trails, already in existence for hundreds of years. At strategic locations the Romans built colonies along the roads in conquered territories, as evidenced at the strongholds in Venafro, Isernia, Alfedena, Boiano,

Sepino, Benevento, Alba Fucens, and Pietrabbondante. With time, the Romans had colonies outside Latin Italy, to the far reaches of their Empire. The colonies had both military and economic significance, as they also acted as trading posts.

Because the Romans were well aware of the fragile balance of power between them and contenders, they developed a worldview geared to strengthen their position and eventually prove their superiority. It was also their dealing with the Samnites that greatly influenced Rome in areas of foreign policy and land reforms. For the Romans to become richer and stronger, a patrician-plebian aristocracy emerged, allowing for the aristocrats to benefit from the sweat of the commoners—and the hundreds of thousands of slaves imported from foreign wars.

The importation of foreign slaves from conquered areas provided cheap labor for massive construction projects. Besides the road system, aqueducts, fortifications, villas, temples, and many other structures were built. The governing system had to adapt to keep the prospering republic and later empire running efficiently. The military kept peace in the peninsula while reaching its powerful arms farther into foreign lands, such as Scotland and Egypt.

The decisions they made early on played greatly on the future of the peninsula. Often, prominent political and military leaders were given lands on the peninsula in reward for their services. They lived luxuriously on their private estates, but at the loss of lands to the commoner. It became cheaper to import foods from foreign lands, and the peasants on the Italian peninsula reached new depths of poverty. Rome and other large cities prospered, especially with growing trade. The growing use of common coinage certainly facilitated it. Those under Roman rule on the peninsula became Romanized in the cities, but the less-accessible highlands retained their agrarian character.

The Empire grew so large that Emperor Diocletian divided it into halves in 285 CE. Rome was the seat for the western empire, while the eastern empire was ruled out of Byzantium (modern-day Istanbul). The latter evolved away from Latin Roman ways, adopting Greek traditions. Over following centuries the eastern empire was subject to its own metamorphosis in history.

chapter 5

Knock, Knock:
Invasions from the North & South

As Rome became excessively rich, corruption grew like a spreading disease, weakening the stability of the empire. For eight hundred years, Rome was an untouchable bastion of strength. So when the Germanic Visigoths sacked Rome in 410 CE, a veil was removed that exposed a decayed government. Forty-five years later, another Germanic group, the Vandals, ravaged Rome. In 476 CE, the last of the Roman emperors in the west was overthrown by the Germanic leader Odoacer, who became the first barbarian to rule in Rome. About ten years later, Attila the Hun came knocking with a mixed group from Central and Eastern Europe. They plundered northern Italy but somehow Pope Leo I talked him out of entering Rome. The Goths—now allies of the Huns—didn't sit around waiting for coins to fall from the sky. They invaded Molise in 535 CE. In his wonderfully written and informative book, Tommaso Astarita states that "Calabria, Abruzzo, and most inner regions—largely mountainous, difficult to reach, and ungenerous to agricultural efforts—remained poor, rural, and culturally and religiously isolated."[1] Marauding groups were certainly pillaging wherever they happened to travel. They devastated lands and settlements, and malaria took a toll on inhabitants in a number of areas as well.

◀ Gold reliquary of Charlemagne (fourteenth century) in the Aachen Cathedral Treasury, Germany. Charlemagne, emperor of the Romans from 800. He united the majority of western and central Europe during the Early Middle Ages. *Photography by Beckstet, CC BY-SA 3.0CC BY-SA 3.*

Why were all these Germanic groups heading south into the Italian peninsula? The various populations in Central and Eastern Europe clashed when food sources were in short supply. The pressures north of the Alps caused groups to migrate into the Italian peninsula in search of a more promising livelihood. What it did was to bring them into contention with the locals present in the Po River Valley and in Rome itself.

Justinian, emperor of the Byzantine Empire, arrived on the peninsula with his military in 553 CE. In order to unite the old Roman Empire, he destroyed many of the political and economic powers on the peninsula, but Papal State opposition held fast. Some territories were being organized under the Pope. In large part, this was in response to the Germanic migrations from the north. Thus the Papal States formed a powerful presence from Rome across the land into modern Emilia-Romagna. The Pope's influence in central Italy increased as the people of the area relied on his power for protection against barbarian invasions. As a summary of this particular era, Astarita writes the following:

> All of Italy suffered terribly in the chaos and warfare that accompanied the dissolution of Rome's rule in the West and continued through much of the fifth and sixth centuries. Different Germanic people fought each other in and over Italy. In the sixth century the eastern empire [Byzantium] under Justinian (ruled 527–65) attempted to reestablish control over Italy and the western Mediterranean. This resulted in long wars, religious divisions, economic catastrophe, and a steep population decline, caused also by deadly epidemics. The long wars over Italy between Justinian's forces and the Goths were especially destructive.[2]

The threats from the north didn't stop. Another Germanic tribe, the Lombards, entered the peninsula in 568 CE. In less than five years, they successfully extinguished the rule brought by Justinian. They were destined to make an everlasting mark on the territory from the north to the south—some factions of the invading group staying in the north while others went farther south to settle. Today we clearly see the Lombard influence in the modern region named after them: Lombardy. Their strong presence in the south is less visible to those without knowledge of Italian history.

After the mid-sixth century, there were thirty-five Lombard dukes on the Italian peninsula who were ruling independently. This included the two "great duchies" of Benevento and Spoleto. It was Duke Zotto who commanded Benevento, after "his partly heathen bands inundated the province of Samnium and spread terror all around."[3] By 571 CE Benevento became the main center of the Lombards in the south. They conquered Molise in 572 CE. Arichis, the duke of Benevento, "consolidated his duchy by gaining nearly all the territories in South Italy with the exception of a few towns on the coast."[4] This included the sacking of the great religious monastery of Monte Cassino in 580 CE.

Eventually the Lombards became highly Romanized. Fortunately for those on the peninsula, the Lombards brought great herds of cattle and swine from their homeland to the peninsula. Stock management and cattle breeding became particularly important in the mountainous areas such as Abruzzo-Molise. As Gattei, et al. write, "With the collapse of the Roman empire, the central-southern Apennines regress to the conditions of a poor and primitive farming and pastoral society shut up in itself and enclosed by the new feudal boundaries."[5]

Meanwhile, near the Rhine and Maas Rivers, Germanic tribes had been uniting into a strong political entity that became known as the Kingdom of the Franks. They brought nearby territories under their control, consolidated, and reached farther out in all directions. The Franks were destined to invade the Italian peninsula.

In 768 CE, the Kingdom of the Franks came under the rule of Charles, usually known as Charlemagne. As his military grip was securing lands from the Pyrenees to the Elbe River in modern Czech Republic and Hamburg to the north, Charlemagne overwhelmed the Lombards in northern Italy. Charlemagne was a devout Christian and even forced conquered subjects to adopt the Christian faith or face death. In part because of his devotion, he took a peaceful approach with the Papal States, offering Frankish protection to the Pope in exchange for a sizable donation. As a result, the Franks' conquest of northern Italy was complete by 774 CE, and southern Italy was left to struggle with its own political developments.

Since the fall of Rome, Western Europe had experienced centuries of chaos. Now, under Charlemagne, most of Western Europe was once again united. One area that Charlemagne failed to bring under his control was the Duchy of Benevento, just over sixty miles south of where Montenero is located today. Duke Arechis II, a southern Lombard, held the seat of power in Benevento. He proclaimed independence for the duchy. He was a patron of the religious centers of Monte Cassino and San Vincenzo al Volturno, which were under the papacy.

At San Vincenzo al Volturno, a Benedictine monastery was founded by noblemen from Benevento in 703, and on those lands the village of Montenero was destined to later take root. The monastery found itself in the path of expanding Frankish-Papal and Lombard powers. Because of its

57

strategic location, Charlemagne waited for the appropriate time to move against Arechis in Benevento. He did so in 787 CE, and Benevento also submitted to the Franks. As the Duchy of Benevento and the Franks established good terms for their borders, the Arabs were of growing concern from the south. The advent of Islam in North Africa came after the fall of Rome, and the Arabs controlled the entire region. In 746 they sacked Rome and made numerous raids around southern Italy.

In the ninth century, as Kreutz writes, "the whole of southern Italy was still sparsely populated, as a result of three centuries of disaster, natural and man-made."[6] The area suffered from low production, and it took another hundred years for the land to become prosperous. It was an opportune time for Arab incursions. Isernia was destroyed in 800, and a dozen years later, the Arabs attacked Ischia. Sicily was a logical target, and a conquest began in 827, with Palermo becoming the Arab capital. From Sicily, Arab groups regularly attacked the southern peninsula. The duchies in the south were growing more unstable.

Beginning as a Byzantium province in the seventh century, the Duchy of Naples became an independent state lasting about five centuries. In 835 CE, when troops from the Duchy of Benevento arrived threatening to encircle Naples, the Neapolitans searched for help and found it by hiring Arab mercenaries from Sicily. The mid-ninth century found a great number of conflicts, with Lombard attacks on Amalfi and a civil war with Salerno. Hiring the mercenaries sounded like a good idea to the Neapolitans. The people of Benevento and Salerno thought it was and soon hired Arab mercenaries too. This was like hiring wolves to guard the hen house. The mercenary work allowed the Arabs to see opportunities on the peninsula. The southern duchies were in conflict and disorder, making the situation ripe for the Arabs to act independently, indiscriminately raiding and plundering the whole southern peninsula. In order to distinguish these Arab marauders from other Arab groups, the term Saracen was usually used in the middle ages. It referred to Arabs who came from desert areas in or close to the former Roman province of Arabia Petraea. It is noted that the term *Saracini* may have derived from a Semitic root with meanings of "to steal, rob, plunder," or a noun to signify a "thief, marauder, or plunderer."

In 846 CE the Saracens attacked Rome for a second time, this time with eleven thousand men and five hundred horses. They robbed a number of basilicas, including Old Saint Peter's. Such raids in the south, plus the strained relationships among the duchies, were of concern to those in the north. Armed forces were sent south with specific objectives, including strengthening Rome with more walls. To illustrate the importance of the southern situation, Louis II, King of Western Franks, went to Benevento in 848. Although his main objective was to support Salerno and increase their power in the western region, he left Benevento to deal with the eastern region and the upper midsection of southern Italy. As Kreutz notes, these eastern areas "included not only places now held by the Arabs but also areas often claimed by the papacy, in the general vicinity of the monasteries of Monte Cassino and San Vincenzo al Volturno. Also, both of these great monasteries, with all their lands, were specifically exempted from the division and placed under the protection of the Caroligian emperor."[7] San Vincenzo al Volturno was protected from the political storm, but the abbey did suffer damage from an earthquake that occurred in 848.

Arabs had been using Benevento as a home base from where they could make raids through the region. They were pillaging from Isernia to the west of Cassino. In 849 CE, Arab pirates met a united Italian league in the naval Battle of Ostia and were defeated. The abbey at San Vincenzo al Volturno was saved from a sacking in 860 CE when the commander of the Arabs in Bari was paid off with a handsome tribute not to attack the monastery.

With the support of Louis II, the overall tide was turning against the Arab marauders. Salerno and Benevento were forbidden to hire Arabs again, and the Arabs were methodically expelled over the following decades. A great reconfiguration of the south was underway in the southern Lombard regions.

The southern contention was not only with the Arabs but included the intrigues involved in civil wars among the Papal States, Naples, Amalfi, Salerno, and Benevento. The latter two, Salerno and Benevento, became autonomous principalities in 849 CE, after a decade-long civil war. A year later, Louis II was crowned emperor in Rome. There was much work to be done as the Arabs continued their raids. Fearing the Arabs, abbots of Monte Cassino and San Vincenzo al Volturno begged Louis for help. He did send troops to attack the Arab emirate in Bari but failed to push them out. The Arabs continued to ravish numerous southern areas.

In 860 CE, Arabs destroyed Isernia, Telese, Alife, Sepino, Boiano, and Venafro. A year later Arabs torched the fortified Ascoli, and the following year, the high valley of the Volturno, including the abbeys at Monte Cassino and at San Vincenzo. From the latter monastery, the marauders from Bari took any treasure they could carry, plus three thousand pieces of gold as a bribe for not burning the buildings. These are just samples indicating a portion of the rampage taking place in the southern peninsula. Since the emperors in the west did not provide help, San Vincenzo looked to Constantinople, which drew the Byzantines back into southern politics. In 869 CE, forces arrived in four hundred ships off the coast at Bari. With their help, Louis successfully drove the Arabs out of Bari in 871 CE.

On the other side of the peninsula during the 870s, thirty thousand Arabs landed in Calabria and entered many towns. Salerno itself experienced a year of siege. Louis and his forces managed to rescue Salerno. Pope John (872–882) devoted much to halt the slide of southern Italy into Islamic orbit, basically emptying the treasury to pay for any assistance received, for example, from Amalfi and Naples, plus paying bribes to the Arabs.

The discord between independent areas on the southern peninsula not only continued to ease the way for marauding Arabs but likewise was conducive to the Byzantines. They drove the Lombards from Bari in 876, and in a relatively short time, they overran half of the lands previously claimed by the Lombards, including the power center of Benevento. However, they could only do so in the face of the Arab bands that were picking over much of the southern peninsula.

A famous attack on San Vincenzo occurred in 881. The monastery complex was almost totally destroyed by a group of the Arabs from Sicily. It seems the abbey was the largest and richest in the southern peninsula— and naturally a prime target. However, it must be noted that those who burned and robbed the monastery were hired to do so under the pay of the Duke of Naples. Naples had earlier hired Arabs as mercenaries to help keep the balance of power among the southern domains, even allowing them to settle just south of Naples. In San Vincenzo's abbey, most of the monks were killed, some at the main altar. This was a coveted gem among other ransacked sites located in the principality of Benevento and the papal territory to Spoleto. Kreutz writes that the "Arab band operating northward from Benevento first took Telese, near the confluence of the Calore and Volturno Rivers, and from there raided up the Volturno to Isernia (on a tributary) and then on to San Vincenzo, presumably floating their loot downstream, perhaps sometimes all the way to the coast."[8]

In the early 880s, a number of efforts were made to expel the Arabs from the south. Naples and Salerno joined forces to clear their territories of the Muslim presence. Unfortunately, the papacy was already a withered power. The pope went to France in search of support, paid bribes and excommunicated others, but his efforts proved ineffective. Overall, the disarray of the south allowed the Byzantines to grab half of what were once southern Lombard lands, building garrisons at strategic sites.

When we think of the Arab attacks in the southern peninsula, visions of burning villages, rape, and robbery paint one horrific picture.

However, a major part of their interventions were made to acquire slaves. The Romans built their empire on slave labor. Now, Christian captives from the Italic peninsula were exported to work in other areas, such as Egypt. Thousands of captured people were shipped away, contributing to a depopulation of the southern peninsula.

The growing presence of the Byzantines, along with actions taken by independent states, kept the political landscape in flux. In 895, for example, Guy of Spoleto drove the Byzantines from Benevento. Only five years later, Capua took control of Benevento. Perhaps in response to recent losses, the Arabs made their largest incursion into southern Italy in 902. Another important three-month campaign took place in 915, as Byzantines, Lombards, and others drove the Arabs out of their base between Rome and Naples. The Byzantines now emerged as the top military power in southern Italy, but they still were not strong enough to keep peace. The Arabs sprang back, demanding tribute from Salerno and Naples in 928. In 937, Hungarians raided areas in Beneventan and Capuan territories and approached Naples.

Some areas that were destroyed in previous years were not worth attacking again. For example, a few monks who escaped the 881 attack on San Vincenzo al Volturno had returned in 914 only to find the abbey's land desolate. They reconstructed a monastery and sought to bring in people to farm and raise animals. To do so, by 916 they offered to lease sections of land located on the monastery's grounds. By 939, the emphasis on rural repopulation and expanded cultivation led to offering leases specifically to "men coming with their families and animals."[9]

How well did the abbey's enticement work to bring people to settle on its lands? One example of its success dates to 972, when a collective group of sixteen to twenty families contracted for a large tract of land in the center of San Vincenzo's territory. It was required that "they must build a castle inside these bounds where they wish, and build houses, courtyards and gardens there, and live there."[10] As an added incentive, "some of S. Vincenzo's incastellamento charters do not require rents for the first three–four years, to give the tenants a chance to build up their crops."[11] Rent was paid not with money, but in goods. The yearly rent consisted of roughly thirty pounds of wheat, "one of barley, and two of wine per house, plus one pig in every eleven, or twenty, was fairly normal for S. Vincenzo tenants, for example."[12]

By 975 the Abbey could boast a population of over seven hundred on its lands. According to the *Chronicon Volturnensis*—an illuminated manuscript of the abbey—one of the rented tracts was originally called Mons Nigro (Black Mountain) and Mons Niger de Sangro and the valley called Malacocchiara. The valley was no doubt named as a cautionary sign for a malarial area: *mal aria* meaning "bad air" in Medieval Italian. Malaria can be fatal. The disease results mainly from mosquito bites that carry a parasite. In an infected human, the red blood cells are destroyed. Over the centuries, malaria has plagued many parts of Italy. On the lands of San Vincenzo al Volturno, the marsh (pantano) sitting below today's Montenero was an ideal setting for mosquitoes. Because of this, areas selected for human settlements were wisely situated on upper heights, above mosquito-infested swamplands. Thus, we find the embryonic growth of Montenero village, which probably consisted of a few families that lived in rustic homes, farmed, and raised livestock.

▼ Monastery of San Vincenzo al Volturno, Molise, Italy.
Photograph by Bryan ©2007. https://creativecommons.org/licenses/by/2.0/deed.it

Chronicon Volturnensis ▶

The first mention of the Montenero settlement is noted in this medieval illuminated manuscript (page 180, seventh line from the bottom) written by a monk named Johannes in the Benedictine monastery of San Vincenzo al Volturno. He utilized materials from the eighth to the tenth centuries, completing this work circa 1130. This image is reproduced here by permission of the Biblioteca Apostolica Vaticana, with all rights reserved. © 2019 *Biblioteca Apostolica Vaticana, BAV Barb. lat. 2724.*

A ul' abbs scilluc sedan xxiiij. Iste
dedita ad habitandu cata de sangto.
hominibus debellir. et in ipso cassto de al
fedena. Similia homines coducere facerat q
habitarerat. et castellu edisi caperat i locu ubi di
eract aluuella. Similia et i locu q dicerat Uaedu
atufpedina. Similia et i locu ubi dicerat hunatot. Similia et i
locu q dicerat castal austera. Similia et i lo cu q dicerat ad ipsa
cansa. ubi casttu catasol une. Quotumi bella huc coumina.

II noie dni nri ihu xpi dicerum. octosimo sedo ¶ [de al fedena]
anno dni perndol s catoh pharicipis. et vij anno pacerparus
dni aendul s s hir eq. ase dig. iij i dieson. I docq nos qsum
pecco. ftamesicui. et anser germani. f hi it aczoni. habitarautes
i comure cau bel uestse. manifestu facerum qa platerpari cutuueuese
libellatp opsdi ne dedita nos secdi leze. donq ptul us ueuaths mo
nost s uine sicui sup uul catru fluminis fonae ipsu unu cassel
lu. et catus ss tur montt i loco al fedena. phos srns. sine bele. et sine
sangto. et sine mona cu nigro. et quomodo ipsa t iaculae i catro
i sangto. et ul catu sangtu mona cu q noiecat germa. I do platerpari
cutuueuese dedita et apardidia nos libellatp opsdi ne ipse ss douus
ptul us uerath s amodo et usq. i xx viij an septecatos. ad catiscudu
et dominandu la dictu castellu cu lam dichsacus. ua debeam nos
et nu hepedes actiete ipse iacetute medicauae de ss castello. cu ipsa
iacetute medicauae de ipsi acus de ipsi hoib q habitarur i ss castello.

The section on page 180 from the *Chronicle* (see previous page) mentioning **Montenero** and the **Zittola River** is translated from Latin into Italian and English [emphasis added in this and following sections]:

ITALIAN: Nella località di Alfedena con quest confini: la terra di Baia, la terra di Sangro, la terra di **Montenero** e come la **Zittola** entra nel Sangro e, oltre il Sangro, il monte chiamato Grema.
ENGLISH: In the locality of Alfedena with these borders: the land of Baia, the land of Sangro, the land of **Montenero** is, like the **Zittola**, enters the Sangro and, beyond the Sangro, is the mountain called Grema.

▶ Detail of verso page 331 from the *Chronicon Volturnensis*. This image is reproduced here by permission of the Biblioteca Apostolica Vaticana, with all rights reserved.

There is also mention of **Monte Nero** and **Mala Cocchiara**. These passages discuss the takeover of monastery lands by the Borrellos and the eventual return of possessions to the Abby of Castel San Vincenzo (original pages numbered 331 and 334):

> **ITALIAN:** I figlie di Borrello gia erano insorti contro i figli di Anserio, e uno ucciso con l'inganno, gli altri fatti prigionieri per garanzia, portarano via Alfedena, **Monte Nero**, Buscurri, **Mala Cocchiara**, Rionero, Cerro con Spina, Acquaviva, Tenzonoso, Licinoso, Colle Stefani e tutte le altre terre.
>
> **ENGLISH:** The daughters of Borrello had already risen against the sons of Anserio, and one killed by deceit, the others taken prisoner by guarantee, carried Alfedena, **Monte Nero**, Buscurri, **Mala Cocchiara**, Rionero, Cerro con Spina, Acquaviva, Tenzonoso, Licinoso, Colle Stefani and all the other lands.

▲ Detail of verso page 334 from the *Chronicon Volturnensis*. Third line down is the mention of Montenero and Malacocchira. This image is reproduced here by permission of the Biblioteca Apostolica Vaticana, with all rights reserved.
© 2019 *Biblioteca Apostolica Vaticana, BAV Barb. lat. 2724.*

ITALIAN: Poi con la sua apostolica autorita sottomise i tiranni sacrileghi alla sua potesta e recuperando castelli, villaggi e diverse proprieta del monastero, li restitui alla giurisdizione di quello stesso monastera, cioe il Castello di Scapoli, Fossa Cieca, i servitori, Colle Sant'Angelo, il Castello di Guado Porcino, il Castello di Fornello. Tutti gli altri possedimenti, cioe Licenoso, Colle Stefano, Tenzonoso, Cerro con Spina, Acquaviva, Rionero, **Monte Nero, Mala Cocchiara** e Alfedena, furono lasciati a loro a tale condizione che, presentati i giuramenti, e obbligando se stessi, in qualunque tempo avessero potuto trovare rifugio per loro nella zona di Valeria, li avrebbero restituiti tutti integralmente al monastero.

ENGLISH: Then with his apostolic authority he subjected the sacrilegious tyrants to his power and recovering castles, villages and different properties of the monastery, returned them to the jurisdiction of that same monastery, ie. the Castle of Scapoli, Fossa Cieca, the servants, Colle Sant'Angelo, the Castle of Guado Porcino, the Castle of Fornello. All the other possessions, that is Licenoso, Colle Stefano, Tenzonoso, Cerro con Spina, Acquaviva, Rionero, **Montenero, Mala Cocchiara** and Alfedena, were left to them on this condition that, having presented their oaths, and obliging themselves, in whatever time they could find refuge for them in the area of Valeria, they would have returned them all in full to the monastery.

During the decades while San Vincenzo was rebuilding and repopulating, great changes were occurring to the far north. As on the destabilized Italian peninsula, Germanic tribes were in conflict too. The Duchy of Saxony under Otto I grew strong as the Carolingian dynasty grew weaker. After uniting the German tribes into one kingdom, Otto I invaded Italy in 961, conquered the north, and then moved easily toward Rome. A year later he was crowned as the Holy Roman Emperor.

In the southern portion of the peninsula there was still a strong Byzantine presence. When Lombard Pandolf, the prince of Benevento, agreed to accept Otto I as the new sovereign in 967, he gained Spoleto and Camerino as fiefdoms. This brought tensions with the Byzantine Empire that claimed sovereignty over Benevento and other principalities of southern Italy. Otto I died in 973, and his son Otto II took his place as Holy Roman Emperor.

Although Otto II married a Byzantine princess, he fought to bring all of southern Italy into his empire. Byzantine and Arab resistance were significant. Otto II conquered and united the southern Lombard principalities, which were under Byzantine rule, but his campaigns came to an abrupt halt in 982 after a calamitous defeat by the Arabs on the southern Calabrian coast. Closer to their Saxon homeland, a revolt by the Slavs forced Otto II to depart Italy. His kingdom fell apart after his death in 983 at the young age of twenty-eight. Otto II's regent successors gave up on trying to subdue southern Italy.[13] Arabs returned to their marauding ways in the south, and people north of the Alps tended to their own affairs.

NORSEMEN STUMBLE INTO POWER

For non-Europeans, the mention of "Normans" is confusing. Of course they are connected to the area in France called Normandy, but some may not know their name derives from "men of the north" (Norsemen). In 911, an exiled chieftain and companions left their homes in Norway to arrive on the northern French coast, where they founded the Duchy of Normandy.

By the eleventh century, Normandy was getting overpopulated. It seems the ol' Viking spirit drove some Normans to southern lands. In 999, forty Normans decided to make a pilgrimage to the holy sites in Jerusalem. When the Norman group arrived in Italy, their objective was to reach Monte Sant' Angelo, a sacred shrine in Apulia and a practical layover on the way to Jerusalem. However, their plans were postponed when the Lombard prince of Salerno asked them to help fight the Arabs. They did their job well and soon found new opportunities in southern Italy. Others in Normandy heard that fortunes were to be made in south Italy and arrived to join forces.

The Norman band was swayed into being independent knight-freebooters. The Norman leader Rainulf Dregnot agreed to help Naples battle neighbors, and in 1013 he was rewarded with a tract of land north of Naples, which the Normans then utilized as a base. A few years later, Lombards in Apulia asked for Norman assistance in their rebellion against the Byzantines. Hundreds of Normans came to their aid and made a second base there for themselves. From their two bases, the Normans began pillaging as they wished, raping and torching as they went. Their power grew gradually as opportunities arose, starting with a victory over the pope's army. After nine months at the table, they arranged a settlement with the pope. The Normans soon created a kingdom in southern Italy which was to last over seven hundred years.

What gave momentum to the Norman grasp over southern Italy were the incessant quarrels among Lombard leaders. "Brother plotted against brother, cousin against cousin, in a seemingly endless cycle of coups and struggles for dominance among the intricately interrelated princely families."[14] Individual Lombard principalities sought Norman assistance to gain advantage over the others. They sorely lacked military leadership, a quality the Normans relished for centuries.

More knights were arriving from Normandy. One example is that eight of twelve sons of a Norman lord, Trancred Hauteville, went to Italy and made easy fortunes. Their arrival coincided with the Byzantine decision to reconquer Sicily. This only served to incite the Arabs, and, in response, numerous militia groups in south Italy organized to ward off the threat. In addition to roughly five hundred Norman knights, even Scandinavian and Russian mercenaries assisted. South Italy became strongly anti-Byzantine, and eventually the Normans took over seats of power. In Apulia, for example, a contingent of roughly three hundred Norman knights arrived with six hundred soldiers. Greatly outnumbered by thousands, how did the Normans ever think they could emerge victorious? A Norman knight punched his horse in the head, killing it at the front gate of the Byzantine fortress. This tactic of psychological warfare routed the Byzantines.

By necessity, the Norman knight-freebooters transformed into political leaders and military strategists. In order to control and protect their conquered lands, the Normans formed new fortified settlements. The eventual unification of southern Italy came after Robert Guiscard's arrival from Normandy in 1046. Because of his military prowess and personal charisma, Robert became the leader of the Normans in Italy. He skillfully conquered southern Italy piece by piece, including Sicily in 1091. His younger brother, Roger, was of great help. "Within a few years the Normans had conquered the major cities of the South and soundly defeated the three groups that had ruled the region for centuries: The Byzantines, the Arabs, and the Lombards."[15]

The Duchy of Benevento switched hands in 1078, after the last Lombard prince died, and the pope allotted the seat to Guiscard. Of particular significance to our book's focus on Montenero, the Norman settlements "seemed primarily concentrated in the areas dominated by the two great monasteries, Monte Cassino and San Vincenzo."[16] Due to the void of any significantly large cities in the Lombard Abruzzo-Molise borderland, actual political control over the region was very weak. Some Norman knights found this a great opportunity to stakeout independent holdings for themselves in accord with their strength of arms.

San Vincenzo al Volturno was located on the northern edge of the Duchy of Benevento, which borders the Duchy of Spoleto. The border area has often been under dispute and suffered from these struggles, particularly between the north and south. One of the rulers of the Italian area in the vast Holy Roman Empire, Ugo di Àrles, indirectly affected the territory of San Vincenzo. Seems he had a favored vassal named "the Frank" Bernardo, who managed to become a count in possessions of fiefs in southern Abruzzo. Bernardo started a family lineage that became a strong presence in the area.

One Bernardo relative named Oderisio I became the count of Sulmona. He married Ruta, who was the sister of the Countess of Spoleto and the sister-in-law of Pandolfo, the prince of Benevento. In part political strategy and in part familial expectation, Pandolfo gave Oderisio and Ruta the country of Pietrabbondante in 1004. Their son, Oderisio II—nicknamed "Borrello" after the area in Abruzzo where he lived—was granted the fief of Trivento in 1020 by Lombard princes of Benevento. Trivento was an important city of the region and had become the Catholic episcopal see in 940. The bishop's ecclesiastical powers covered a large area, which came to include Alfedena and Montenero. The powers of authority, both spiritual and secular, often intermingled. In the case of the family now referred to as the Borrello, the lands associated with them are often referred to as "Terra Burrellensium" or "Terra dei Borrello."

Today on Montenero lands there is a church dedicated to Saint Ilario. Perhaps it was named after Abbott Ilario, who in 1011 granted lands to descendants of a knight, the viscount of present-day Pietranseri.[17] The land concession included Alfedena and Montenero. Along came the Borrellos, who invaded the area in 1044. Under threat of death, these lands were taken over by the Borrellos. Allied with Landolfo di Capua, they conquered and sacked the monastery at San Vincenzo al Volturno. The Borrellos' grasp came to include "the abandoned settlement of Malacocchiara to the east of Montenero, and Rionero."[18] Records state the Benedictines gave Montenero to a family named Filangieri, but the Borrellos usurped it in 1064. After the power of the Borrellos had waned, San Vincenzo returned into the hands of the monks. Quiet days ensued, for we do not hear anything about Montenero or San Vincenzo until 1166. The monastery certainly became prosperous again in large part because of the new settlers, even producing luxury items such as silk.

While the Borrellos were making their mark on lands in modern southern Abruzzo and at the northern Molise border, the Normans continued to terrorize the south as individual knights tried to acquire personal wealth and land, including high mountainous areas. As Brown states, "Most of the interior was mountainous, either heavily forested or badly eroded, and in both cases unsuitable for more than subsistence agriculture. The coastal plains were underdeveloped as a result of malaria and centuries of Arab pirate raids that had driven much of the population to inland mountain towns."[19] The time was ripe for small mountain villages like Montenero to develop.

In 1051 the pope urged the Normans to stop raiding. Drogo, the politically savvy head of the Normans, "controlled the behavior of a few of his nominal barons, who had spread their private wars throughout the province of Apulia and even, to the north, into lands belonging to the state of Benevento and the Lombard gastaldts [Eng., *gastald*; It., *gastaldo*; an official in charge of a piece of the royal lands] of the Abruzzi region."[20]

Unfortunately, Drogo was assassinated and aggressions resumed. In the end, Pope Leo and his allies lost the great Battle of Civitate in 1053, giving the Normans total victory. The Norman lands were fortified for added security, but much of the southern realm remained politically fluid under expanding and shrinking influences of the Greeks, Romans, Lombards, Byzantines, and Arabs. According to Brown, "Borders were not fixed and fringe areas changed hands frequently; the rulers often controlling little beyond the areas around the major towns, and exerting their rights in the often mountainous hinterland largely through periodic tax gathering."[21] Between 1000 and the 1400s, independent city-states were formed, including the Lombard states of Benevento, Capua, and Salerno, and three others on the east coast: Naples, Amalfi, and Gaeta.

As the Norman knights continued to carve out independent holdings in southern Abruzzi, some sought out richer areas such as Sicily. They helped the Arabs fight off Byzantine invasions. As Sicily became stabilized, there were revolts in Apulia in 1065. Despite plots by the pope and other leading rulers in south Italy against the Normans, Norman leader Roger II succeeded in forging Sicily and the south into one political unit. In the Abruzzi area, the Norman knights competed with each other to seize lands, including papal lands. In the Abruzzi, "it was already clear that neither the pope nor Landulf had sufficient power or clear authority to stop the Norman expansion there."[22]

An even greater problem arose for Pope Gregory. He feared that Henry IV, king of the Germans, would invade Rome, so he sought support from Norman leader Robert Guiscard. King Henry offered Guiscard a vassalship in the Abruzzi, which Robert refused. "Robert intended to push forward, to reinforce and expand his domain by controlling more of the Abruzzi, and he considered that he needed neither the pope's acquiescence nor the emperor's license to continue his piecemeal advance."[23]

King Henry took Rome, installed a new pope, and became the Holy Roman Emperor. Although Robert Guiscard protected Pope Gregory, Rome was looted. When Robert died in 1085, barons in the Abruzzi became increasingly independent. Norman power fell to Roger II, who now found "his priority in promoting the security and prosperity of the lands he had already conquered."[24] He forbade all private war. Borders established at this time by the Normans remained until the nineteenth century. Plus, "a cultural and official eclecticism took root that would mark Norman rule for centuries."[24] The Normans should receive great respect for their evolution of political organization. In conquering Sicily, for example, they took measures to refrain from looting and gave respect to people and property.

In the meantime, the church had a different political agenda. In 1095, Pope Urban II called on all European Christians to join together in a great military campaign to reclaim the Holy Land from Muslim control. The first Crusade of 1097 was organized under the ruler of the Christian Kingdom of Jerusalem. This was followed by six other campaigns over two centuries. The sizzling consequences reverberate today.

Papal powers continued to contend with the Normans. For example, in large part in response to Muslim threat, the abbey at San Vincenzo al Volturno was relocated to a new position that afforded better defense. The pope consecrated the new abbey in 1115. However, the Norman conquest of Abruzzo in the twelfth century eventually weakened the power of the monastery at San Vincenzo al Volturno. Norman rule was strong from Abruzzo to Sicily.

By 1130, the southern mainland and Sicily were now referred to as the Kingdom of Sicily, under Roger II, who became the uncontested ruler of the Normans. "The government was among the most efficient and tolerant of its age,"[25] allowing learning and the sciences to flourish. "The rich, cosmopolitan culture that developed in the kingdom . . . distinguished it from much of the rest of Europe, and provided a bridge between east and west, north and south."[26]

Norman influence reached into the mountainous interior. "Between 1139 and 1156 a series of agreements with the papacy gave Roger control of the border region of Abruzzo and settled the borders of the kingdom with the Papal State, which then remained unchanged for seven centuries."[27] Montenero was slowly emerging during this time. As Tommaso Astarita points out:

> Under the Normans the southern landscape acquired features that are still apparent. . . . villages developed on hilltops or mountains, where they were better protected from attackers (pirates or soldiers) and the malaria that lurked in the plains. This pattern was greatly reinforced by the vast estates that grew with the introduction of the feudal system.[28]

A major factor forming the brickwork for Italy's social structure came from the Normans as they transplanted feudalism to south Italy from France. But what does feudalism entail? Being the dominating social system in medieval Europe, feudalism evolved around military service. Successful knights were usually rewarded with village land or even a group of villages. In addition, they were given titles of nobility. The noble lifestyle was supported by tenants who rented land, and lowly peasants who did all the manual labor. The relative security of the peasant to live and work on the land, and to receive a share of the produce, was in part balanced by the military protection provided by the nobles. Such a hierarchy was tied together by many hereditary obligations.

No doubt the peasants' work was grueling. Their work patterns remained unchanged for centuries to follow. According to Astarita, "Well into the twentieth century many southern peasants left their villages before dawn to reach their fields and returned home after dark. This labor and residential pattern became established in the first centuries of the southern kingdom."[29] He goes on to add that, "Even after its military function declined, feudalism continued to dominate southern society until well into the nineteenth century, and its effects have yet to disappear entirely from southern life."[30]

Nine important countdoms were in existence in Molise: Venafro, Larino, Trivento, Isernia, Campomarino, Termoli, Sangro, Pietrabbondante, and the most powerful, Boiano. In 1095 the latter was under the Norman noble Hugo I of Molhouse, from which many believe the name of the Molise region was derived. In 1144 Hugo was succeeded by Hugo II, known as the Count of Molise.

As the villages and political boundaries started to take shape during this period, some nobles governed well while others found it difficult to maintain peace and order. Protests could become violent, especially in cases where peasants were abused by being forced to live and work in overly harsh conditions. Between 1150 and 1155, for example, Mario Borrello led a revolt against the Normans. Fortunately, some villages prospered, as in the case of Montenero. In 1182 Pope Lucius III sent a letter to the Bishop Rainaldo of Isernia mentioning that a church and parish were active there. So, in addition to the religious presence stemming from the abbey at Castel San Vincenzo, Montenero had a spiritual center of its own to serve the needs of the faithful.

Many changes came during the latter half of the twelfth century. By 1176 the Normans occupied lands that for roughly six centuries had been in Lombard and Byzantine possession. They eliminated both powers from the peninsula. When Frederick I "Barbarossa" had arrived in northern

Italy from Swabia—a very large principality in southwestern Germany—his main goal had been to squelch the Normans. His progress was delayed because he was occupied in northern Italy as well as Germany, Poland, Hungary, and elsewhere. His six military campaigns pressured northern cities into submission and led him to Rome, where he was crowned Holy Roman Emperor in 1155. Frederick introduced a nonfeudal tax system by placing direct taxes on income and property. He changed the mode of currency by establishing a mint and developed the customs service.

Frederick Barbarossa died in 1190 while leading an army in the Third Crusade, proving to be one of the great medieval emperors. His son Henry VI carried on his father's hope to subdue southern Italy. While the Normans fell into political discord, Henry marched onward to Palermo and was crowned king in 1190. It took time for the Swabian rule to adapt to situations in the lower peninsula and Sicily. The Kingdom of Sicily fell into disarray for some decades, experiencing an upsurge in violence, such as the 1199 sacking of Isernia by the count of Molise. Great changes are seen in future decades after Henry's half-Norman son, Frederick II (a birth of questionable legitimacy), was crowned king of Sicily in 1212. Regardless of DNA, Frederick proved to be a great intellectual and an exceptional ruler in all of Europe.

Frederick II's influence was pervasive. Although he was also crowned king of Germany, he lived most of the time in Italy. His knowledge was highly encyclopedic, and he placed emphasis on building great continental cities, especially Naples. For example, in 1224 he established the University of Naples, the oldest public nonreligious university in the world. Its very practical purpose was "to train the legal personnel necessary to strengthen royal law and administration."[31] For maintaining political order, the evolving bureaucracy was important for growing populations in large cities as well as being capable to reach remote areas. Famous scholars such as Thomas Aquinas taught at the university.

Many credit Frederick II as being the greatest figure of the century. According to Astarita, "He arguably made the South the center of European life. Yet his reign also continued trends that damaged the southern economy. The spread of the feudal system in the countryside increased peasant subjection and dependence and reduced the chances for more innovative agriculture."[32] Again, we see strains in the feudal system resulting from struggles between rich and poor. Governing bodies certainly had their disagreements too, and violence erupted. An example of this is seen in the 1223 torching of Isernia by Frederick II's soldiers. Even the spiritual realm was shaken by the start of the Inquisition in the 1230s, established for the suppression of heresy.

Although Frederick II gave much to Italy, there were tremendous growing pains in south Italy and throughout Europe that placed numerous challenges on leaders and the populace. German lands became fragmented as the Swabian power waned, which resulted in a weakening of their rule in Italy. After Frederick died in 1250, other relatives sat on the throne, holding northern and southern lands on mainland Italy. In between were the Papal States. The papacy was feeling a pinch and declared the kingdom a papal possession. It only needed to figure out a way to enforce the decree.

Popes Urban IV and Clement IV both discussed invading Sicily with the help of the French Count, Charles of Anjou. They befriended him as a counter to Manfred (1258–1266), whose fate was to be the last Swabian regent to rule Sicily. Manfred was beaten by Charles of Anjou in the Battle of Benevento in 1266. Manfred's relative Conrad II—the actual king of Sicily living in Germany—made a strong effort to regain control of the kingdom by battling Charles at Tagliacozzo in 1268. Conrad failed. Thus entered a French influence in southern Italy with Charles having support of the pope.

During the ensuing years the feudal system spread, not only making the south poorer but forging a very polarized society and a more rural one. The Battle of Benevento also marked a political change for Montenero, which is less than seventy-five miles from the site of the conflict. The Borrello family that had dominated the village was stripped of the land when the French took over. In the late thirteenth century, Montenero became "a possession of the Collalto family, who later sold half of it to the Carafa family and the other half was donated to the Casaluce Monastery of Aversa."[33] Regardless of what noble family was in seat, peasant life in the rural villages like Montenero in the High Molise remained much the same. Daily work allowed families to live at the minimum sustenance level, with a good percentage of production going to pay taxes.

It didn't take long for the locals in the Kingdom of Sicily to resent their French sovereigns. French officials benefited by their positions in many ways, one being by heavy taxes and military service imposed on their subjects, in part to help pay for wars outside the Kingdom of Sicily. Spanish and Byzantine operatives added fuel to smoldering embers, igniting a violent rebellion. The uprising, known as the Sicilian Vespers, erupted in 1282 against the French-born King Charles, who soon lost control of the island. The rebels were successful in ousting the French, but who could replace them and successfully rule? An alternative with the papacy failed, so the rebels asked Peter III of Aragon, Spain, for help. They needed Peter III's force to counter a planned return of Charles. Repulsing Charles, Peter held ground and became the new king of Sicily. Thus enters the Spanish influence in Italy.

From the initial uprising, the War of the Vespers dragged on until 1302. The result was to break the Kingdom of Sicily into two. Even with the support of the papacy and French kings, Charles of Anjou could not regain any hold on the island of Sicily. Tensions were only resolved when Frederick—a son of Peter III of Aragon—became king of Sicily in 1295 and made significant constitutional reforms. The Spanish house of Aragon continued to rule Sicily as an independent kingdom for over one hundred years. The southern peninsular territories remained in French hands under Charles II, and this land is usually referred to as the Kingdom of Naples.

▲ Castel Nuovo (New Castle) was first erected in 1279, a main architectural landmark of Naples. It served as a royal seat for kings of Naples, Aragon, and Spain until 1815. © Mstyslav Chernov. https://creativecommons.org/licenses/by-sa/3.0

BORDERS OF MOLISE

If you wish to send a letter to someone in Montenero Val Cocchiara today, it's necessary to add that it is in the province of Isernia, in the region of Molise. We see from the previous pages that Isernia had been inhabited by Samnites and known by the Romans as Aesernia. Montenero falls under the administration of Isernia. When does the provincial name Molise come into existence? There are a few theories.

Some say the name Molise derives from the Latin word mola, which means "mill." There certainly is a similarity in pronunciation, but little logic for naming a relatively large region after a grain-grinding mechanism. Perhaps it took its name from an ancient Samnite city.[34] Another theory is much more plausible.

During Norman times, a number of knights were establishing personal strongholds in the areas we now call Abruzzo and Molise. One of the nobles arrived in 1053 from northern France. He was Rodolfo de Moulins, known in Italy as Rodolfo de Molisio. He claimed an area for himself and became the first count of Molise, which was based in the county of Boiano. The territory was divided into two:

1) Molise County (1055), being the innermost area, and
2) Loritello County (1061), the lower coastal areas.

Rodolfo's descendants expanded the territory:

[T]he boundaries of their county widened into the territories of . . . Venafro, Isernia, Trivento and part of that of Larino, creating the vast and important county of Boiano that, starting from the year 1142, for want of King Roger II of the Norman kingdom of Sicily, it was called the County of Molise.[35]

In 1140 royal authority was consolidated over southern Italy. The County of Molise was in the hands of Ugo II in 1144. A chronicle states that six years later the County of Molise was given to Norman noble Riccardo di Mandra, count from 1170 to 1196. In 1166, Riccardo's son Ruggero di Mandra followed in his footsteps. He was destined to be the last owner of the County of Molise.

When the Swabians invaded, they took over rule of Molise and slightly changed its boundaries. Their hold on Molise was lost when the French arrived. In 1270, Charles of Anjou placed the County of Molise under direct control of imperial sovereignty. After a major rebellion, Molise was placed under the administration of the *Terra di Lavoro*. The name *Terra di Lavoro* (Land of Labor) is a misnomer for an ancient tribe called the Leborini. As part of the reorganization, the Loritello (the eastern county of the principality of Benevento) was added to the Capitanata, a district seated in Foggia.

On previous pages we've seen many varied groups coming into the Molise area, either to invade or to establish residence. The area's importance was tied to travel routes through mountain passes, especially of the Matese range. As noted:

> Molise may be considered a "land of passage", a region that, in the
> course of history, has been repeatedly involved in historical events
> that have deeply affected it; a region that, partly because of this, has
> always shown a marked vocation to be a "land of castles". Towers,
> enclosing walls and castles are always associated with the territory
> in a number of ways: they control and subject it, but at the same
> time they depend upon it.
>
> The presence of fortifications in Molise is a constant feature
> throughout its history: enclosures from the Samnite age; fortified
> camps and walled cities from Roman times; [Lombard], Norman,
> Swabian and Angevin settlements, installations and defensive
> works; fortified buildings dating back to the Aragonese period.[36]

SOUTH ITALY BECOMES MORE SOUTHERN

Often Molise's boundary lines were not clear or consistent over past
centuries, but the general outline remains to this day. As part of the unified
kingdom, Molise experienced a revival that benefited the populace in
the later thirteenth century. Montenero, situated on the northwestern
Molise border abutting Abruzzo, played into the historical developments
of the region, reflecting the interchanging religious, political, and military
tides for each epoch. Entering the Avengin period of French rule from
Naples, we will see great influences taking root that came to affect the
future of Montenero and Italy.

> The decline in the political autonomy and economic vitality of
> southern cities represented a significant shift from the previous
> history of the South, and presaged later problems. In many areas
> of northern Italy the twelfth and thirteenth centuries saw the
> expansion of urban economies, the growth of civic institutions, and
> the increasing power of city interests over rural ones. At the same
> time, rural society in the South became more rigidly stratified, rural
> people became more dependent on their lords, and feudal interests
> prevailed over urban ones and dominated the kingdom's life.[37]

Although Sicily became an independent kingdom under the
Spanish house of Aragon, the Kingdom of Naples on the southern
peninsula took on the French style of government. As a capital city,
Naples had spectacular growth, becoming the largest city in Italy, with
over fifty thousand inhabitants, and a major European city noted for its

▲ *Triumph of Death* by Unknown artist, cir. 1446. Regional Gallery of Palazzo Abatellis in Palermo. Epidemics will recur regularly over the centuries.

culture and intellectual brilliance. A high point was under "the Wise" King Robert, who ruled from 1309 to 1343. He was called wise perhaps for his sponsorship of great scholars and artists, such as Petrarch. The flourishing of Naples reverberated throughout the southern peninsula.

After King Robert's death in 1343 came decades of political contentions for power among different Angevin lines. For example, the kingdom was captured a few times by the Angevin king of Hungary. In 1383, the ruling queen was murdered by her own cousin for the throne. As if these political strains were not enough, the plague epidemic, called the Black Death (1347–1350), hit Europe, killing over 40 percent of the population. In 1346 the epidemic terminated half of Montenero's estimated total population of less than two hundred, forcing the survivors to burn and abandon the village that reportedly was on the hill now known as Mount Calvario. They rebuilt on a neighboring hill, which is the present location. Astarita writes, "The losses inflicted by the Black Death and by a century or more of warfare and social and political turmoil had damaged all aspects of southern life."[38] It would take many years to recover from the terrible toll on Europe during the fourteenth century.

Detail of the Triumphal Arch at the Castel Nuovo, Napoli, commemorates the arrival
of Alfonso I to Naples in 1443. https://creativecommons.org/licenses/by/3.0/deed.en

chapter 6

Spain Transforms a Kingdom into a Colony

The Kingdom of Naples faced other internal and external problems, such as competing Angevin lines for the throne, a childless queen, murders, and politically arranged marriages. By the time of Joan II, Queen of Naples (r. 1414–1435), the political tangles were as convoluted as her promiscuous affairs. Faced with the claim to the thrown by Louis III of Anjou, she called on Alfonso, the king of Aragon in Spain, for help. Alfonso arrived in 1421 and was accepted as a liberator. The erratic behaviors of the queen soon put him at odds with her, and he left Naples only to return in 1441 to place the city under a six-month siege, utilizing the foremost artillery of the day. Within two years he had pacified the Kingdom of Naples and come to rule both Naples and Sicily.

Alfonso "the Magnanimous" was a leading figure of his time. His military campaigns took him through the Mediterranean from Spain to Egypt. In Italy during the mid-fifteenth century, his influence was profound. Besides pacifying the kingdoms of Sicily and Naples, Alfonso changed the political-social life in south Italy by building a new infrastructure and transforming the government. Moving from a time of warfare, the military barons were converted into a landowning aristocracy with both civil and criminal jurisdiction over their vassals.[1] Fiefs became tied to barons by hereditary right.

Regarding the barons' fiscal obligations, Benedetto Croce notes that in 1443, the general way taxes were collected was replaced by a tax on each family unit (hearth tax), "which the barons undertook to pay on behalf of their serfs but which was, to all intents and purposes, imposed upon the communes."[2] Many of the governmental changes were made in quest of making tax collection more efficient. By necessity, recordkeeping improved along with laws for guidance and enforcement. "Royal appointees were sent to the provinces as governors with appeals power over feudal courts and to supervise the collection of taxes."[3]

One lucky result for Montenero is a rare census record for the Sangro River Valley:

> In March 1443 King of Naples Alfonso I of Aragona ordered a tax reform, based on a per head tribute called "focatico" [hearth tax] that required a census of all the families with their members. The only books left of that census seem to be one for the Valle di Sangro [over six hundred pages] and another for Calabria Ulteriore.[4]

The list of surnames provided below is from Faraglia's 1447 census record for Montenero, which states that in the municipality there were forty-six different family groups (*fuochi*) composed of a total of 228 individuals (*anime*).

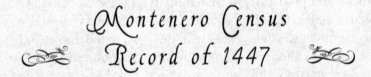

Montenero Census Record of 1447

Surnames in Latin

Antonij, Andree

Bucij, Bartholomei, Baronus

Cocci, Cerri, Cicci

Dorisii

Falzi

Ioannis, Jacobelli, Jacobi, Joannucij

Malepecie, Mariani, Marini, Mancini,

Magistri Petri, Pedis, Petrii Andree Nicolai

Rubeus

Scurcuglye

Urbandi

Zacha

Delegate Names

Latin	Translation
Dei VII eiusdem meij (deputati)	Seven deligates
Domnus amicus Cole Antonij archipresbiter	Dom friend of Cole Antonio, archpriest
Amicus Antonij Magistri	a friend of Antonio, teacher
Petri Cameraius	Pietro Cameraius
Rainaldus Petrii Andree (massaro)	Rinaldo Petrii Andree (farmer)
Cole Malepecie (massaro)	Cole Malepecie (farmer)
Petrus Mancinus	Pietro Mancini
Angelus Antonij de Acquaviva	Angelo Antonio de Acquaviva

Croce's writings indicate how people in a village like Montenero would have been subject to the nobility: "Villagers owed dues to their lords and were subject to the latter's growing jurisdictional authority, but they rarely owed labor services, they could sell their own land, and they could leave the village."[5] In theory all would benefit, but in practice there were faults in the method. The peasants were poor, and in many cases so were the feudal barons, who were usually uncooperative and ineffective when it came to fulfilling their job descriptions. "The barons never even attempted to build up a policy, foreign or domestic, for the good of the Kingdom . . . . Their concerns were strictly materialistic . . . self-interest."[6]

Taxes and rents were paid in money or in kind. The peasants worked their fields and tended their flocks to eke out a living. As part of the High Molise, Montenero relied heavily on animal husbandry. Alfonso's decision to form a bureau called the *Dogana of Foggia* facilitated work with animals, especially for the seasonal run of live-stock from one grazing ground to another along the sheep trails (tratturi): "This royal agency . . . regulated the interactions between landowners and sheep-owners and ensured the smooth working of one of the kingdom's most important economic activities, moving millions of sheep from winter to summer pastures."[7] This  agency functioned for over 350 years. In 1496, for example, there were 1,700,000 sheep to be transferred for pasturage and thus taxable. By 1580 the number had increased to 4.25 million.[8]

The latter half of the fifteenth century brought some important changes for south Italy. Before he died in 1458, King Alfonso divided his lands, giving Aragon, Sicily, and Sardinia to his brother John, and the Kingdom of Naples to his illegitimate son Ferrante (1423–1494). Ferrante soon faced war with his uncle, serious revolts of the barons, and plots from all directions. He had to rule with an iron hand. The quest for control involved both military and political actions.

▲ View of Naples in 1472.
Museo di San Martino, Naples, Italy.

Ferrante faced disruptions in Naples as well as in rural areas. He gave Benevento to the pope, but this didn't alleviate the problems festering in that fiefdom or the surrounding areas.

Rural crime was much harder to control. Bandits attacked travelers, pillaged castles and villages, and exacted protective payments from the population. These organized armed groups emerged from widespread poverty and discontent of the rural population and at times received the support of the local people. Many nobles also entertained profitable relationships with bandit groups, while the Spanish government struggled to control them. Banditry increased in times of heightened economic crisis, famine, or especially harsh taxation. The papal enclave of Benevento with its porous borders was often a haven for bandits.[9]

Abuses by the aristocracy pushed the peasants toward insurgency. To relieve pressures on them, Ferrante I issued a decree in 1466 that would check the misuses of high offices. For those involved in produce "he gave every man freedom to sell the fruits of his land without hindrance from prelates, counts, and barons, who were wont to arrogate their

purchase to themselves and fix the price."[10] In 1480, in order to facilitate internal and international trade, Ferrante declared that the only legal system of weights and measures was the one standardized in Naples.

In service sectors, we see another example of how more avenues opened up to lower classes. The number of inns and taverns grew after 1483, when a new law put an end to a monopoly previously reserved for barons. More than half of the laws written for the communes went into the books because of King Ferrante.

The mid-fifteenth century also benefited by the advent of movable type for printing and the spread of Humanist thought. This philosophy emphasized the central importance of the human over the supernatural. It elected to face the problems of the world by looking at the human condition and needs with a quest to solve problems in a rational way. The ideals of Humanism influenced intellectuals but certainly didn't bring immediate change in social conditions.

Despite all Ferrante did to help the Kingdom be more functional, destructive forces became overwhelming. In 1484 a feudal revolt flamed up against the monarchy in Naples. A year later another revolt was ignited with the spark of papal support. When Ferrante died in 1494, the Kingdom of Naples was far from stable. His death ushered in a chaotic period known as the Italian Wars—an apt description of the next sixty-five years. Most of the city-states on the peninsula were at war with each other, with major Western European and Turkish Ottoman empires also involved.

The start of the Italian Wars is seen with King Charles VIII of France, who arrived in Naples in 1495 with an army of twenty-five thousand men. The Kingdom of Naples was so weak that there was little opposition, and he was coronated that same year. Charles started to give more representative power to the commoners, but eventual uprisings by noble barons and a league of Italian rulers quickly united under the threat of Charles's rapid advance, forcing him to flee not long after his coronation. Ferrante's grandson King Ferdinand II was placed on the throne, only to rule one year. The following decades are aptly described by Benedetto Croce:

> Wars among pretenders, plundering, slaughter and devastation on the part of mercenaries, depredation by brigand bands, the betrayals of the barons, the inconstancy of the people, the continuous passage of power from one faction to another, the sudden and grandiose catastrophes which involved single persons and entire noble houses, poverty, idleness, and the last of any artistic development, a decline of morality in all classes of society, all these characteristics of the Kingdom—when it was one—gave southern Italy a bad name, though it had never enjoyed a good one.[11]

For the next sixty years the French and Spanish were the main contenders for the throne in Naples. The French eventually abandoned their interests. Spanish power was on the rise on the world stage, and in 1503 Spain took over most of the Italian southern peninsula. Its viceroys sat on the throne for the following two centuries. "The Spanish army went on to dominate military events across Europe."[12] Such a strong presence would leave a lasting imprint on the peninsula.

The sixteenth century fell under the shadow of Charles I of Spain. He's been described as a megalomaniac who brought many of his dreams to fruition by becoming king of Spain, archduke of Austria, and emperor of the Holy Roman Empire. Being no friend to Pope Clement VII, Charles sacked Rome in 1527. He eventually placed much of European lands under his rule, from Austria to Spain and the Netherlands, south to the kingdom of Naples and Sicily, and across the ocean to Spanish America.

For nearly two centuries the Kingdom of Naples was ruled through forty-six viceroys. These rulers exercised their authority on behalf of a Spanish king. The "Kingdom of Naples" was, in reality, a colony. A large number of viceroys "were conspicuous only for their ineptitude or their ability to grow wealthy at the expense of their subjects; nevertheless, in the first century of the viceroyalty, a handful stood out either for their excessive honesty, or, more usually, for their attempts to establish order and justice in the city and the southern regions."[13]

The viceroys had their hands full. By 1500 Naples's population was about one hundred thousand and growing rapidly. Beyond the common problems of urban housing, crime, and food distribution, additional dangers abounded. Turkish raids captured people in the south for sale in the slave markets of Constantinople and North Africa. Epidemics hit in 1529 and 1530, with some comfort coming from a patronage of saints and their relics, such as St. Gennaro in Naples. Barons and peasants revolted in protests, at times against religious inquisition, and more often against the burden of taxes and military service.

Plans were made for how the Spanish would administer the Kingdom of Naples. None of the new regulations would be effective without better political organization. In 1519 Charles I implemented an encompassing restructure of geopolitical boundaries. "The kingdom was divided into twelve provinces, each governed by a *preside* (governor) who commanded local military forces and who, if he had a law degree, directed the provincial *udienza*, or tribunal. The territory of each province was divided into *università*, or communities, each based on a city or village. These were the basic units of the tax and justice systems."[14]

By the end of the sixteenth century there were about fifteen hundred communities in the Kingdom. In theory, the administrative structure was set to implement the orders throughout the kingdom as directed by the viceroys. In the sixteenth century Molise was included to the province of Capitanata (Apulia).

Enter Don Pedro Álvarez de Toledo. Clearly, he was the first effective Spanish viceroy. Serving from 1532 to 1552, Toledo was a prime mover for social and economic advancements that benefited urban living conditions. These developments also helped the rest of the kingdom. He was a city builder. Under him, building and fortification projects continued for years because Spain was rich. In large part, Naples prospered in the sixteenth century because Spain grew wealthy from other ventures, such as profiting from silver mines in American colonies.

A major goal was to bring peace and order to the kingdom. Toledo ruthlessly handled defiant barons and peasants, utilizing military might and judicial means. Barons who had previously sided with the French, organized rebellions, and occupied lands were targeted. Many of them were rich and powerful. The Neapolitan nobles were believed to be among the richest in all Europe.[15] Toledo moved swiftly to take away their powers. From urban centers to the countryside, measures were made to ensure social and economic control. A bureaucratic necessity spawned a new elite of lawyers who could mold the land to fit the Spanish regime. They had a monumental task since Naples was the largest city ruled by Spain and the seat of power for the kingdom.

In order to raise the manpower to enforce the government directions, an institute of local militia was created in 1563. It called for every hundred households from all localities to support five men in arms. In the Kingdom of Naples at this time, thirty-one fortresses were manned, including the magnificent fortress in L'Aquila that was built in 1528 and today serves as a museum. Despite its intended purpose, the system of local militia was quite ineffective.[16]

Viceroy Toledo was successful in combating criminal activities in Naples proper. Outside the city, royal policies could not be enforced efficiently, mainly due to limited finances to fund such an enormous task.[17] Stemming from an earlier period of Catholic resurgence initiated in response to the Protestant Reformation, Toledo introduced the Spanish Inquisition.

"Religious conformity—and often ethnic homogeneousness—became a high priority for both Church and state."[18] Although a Humanistic philosophy was spreading to benefit some, there was a backlash against specific groups harboring superstitious beliefs and ancient pagan traditions. Gypsies, Jews, and other religious minorities were expelled from the kingdom. However, armed revolts soon tempered the zeal of the government crackdown. Benedetto Croce looks at this time of revolt in Naples against the Spanish as the "last evidence of Neapolitan independence and political vitality."[19]

By the time Don Pedro Afan de Riviera was appointed viceroy in 1559, Naples had a sprawling population of two hundred thousand. In all of Europe, it was second only to Paris. The overcrowding fostered problems related to poverty, such as crime and noise, and insufficient hygiene, food, and water—all amid growing frustrations and chaos. The dreadful crowdedness and heat of city life led to a habit for many to be outside as much as possible, contributing to a theatrical character now associated with Naples. The city was also dealing with hardships associated with famine, epidemics, and earthquakes. Life expectancy in the Mercato neighborhoods of Naples was only twenty years. In 1570, edicts were designed to alleviate some of the problems. For example, the viceroy ordered Neapolitans to sweep their streets once a week. Other edicts tried to deal with prostitution and gambling, and even prohibited the kidnapping of children by sailors who would sell them as slaves. As Astarita writes, "In 1573 an edict tried to stop an illegal racket that forced prisoners in the Vicaria [neighborhood in Naples] to buy oil for lamps at inflated prices, in one of the earliest signs of organized criminal operations."[20]

▲ Travelers attacked by brigands. The reality of outlaws being present in rural south Italy, including Abruzzo and Molise, kept many from risking travel through the fear of attack. Painting by Bartolomeo Pinelli (1817).

Outside Naples roamed many brigands—gangs leading a life of robbery and plunder. Noted brigand leader "King Marcone," for example, had a force of fifteen hundred that delivered significant losses on the Spanish soldiers ordered to stop his gang. And there was the legendary brigand of Abruzzo, Marco Sciarra. In 1585 he had an army of a thousand men. During that same year in Naples, an increase in the cost of bread caused a massive revolt against Spanish rule. In the Abruzzo area at this time, there were ten brigand groups known to be active. Mariano states that in 1682, more than 25 percent of the kingdom's bandits were in the Abruzzo area; together with Molise, it would be nearly one-third.[21]

In large part the emergence of brigands was in protest to abuse by the nobles and ignited by famines and diseases that left the peasantry impoverished and malnourished. Plague epidemics that started in 1575 continued until 1630, especially typhus that is usually transmitted by mites, ticks, and lice. Such conditions fostered banditry, particularly in the mountainous areas. In theory, the feudal barons with their private armies provided security for the peasantry from such marauding bandits.

Many of the problems facing the Spanish viceroys continued or grew worse with time. When Count Olivares Enrico di Guzmàn served as viceroy (1595–1599), he "continued in the task of battling criminality and trying to contain the demands of the barons. This viceroy managed to carry out a degree of reform and initiated a programme of rebuilding (roads, customs houses, public building, grain deposits) but, unfortunately, fell foul of the city's clerics and found himself in the middle of a war between Spain and France."[22]

Montenero Aristocrats

From the birth of Montenero on the lands of San Vincenzo al Volturno, the Borrello takeover in 1064, and the eventual return of the village to the abbey, the small population there seems to peacefully prosper for over a hundred years. Montenero took root in a feudal time when society revolved around the relationships among lords, vassals, and fiefs. In general, a king or queen rewarded prominent people with lands (fiefs) for their services, which were usually military related. A single rich, powerful noble could have a dozen or more villages and cities under his rule. In theory, the peasantry owed their allegiance, labor, and part of their produce to the overlord in exchange for military protection. Those living on Montenero land worked to serve the landowner, who usually also had other lands or fiefs under his control. What we find is that Montenero thus had ties to a number of other villages in the region, one being Agnone.

Agnone was taken over by the Borello in 1139 and became the most important center in Molise. It was a fief under such famous noble families as the Caracciolos and Carafas. So powerful were these families that many other fiefs came under their control. The Caracciolos, for example, ruled about fifty-six fiefs, including Montenero. The Carafas had eighty fiefs under their family, including Montenero. Although the surnames are different, in actuality the two derive from the same bloodline

Representing possibly the oldest of Neapolitan noble families, Giovanni Caracciolo lived in the twelfth century. His sons started to distinguish four family branches by slight name changes: Caracciolo Rossi, Caracciolo Canella, Caracciolo of Capua, and Caracciolo Carafa. The latter is associated with son Gregorio, who added "Carafa" because he held the exceptionally lucrative position of taxing wine production.[23] Purchasing a carafe of wine in a Montenero bar today should always bring this story to mind.

Andrea Carafa, a Neapolitan aristocrat and knight, purchased half of Montenero in 1365 from Robertina de Collanto. The Caracciolos, a family of French origin, took over many fiefs from the Carafa. Giovanni Caracciolo (c. 1372–1432; a.k.a. Sergianni) was a favorite of Queen Joan II of Naples. He became so powerful and rich that she turned against him, having him assassinated, stabbed by four knights. Montenero then passed into the hands of the Collalto family for a short time before going to the Cantelmo family as one of their eighteen fiefs. In 1442 the fief was under Giacomo Cantelmo.

It seems a close friend of Giovanni Caracciolo, Giacomo Caldora (1369–1439), took over a number of fiefs simply by intimidation. It was written that "he was magnanimous and never wanted to be called either Prince or Duke," although in reality he possessed enough land, money, and power to equal a king. Eventually he was forced by Queen Giovanna in Naples to give up about thirty-five fiefs. Giacomo Caldora continued to hold Montenero until Alfonso I ("the Warrior"), king of Aragon, defeated him and in 1445 placed the village in the hands of Carlo (d. 1517) and Alfonso Di Sangro.[24] One source states that Montenero Val Cocchiara was granted to Ludovico Malvezzi in April 1467.[25] If so, it eventually returned to the Di Sangro family.

The Di Sangro family held the fief until 1536, when it became the property of the Bucca family. The Bucca family had also possessed Montenero's neighboring Cerro al Volturno, Colli al Volturno, Pizzone, and San Vincenzo al Volturno. One of the descendants of this family, Ludovico Bucca, who served in the battle of Lepanto (1571), was rewarded with the title of Marquis of Alfedena by King Philip II of Spain.[26] Ludovico also took over as lord of Montenero. Both Alfedena and Montenero were eventually inherited by Lucrezia Capece.

Because Alfedena and Montenero are neighbors, there were numerous disputes over the agrarian boundaries between them. A document from 1588 concerning one such dispute mentions Ludovico Bucca.[27] Stone markers have long delineated the boundaries in and between fiefs. In Montenero's valley marsh, the pantano, stone markers indicating land ownership can be seen to this day.

Bonaminio et al. point out that "At the beginning of 1591, Montenero became a fiefdom of the Greco family of Isernia. To this family we owe the enlargement of S. Maria di Loreto church and the realization of the central altar."[28] It was recorded that in 1596 there were sixty-nine families living in Montenero. With a birthrate of four to five children per family, we can estimate the total population being about 310 individuals. Cesare Greco came to possess the village, and when he died in 1615, his son Francesco Greco inherited it. Besides being the Duke of Montenero, Francesco provided for a new refectory and dormitory for the Santa Maria degli Angeli Church in Isernia.

Upon his death fifteen years later, the fief went to his son Carlo Greco. A document in the Michele Romano Library states that Carlo briefly controlled Isernia,[29] which he sold to Diego D'Avalos from Vasto in 1644 for 28,000 ducats.

The mid-seventeenth century saw the return of the Bucca family to Montenero with Giovan Battista Bucca. After his death in 1648, his son Raniero Bucca d'Aragona (1642–1667) became Duke of Montenero. Because Raniero did not have a son, it went to his first daughter Maria Beatrice's husband, Giacomo Pignatelli. Thanks to this marriage, Pignatelli's aunt, Beatrice Bucca (1631–1688), came into possession of the fief in 1667 as the third Duchess of Montenero. She married Alfonso Carafa (1626–1668), and they had a son to inherit the fief, Giovan Battista Carafa (d. 1735), who became the sixth Duke of Montenero (1760–1762). He purchased Rionero for 17,000 ducats and became its baron. When Alfonso died, his brother Muzio Carafa (1723–1764) became the seventh Duke of Montenero and Baron of Rionero. In 1763 Muzio placed commemorative plaques in memory of his father and brother in St. George Church in the commune of Petrella Tifernina in Molise.[30] Muzio died without heirs.

Over the centuries, other noble families had a hand in Montenero's affairs. By the start of the nineteenth century, the feudal system was evolving into a more modern political system. Montenero was placed under the jurisdiction of larger centers. In 1799 the village was under Castel di Sangro and in less than ten years under Rionero, Forli, and finally under the District of Isernia.

Since land was given to many nobles who had formerly provided military service, there were often conflicts between them and government officials as well as among themselves. The allocation of property disrupted the work of local farmers. Fiefs often changed hands when nobles moved, the family line died out, or the land was simply taken by the victor in conflicts between nobles. Montenero's population toiled under the nobility and felt the effects of their political-economic dealings. A brief overview of the village's nobility offers a good example of the complex feudal system.

What does this brief overview of Montenero aristocrats actually tell us? Without getting confused by the complexity of the feudal social system, it is clear that the rich and powerful controlled lands and that peasants served them through hard labor and paying taxes. The noble families had land, money, and military power, giving them further opportunities in the political realm as well as for further economic advancement. They cemented their positions through warfare, purchase, political marriages, and social connections. Fortunes varied according to ever-changing circumstances.

In essence, feudalism worked as a business template with a relatively small number of privileged people of noble rank controlling various sizes of property and the people working the lands. For example, during the Kingdom of Naples, the capital city, of course, had the most power. But kings, queens, and viceroys were always occupied by the threats posed by dukes and others who possessed large tracts of lands. Money and power rested in the balance between the social and political connections between prominent people. Like today's business competition, nobles profited by their control of fiefs, drawing their income from the peasants' work. Each village resembled a factory with laborers producing their quota for the noble. A grand duke may have run fifty such "factories" or fiefs.

Because of their political positions, a noble house such as the Carafa placed Montenero within their overall enterprise. For example, peasants in Montenero would need to pay taxes to a marquis, who in turn paid his due to a noble headquartered in Agnone, who would be obliged to pay a share to the viceroy in Naples, and eventually to the king in Spain. During the seventeenth century, Agnone was the largest town in Molise.[31] Over the centuries, the common people living in a small village like Montenero were at the bottom of any such pyramid. They had an affinity with neighboring villages such as Alfedena, Rionero Sannitico, or Forlì del Sannio. During various times, these villages were bonded to other regional centers that included Isernia, Cerro al Volturno, Vastogirardi, Pescocostanzo, and Campobasso. It seems Montenero was never an idyllic village Shangri-la set apart from the realities of southern Italy.

The preceding overview of noble families of Montenero serves as an example of the feudal system existing in Italy over many centuries. There were many noble families, but a few stood out as families welding the greatest power and having the most influence. The highest ranked are these six, all who happened to be associated with specific city districts (*seggi*) in Naples: Carafa, Sanseverino, d'Avalos d'Aquino, Pignatelli, Caracciolo, and Orsini, who "controlled 417 communities and 32 percent of all subject vassals."[32]

The Spanish had rewarded Italians with land and offices for their services to the kingdom. Feudal lords received licenses to establish new communities.[33] As a result, the number of cities and large villages under barons greatly increased. As a ruling policy on the Italian peninsula, the Spanish did not attempt to consolidate the various territories into one realm. Perhaps they realized such a goal would be impossible to reach. Instead they sought "to construct unity in diversity and to respect the autonomy and traditional law system of each territory.[34]

It is predictable that the growing power of individual barons would come into conflict with the Spanish government based in Naples. "In 1531 out of 1,563 such communities" under the barons, "only 55 were royal cities under direct royal jurisdiction. The Spanish rulers increased the number of università [villages] to about 2000, but only 50–60 of the most important in size and strategic location were royal. . . . Then about one million out of the 4.8 million population lived in royal communities."[35] By 1557, the feudal lords controlled the lion's share of land and population. Muto presents these statistics:

> The [noble] houses with title to feudal holdings are a social body of 558 lordships corresponding to 1,592 [properties], divided among the cities, landholdings [and] infeudaled villages, for a population of 329,102 vassals, representing 78 percent of the population of the Kingdom.[36]

Some of the so-called cities under the barons were certainly small. Those with a population of under a thousand, such as Montenero with just over three hundred inhabitants, really didn't fit the definition. If we disregard those with few inhabitants, the Kingdom of Naples had about 144 cities total, with 40 percent of these around the capital of Naples.[37] The area of today's Abruzzo had about ten cities, while the Molise area only had about four. The number of communes was actually greater in previous centuries. In 1268 there were 2,356 communes, but by 1505, that number had dropped to 1,462—a difference of 894, primarily due to epidemics and warfare.

There was a tenuous balance of power between the Spanish viceroy and the barons who continued to pose a threat to political stability. We can see the government cracking down on the barons whose actions went outside the law. In one case, they "jailed a number of barons for illegally using the papal enclave of Benevento as a clearing house for illegal grain exports from the kingdom."[38] Many such conflicts occurred between those who had power and money—and those who had more power and money.

MUNICIPALITIES IN THE PROVINCE OF ISERNIA *Source: 01/01/2019 (ISTAT).*

	Comune	Residents	Surface km²	Density inhabitants km²	Altitude m s.l.m.
1	Acquaviva d'Isernia	402	13.51	30	730
2	Agnone	4,897	96.85	51	830
3	Bagnoli del Trigno	691	36.80	19	660
4	Belmonte del Sannio	708	20.32	35	864
5	Cantalupo nel Sannio	745	15.64	48	588
6	Capracotta	864	42.55	20	1,421
7	Carovilli	1,312	41.56	32	860
8	Carpinone	1,100	32.43	34	636
9	Castel del Giudice	312	14.81	21	800
10	Castel San Vincenzo	485	21.98	22	749
11	Castelpetroso	1,618	22.71	71	872
12	Castelpizzuto	159	15.39	10	836
13	Castelverrino	102	6.20	16	600
14	Cerro al Volturno	1,240	23.79	52	572
15	Chiauci	213	15.85	13	868
16	Civitanova del Sannio	920	50,47	18	655
17	Colli a Volturno	1,324	25.25	52	408
18	Conca Casale	179	14.43	12	657
19	Filignano	626	30.88	20	460
20	Forlì del Sannio	673	32.56	21	610
21	Fornelli	1,883	23.17	81	530
22	Frosolone	3,084	49.89	62	894
23	ISERNIA	21,749	69.15	315	423
24	Longano	675	27.38	25	700
25	Macchia d'Isernia	1,093	17.71	62	360
26	Macchiagodena	1,799	34.35	52	864
27	Miranda	1,011	22.15	46	860
28	Montaquila	2,332	25.45	92	460
29	Montenero Val Cocchiara	513	22,02	23	950
30	Monteroduni	2,118	37,22	57	468
31	Pesche	1,641	12.96	127	732
32	Pescolanciano	843	34.73	24	819
33	Pescopennataro	253	18.84	13	1,190
34	Pettoranello del Molise	441	15.58	28	737
35	Pietrabbondante	707	27.44	26	1,027
36	Pizzone	305	33.49	9,11	730
37	Poggio Sannita	625	25.74	24	705
38	Pozzilli	2,297	34,66	66	235
39	Rionero Sannitico	1,095	29.22	37	1,051
40	Roccamandolfi	923	53.67	17	850
41	Roccasicura	520	28,61	18	758
42	Rocchetta a Volturno	1,082	23.34	46	540
43	San Pietro Avellana	484	44.95	11	960
44	Sant'Agapito	1,443	15.93	91	547
45	Sant'Angelo del Pesco	359	15.59	23	805
46	Sant'Elena Sannita	298	14.08	21	780
47	Santa Maria del Molise	705	17,20	41	650
48	Scapoli	663	18.94	35	611
49	Sessano del Molise	717	25.32	28	796
50	Sesto Campano	2,254	35.32	64	323
51	Vastogirardi	679	60,71	11	1.200
52	Venafro	11.218	46,45	241	222

Peasantry

chapter 7

Nobles, Peasants, Rebels, and Relics

EFFORTS TO CONTROL THE BARRONS

The Spanish tried to control the barons in a number of ways, such as through intermarriages of noble families. By doing this, they had hopes of building stronger loyalty to the government. Credit should be given to this policy because, according to Dandelet and Marino, "the Spanish imperial system served to bring together families and territories from different parts of Italy in a mutually beneficial alliance that was more pervasive, peaceful, and long-lasting than any political system in Italy since the time of the Roman Empire."[1] However, those living outside the direct reach of the royal arm of government, such as in Montenero, had to bend to the individual personalities of the local barons. As Musi writes, "[A]lliances, flexible matrimonial strategies, interplay among factions, and the concentration of the representation of interests of the community in the hands of feudal lords (political mediators par excellence) conditioned local government and its relations with the central government."[2]

When Juan de Zuniga was serving as viceroy of Naples (1579–1582), he prepared the next in line for his position with some prudent counsel. He believed there were five main concerns for governing the Kingdom of Naples: 1) food provisioning, 2) administration of justice, 3) fiscal resources, 4) billeting of troops, and 5) brigandage.[3] The kingdom functioned with the help of strong arms. The threats of uprisings forced the government to allocate more than three-quarters of state expenses to the military during its early rule; by the end of the sixteenth century, due to the reduction in number of threats, that spending diminished to around one-fourth of state expenses.[4]

◀ Indianapolis Museum of Art.
Painting by François-Alfred Delobbe.

The Spanish troops also had to face incursions by Turkish pirates on the coasts of both Sicily and the Kingdom of Naples. If they had failed in warding off the Turks, the course of Italian history would have resulted in a greatly different culture in Italy in later centuries.

For centuries, pirates attacking southern Italian coastal areas were attracted to places where they could loot and abduct inhabitants. Slavery was profitable, as shown in the Barbary cities, extending from west of Egypt to the Atlantic Ocean. In 1600, there were over thirty thousand Christian slaves, of which about 65 percent were from southern Italy. At the same time, there were Muslim slaves working in southern Italy. "Until the eighteenth century, Muslim slaves were common in the region, from elite households in the capital to feudal castles in remote villages."[5] Some slaves also came from the Slavic East and sub-Saharan Africa.

Success in keeping the military and other government departments functioning rested in the viceroy's obtaining detailed information of the land and people under his realm. For the Spanish to rule properly, it was necessary to gather information on all cities, large and small. Along with the administration of the kingdom, records were maintained in order to implement taxation, in part to pay for the Spanish military activities in other foreign lands. The records also gave the viceroy and rulers in Spain a window for viewing the financial status of the barons and their holdings in the Kingdom of Naples. Professor John Marino writes the following:

▲ Two-scudi gold coin. Carlo V of Spain (1516-56).

Provisions include a *libro major* [major book] in every commune for income and expenses (both ordinary and extraordinary) and for local resolutions, a cadastral survey of individuals' goods and baronial holdings, two sets of books (one for the parish, the other for the *mastredato della terra*) of baptisms and burials to avoid the expense and labor of numbering hearths, which were counted for direct taxes and provided the largest source of revenue for the kingdom.[6]

These records would have included details about Montenero. Unfortunately, the books have not survived over the centuries. When available, the records allowed government officials to sense the pulse of the barons and the value of their lands.

During the seventeenth century in the Kingdom of Naples, "there were no less than 119 princes, 156 dukes, 173 marquises, and hundreds of counts, with titles that often did not go with a fief but were attached to mere fields and farms."[7] A great number had wonderful-sounding titles but no substance, and the peasantry despised the barons for their conceit and strong-arm tyranny.

In trying to maintain or expand their own status, barons always fell under the pressures exerted by their overseers in Naples. On a different level, the barons operating from their own self-centeredness were also often at odds with the peasantry, who lived with bare sustenance. A quote from a Venetian ambassador to Spain in 1559 gives a frank and figurative view on the numerous schisms between social layers, particularly as embroiled between the peasantry and privileged nobles: "An ancient hatred is like a poisonous disease spread throughout the whole body; if medicines or plasters soothe one affected part, the disease breaks out in another where it was least expected."[8]

In general, feudalism during the Kingdom of Naples functioned, although there were strains on the social order. It didn't take much to become dysfunctional. Some causes that brought disruption were uprisings by barons or peasants (sometimes both), earthquakes, and famine. The government tried to be prepared for such catastrophes by initiating a number of programs. An example is a program started by the viceroy in 1638 calling on all the communes to stockpile grain for emergencies.

Unfortunately, successes in some areas were met with failures in other areas. Between 1570 and 1620, foreign producers of woolen goods caused a collapse of wool production in the kingdom.[9] It took time to adapt to market changes by methods that became the norm, such as bribery. In the wool market, for example, "the sale of offices permitted the bureaucratic rise of families engaged in transhumance and linked to the interests of the sheep owner's guild, the Mesta."[10] Bandits sometimes robbed customhouses stationed to collect tolls on sheep. The government accepted no disruption to its flow of income. Military personnel was stationed to ensure that citizens met financial obligations to the state. As the Venetian ambassador Michele Suriano wrote:

> The kingdom of Naples yields revenues of a million in gold and has expenses of a million and a half. They make up the differences with grants, assessments, subsidies, new taxes and increases of old ones, confiscations, and other unusual methods. You can't imagine a method of extracting money from subjects which has not been used in this kingdom.[11]

The Spanish intervention in the Thirty Years' War (1618–1648) brought demands for money, goods, and men from the Kingdom of Naples, an unbearable burden on the people. Many wealthy aristocrats were likewise driven into poverty. Little wonder why corruption was rampant at all levels of society. "Urban disorder, rural crime, and aristocratic violence resisted repression and became almost endemic in southern life."[12]

In a number of areas, others stepped in to help where the government failed to contribute to the welfare of Naples and the kingdom. The sixteenth century saw a growth of welfare institutes to help serve the commoners. There are a number of worthy examples. The first permanent hospital was founded by Maria Long, and a convent for repented prostitutes founded by Marie de Ayerbe, the Duchess of Termoli (Molise). Many hospitals and orphanages were built and filled to capacity. Abandoned babies were cared for and given the family name Esposito (derived from *esposto*, to place outside; expose). Esposito is now the most common surname in Naples. A charitable brotherhood called the Redemption of Captives also came into existence to deal with the personal turmoil of those enslaved by pirates. To help ease financial strains among the poor, a Christian bank called the Mount of Piety offered loans at low or no interest in exchange for pawned goods.

Naples's population had doubled since 1550, reaching three hundred thousand inhabitants by 1600. It now ranked first in population among the cities of Western Europe. In the early seventeenth century, the church was burning books under strict rules of censorship. This gave way to much freer thought as the viceroy in Naples and power nobles came to support a highly intellectual and cultural environment. Splendid gardens and courtyards added to the beauty of architectural masterpieces. Various forms of art and music flourished, and Naples became known as the center of Baroque art in Europe. To honor the artists, many statues were made of famous painters who lived in the city. "By the end of the century [1600s], in fact, Naples probably became the leading school of Italian painting, and [Luca] Giordano [1634–1705] and later Francesco Solimena (657–1747) were arguably the most successful Italian painters of their generation."[13]

It was not only the rich nobility who were known for architectural works. "Religious orders surpassed noble families in their building patronage."[14] Just as used by politicians, religious orders utilized their own buildings and lands for staging events. In Naples, the flamboyant excess became an inbred trait of the people, often shocking to visitors from the outside. Under religious patronage, confraternities and guilds were formed for specific professions, such as bricklayers, barbers, weavers, and even the makers of playing cards! These organizations gave those involved a sense of identity and social solidarity.

For all the wonderful things that could be found in Naples under the Spanish, the outlook on life was stained by the poverty of the peasants and discord among those in power. This led to the well-known cliché that the city was "a paradise inhabited by devils."[15]

Because of the ever-increasing population, the government tried to expand with housing projects, but it could not allocate the funds. In the early seventeenth century, Naples experienced an economic depression, forcing the viceroys to impose higher and higher tax hikes. This followed from a crisis in Spain, which had previously dominated affairs in Europe but fell sharply into decline by 1643. French power was on the rise. France had a fleet poised in the bay of Naples in 1647 and 1648. Overall insecurity in the Kingdom of Naples led to mounting corruption. Revolts began in Palermo in 1647, then spread to Naples.

▲ Portrait of a woman by
Francesco Solimena.
Museum of Augustins, Toulouse.
Photograph by Daniel Martin.

The lower and middle classes could not bear the burden any longer and rebelled. The most famous uprising was the Revolt of Masaniello that occurred in 1647 only to be put down by the Spanish and loyal barons by the following year. The riots in Naples incited people in other areas. Astarita writes that "Authority broke down throughout the kingdom, rural areas exploded in antifeudal rebellion: peasants sacked the castles, attacked feudal agents, looted feudal property, and gruesomely killed a few nobles."[16] Because there was no real alliance between rebels in Naples and those in the provinces, the end result was anarchy. Many barons resorted to brutally suppressing their vassals from any attempt at antifeudal rebellion.

Masaniello

Drawing by
Aniello Falcone, 1647.

Tommaso Aniello (1622–1647), known by the abbreviation "Masaniello," was a fisherman turned rebel leader. His 1647 revolt in Naples "was the most dramatic crisis during the period of Spanish hegemony in southern Italy."[17] He inspired thousands to revolt and riot in the streets. His initial success was acknowledged by the viceroy with great dignity, but soon soured when Aniello started acting mad, perhaps due to poisoning. Extremists proclaimed a Neapolitan republic that ended in less than a year, when the Spanish reclaimed the seat in Naples.

How should Masaniello, the handsome hero of the people, be treated by his fellow brethren? In seemingly contradictory fashion, his life ended by decapitation. His head was given to the viceroy and his body buried separately. Then emotions led the locals to later dig up Masaniello's body to be buried respectfully with a resplendent funeral. There is a well-known statement regarding this southern hero:

"He was honored by the people like a king,
killed like a criminal,
and adored like a saint."

Spanish viceroys had to perpetually struggle with rebellious barons and peasantry. In the aftermath of Masaniello, "a ferocious repression was under way in the provinces, where armies led by feudal barons looted, burned, and killed rebels and peasants."[18] The count of Onate, who served as viceroy in the mid-seventeenth century, was noted for his role in putting down the Masaniello revolt of 1647. After the revolt he labored to help the populace by lessening taxes. He also worked to decriminalize the barons. The crackdown on the barons and peasantry continued over the next decades.

Under the viceroyalty of Marquis del Carpio (1683–1688), as Croce brings to light, "brigandage was definitely weakened in all the provinces, including the rocky fastness of Abruzzo, and because of new political and social factors, did not reappear until a century later."[19] However, some of the thoughts, emotions, and methods were to manifest in future centuries. The examples of the barons' private forces laid "the roots of Mafia-style intimidation and protection."[20]

In overpopulated Naples, the Spanish viceroys did make attempts to improve living conditions. As mentioned earlier, life expectancy was very short. On average, adults lived only into their early twenties in some neighborhoods. Basic cleanliness was a priority, so streets were widened, opened to sunlight, and swept once a week. Laws were created with hopes to forge some moral guidelines, such as prohibiting nude bathing on specific beaches and prohibiting prostitutes from vending their talents in certain locations. There were bans on gambling, although the government did start a lottery in 1672. Many of the city's vices continue today, but a few simply fazed out with time. An example would be the outlawing of kidnapping by sailors who sold children into slavery.

In addition to the regulations, a more enlightened mode of thinking was developing as a conviction in progress and science took hold in Europe. In order to learn the demographics of the kingdom, a thorough census was taken in 1669, gathering population details from the largest cities to the smallest villages. Montenero, of course, was included in the study and was found to have 1,285 inhabitants. The quest for knowledge led to the first public library being opened in Naples in 1691. A major field of learning was law, which was seen as a necessity for governing.

As the legal field grew, the medieval notions of nobility went into decline. Change was necessary—but also feared. Some of the brightest minds of the time were punished for their forward thinking. In his quest to help the masses, Carlo Antonio Broggia produced writings concerning taxes, finances, and sanitation, but he was banished as a threat to the kingdom. Pietro Giannone was simply put into prison for writing about the clergy. Toward the end of the seventeenth century, the kingdom stagnated under thought numbed by superficial and sensual drives. Historians of the time were uncritical, with the exception of Antonio Serra, who labored to find solutions for catastrophic social, political, and economic problems that flourished under the Spanish viceroys. He was thrown in jail.

As the Kingdom of Naples stagnated, the Spanish remained in power simply by withdrawing demands upon the populace. Almost all the old troubles remained, such as city crime and banditry in the mountainous areas. Regardless, during Spanish rule, Naples did become a major European capital. Unfortunately, it also sowed seeds for its own downfall. As a city, Naples could boast some great accomplishments and exhibit wonderful achievements in areas such as art, architecture, and civil development. However, the viceroys failed miserably when we look outside Naples to the rest of the country, where the majority of the population lived. In particular, those living by cultivating land and breeding animals became impoverished under feudal oppression by nobles of huge estates. Taxes collected were not used for agrarian reform. The Spanish exploited the peasantry as a source of revenue that would primarily benefit themselves.

The death blow to the Kingdom of Naples under the Spanish came about after a horrendous plague of 1656. At least half of Naples's population, the total estimated to be between four hundred thousand and 450,000 at the time, perished. The viceroy didn't do anything to improve the situation. To the contrary, his main obligation was to extract as much money as possible from the Kingdom of Naples to aid the Spanish Habsburg Empire. The economy plummeted during the second half of the seventeenth century. The southern peninsula was not only one of the most exploited areas in Europe, but it also became one of the most backward.

THE 1685 ASSESSED VALUE OF MONTENERO[21]

After the Masaniello Revolt and the plague of 1656, villages were being abandoned. Many nobles saw their feuds devalue. They obtained permission to get royal assessments of their feuds, often with the objective of selling them. A full report was done for Montenero in 1685 by Gennaro Pino, which he presented to the royal councilor Scipione de Martino.

Assessor Pino's descriptions of Montenero offer a rare glimpse of the village at such an early date. His report on the exact location of Montenero includes the mileage from a number of other cities and villages. He notes that one could enter the village through three gates: the Door of the Church (south side), Portanuova (north), and the Portella of the Palace (east). The alleyways were stony, and some were impassable on horseback.

At this time the boundaries of Montenero were clearly marked by carved stones, often in the shape of a cross. The resulting lines indicated where other fiefs began, including Brionna, Scontrone, Alfedena, and Pizzone. Every hill and dale had a name and was noted for what type of trees and plants grew on the land, be they woods or grasses.

Pino states that S. Maria del Rito was the main church and had an interior of eight chapels on the left and right. Behind the altar was a choir. Near the sacristy was a baptismal font and pulpit, and religious ritual items were of fairly high grade. One painting stood out for its quality.

Next to the church was a bell tower with four bells. An archpriest was the officiant assisted by four other priests, a deacon, and four clerics. The church in Montenero was under the ecclesiastical jurisdiction of the Cathedral of Trivento. In addition to the main church, Pino lists three other chapels: S. Maria Lambierto, S. Antonio, and S. Lionardo.

The baronial palace atop Montenero was in near ruin. In many rooms the ceilings had caved in. Pino describes the town's inhabitants as "low people," without doctors, medicine, or artists. The archpriest conveyed that there were eighty-three hearths for the population, estimated to be five hundred. Although the people dressed poorly, in general they were "in no bad appearance," with good complexion and longevity. They made abundant quality bread and had excellent water from several springs. Also plentiful for hunting were animals of "hair and feathers." Women did the weaving, spinning, and sewing. Men tended about sixty cattle, eighty horses, and three hundred goats and sheep. Wine, fruit, and other items they obtained at fairs and markets outside Montenero. Despite certain assets, living conditions were generally miserable, and only a few could afford to sleep on woolen mattresses.

Montenero functioned under the feudal system. Appointed by the noble who owned the village, a chamberlain acted as a manager of the estate. There were two majors plus a chancellor who handled the legal matters. Taxes were part of the local administration. Amounts due were adjusted according to the year's production and quality of produce.

In order to assess Montenero, Pino took into account all the factors discussed above: location, number of inhabitants ("qualities of vassalage"), quality of land, buildings including the religious structures and the baronial palace, animals, wheat and hay production, water mills, and fishing. Rents were tallied, such as the use of a water mill and farming and grazing lands. Montenero had some common lands, while parts of the territory were rented by locals, including the following:

Fulvio Bruno	Giovanni Gabriele
Angelillo de Filippo	Angelo Giolietti
Cosmo de Fiore	Giovanno Iacovazza
Sabastiano de Fiore	Benedict Orlando
Francesco de Marco	Orazio Pede
Livia de Martino	Leonardo Pellino
Pietro Antonio del Forno	Carlo Ricchiuso
Ara delli Mantiarielli	Vincenzo Sabiano
Sebastiano di Fiore	Cosmo Sansone
Vincenzo di Massa	Giovanni Battista Scalzitti

Marc'Antonio di Marco	Agostino Scalzitto
Vincenzo di Nicola	Francesco Valleo
Maiorano di Orlando	Franscesco Velotta

Assessor Pino equated value in terms of ducats, the gold coin in use at that time. The Baronial Palace, for example, was valued at 500 ducats, and the feud's value at 8,145. His report gives a lengthy list of everything of worth and arrives at a total sum for the value of Montenero: 20,729 gold ducats.

Chavarria and Cocozza let us know that "Montenero was sold in 1689 at the request of the then Duchess of Montenero, Maria Beatrice Bucca d'Aragona, widow of Giacomo Pignatelli. Thus, once the valuation was performed in 1685, the feud of Montenero was purchased by Ippolita Maria Muscettola for 18,371 ducats."[22] For reference, Pizzone sold for 15,897 (1663) and Campobasso for 70,316 (1688).

Dispersion of Relics

The crisis in the southern Italian peninsula accompanied Spain's political, economic, and military problems. In addition to disasters caused by humans themselves came natural catastrophes. Focusing on Naples, we find a number of plagues hitting the city, as happened in 1624. Vesuvius erupted in 1631, killing over three thousand people. Of even greater significance is the plague of 1656 that claimed 50 percent or more of Naples's estimated 220,000 residents, plus thousands more outside the kingdom. Earthquakes hit Naples in 1688 and again in 1694. How did the politicians respond to these earthquakes? The "government's actions proved hesitant and haphazard."[23] Would those in power be better prepared for future calamities? After the earthquake in 1694, it was noted that "No significant reform or policy shift resulted from the disaster."[24]

The crippling disasters of the seventeenth century were seen as divine punishments. With such a bleak situation in the physical world, the main comfort for people came from the spiritual realm and faith in holy powers. Individuals invoked divine forces for protection and help utilizing "incantations, potions, amulets, magic formulas, and a whole array of other methods to bring supernatural forces to bear on daily life."[25] This aspect of the human psyche was manifested in numerous ways, with the cult of saints becoming one of the most profound expressions. As intermediaries between the human and divine realms, their relics were thought to possess special powers to aid the faithful.

In the seventeenth century the Kingdom of Naples experienced a "growing number of official patron saints across the South."[26] At the start of the century, over thirty patron saints could be counted in Naples alone, including saint Thomas Aquinas. The heights of religious fervor shown in the number of dioceses can be better understood when compared with those of other countries. There were fifty-five dioceses in Spain and just over a hundred in France. Italy boasted 315. While Naples had a full arsenal of protective patron saints, relics continued to be dispersed to churches of every diocese across the peninsula into the mid-eighteenth century. During this period, the relics of 410 patron saints spiritually empowered 225 southern communities, including the transfer of Saint Clemente to Montenero. "To this day," Astarita writes, "southern popular beliefs reflect this intense search for the protection and help of divine forces."[27]

The story of Giulia De Marco serves as another example of the religious climate of the seventeenth century. She was born of a Molise peasant and a Turkish slave and was credited with mystic powers helpful when offering spiritual guidance. Giulia went to Naples in 1612 with her special gifts. She caused such a ruckus that in 1615 she was questioned under torture by authorities. She eventually "confessed to heretical views and promiscuous sexual behavior" and was jailed for life.[28] Many peasants certainly blended ancient pagan practices with Christian practices, as she did. The dark days of the kingdom caused the religious pitch to peak in the seventeenth century and mellowed by the eighteenth century's intellectual influences of rational sciences.

Austrian Rule (1707–1734)

King Charles II of Spain died in 1700. Because he was childless, there was great apprehension over who would gain control of the various Spanish territories. The War of the Spanish Succession (1701–1714) broke out between Spain and France. King Charles's closest heirs were members of the French House of Bourbon and the Austrian House of Habsburg (the main line of the Holy Roman Empire), who wrestled for control of the Kingdom of Naples. Despite conflicts and conspiracies, the Austrians came to control the kingdom under the hands of viceroys from 1707 to 1734. Horner concludes: "Nothing remarkable occurred in Naples . . . from 1720 to 1730, except earthquakes, volcanic eruptions, floods, and other destructive phenomena."[29]

King Charles

chapter 8

Spanish Attempts to Renovate the Kingdom

The Habsburgs didn't remain long in Naples. In 1734 the Spanish army defeated the Austrians and took over both the Kingdom of Naples and Sicily. The commander of the Austrian army was Giovanni Carafa, a family name we remember being associated with the Montenero fief. In the following year, King Philip V of Spain installed his eighteen-year-old son Charles VII as king of both Naples and Sicily (r. 1734–1759). Charles received a blessing from the local archbishop, Cardinal Pignatelli—another surname associated with the Montenero feud. Alfonso Carafa, the Duke of Montenero, held the post of "chamber gentleman" of King Carlo III. His duties were, "waiting on the King when he ate in private, helping him to dress, guarding the bedchamber and water closet, and providing companionship."[1] In 1743, Alfonso became commander of the provincial military regiment of Molise.

Before the installment of Charles VII, Naples did not have a resident king for 230 years. An actual king took over after two centuries of rule by viceroys. How the Kingdom of the Two Sicilies developed over the eighteenth century was largely due to Charles and his son Ferdinand IV, who ruled from 1759 to 1816, with two disruptions by the French in 1799 and from 1806 to 1815. Under the new leadership of the Bourbons, Naples experienced a metamorphosis that made it the most ostentatious city in Europe.

◀ Eleven-year-old Charles—the future king of Naples
and Sicily, and the king of Spain and the Spanish Indies.
Oil on canvas painting by Jean Ranc (1674–1735). Museo del Prado.

When Charles took his position as king, Naples was Europe's third-largest city. Its population of about 315,000 in 1742 grew to over four hundred thousand by the end of the eighteenth century. No other city in the Kingdom of Naples came close to this figure, since other cities had populations of less than twenty thousand. To rule over such a population, King Charles inherited eleven different codes of legislation,[2] illustrating a need for standardization of laws to improve equitable implementation. He continued to reform and build upon plans formulated by the Austrian viceroys. At the same time, "a check was put on the nobles by buying back fiefs and offices."[3]

A kingdom cannot be functional without practical communications with the provinces, including villages located deep in mountainous areas. Therefore, by 1741, attention was given to the road system to expand "the capital's links to the provinces."[4] A new Royal Road of Calabria was being built while existing roads to Puglia and Abruzzo were improved. The interest in the countryside was of course tied to the overall economics of the kingdom, inspiring scholarly studies in old and new areas. "Young thinkers produced concrete studies of the capital, the provinces, and economic trends."[5]

When we think of the kingdom's economy, we must take into consideration the influence of the church. The church had long possessed much tax-exempt land in the kingdom, diverting potential income from the capital. The 112,000 ecclesiastics living in the kingdom were seen as being nonproductive. Also, the quality of religious services in the provinces was far from praiseworthy. Religious practices of the rural population shocked the Jesuits. "An inquiry near Benevento in the early eighteenth century found that four-fifths of the local priests could not properly conduct the mass."[6]

Like Montenero, "many villages were remote, and their isolation posed great obstacles to the spread of new standards of piety and devotion. Missionaries and bishops found customs and emotions that struck them as violent and unchristian."[7] A missionary visiting shepherd communities wrote that the people he had visited were not too "different from the very beasts they guarded."[8]

According to Professor Astarita, "Wild rural customs were one expression of a trait that marked all of southern religion in the early modern period and beyond: its performative, dramatic aspect, apparent in peasant funeral customs as in urban processions and feasts."[9] Ancient pagan beliefs and practices remained infused in religious expression, including dramatic gestures such as pounding the chest, cutting off one's hair, lacerating the cheeks, and wailing in grief.

Professor Astarita sees a connection between religious expression and southern culture in general, as influenced by artistic passion and Catholic revival: "its theatrical fervor, its ardent faith in the supernatural, its practical search for powerful protection. These traits flourished in urban and rural settings, contributed to an artistic boom that still gives many southern cities their dominant look, and shaped southern mentality and behavior in long-lasting ways."[10] The longstanding weight of political instability, warfare, plagues, poverty, and discord of thought certainly shaped the character and behavior of the people of the southern peninsula, including their perplexing religious practices.

As the government views of the church changed, the Bourbons took action. A major change was to start taxing clerical wealth and taking over some of the lands previously under the church. The Bourbons foresaw an evolution in government in which both the presence of the church and nobles could be restrained from interfering in the governance of the kingdom. As a count of the Holy Roman Empire noted from his travels: "The people of Molise complain as bitterly as their [Abruzzo] neighbors of the abuse which some of the barons make of their feudal privileges; nor do they boast of the learning and morality of the greater part of their clergy."[11] The Bourbons were systematically weakening the powers of both the church and the feudal nobility.

The Bourbon decision to abolish feudalism came after all other Western kingdoms did so. A turning point for the old noble houses came with a law put into effect on 4 October 1740 by King Charles. The law called for a "complete fiscal and demographic survey of the kingdom: All citizens were listed by household, and all real estate, livestock, investments, and other assets were to be reported, with the goal of establishing a more accurate and fairer tax system."[12] Known as the *Catasto Onciario* (1741–1754), this land registry made it possible to implement a tax reform that ignored the old feudal structure. Nearly a decade of work resulted in over nine thousand volumes of handwritten documents. A full record was to be kept in each location being studied, and a duplicate was to be kept in a special library in Naples. Many registries were destroyed over the years, such as from bombings during World War II. Luckily for Montenero, a copy survived in Naples.

Catasto Onciario

The 1753 Tax Registry for Montenero Val Cocchiara[13]

In conducting research for this book, I ordered a digital copy of the registry for Montenero from the state archives in Naples. The cost was over $700, paid for with the thoughtful donations received through a GoFundMe page. Thanks goes to thirteen people with Montenero roots, all living in the United States or Canada, for allowing the registry to be available in the Montenero library: Fred (Mannarelli) Bove, Elizabeth (Gasbarro) Bucarelli, Amina DiMarco, Gayle (Fabrizio) Davis, Dora (DiMarco) Garcia, Marilyn Fabrizio, John (Bonaminio) Fiorenzo, Vivian Jacobozzi, Lucina (Tornincasa) Gibson, Lisa (Donatucci) Lopez, Nora (Caserta) Olds, Linn (Donatucci) Rater, Susan Presogna, and four friends.

A handwritten document of 701 pages, the *Catasto Onciario* for Montenero provides details on all inhabitants, their work, and possessions. Also included are details on political and religious individuals serving in the village, such as priests and religious establishments, and Montenerese living in other cities (Alfedena, Castel di Sangro, Naples, Pizzone, and at the Abbey in San Vincenzo in Volturno) who had financial obligations to the home village. Most of the writing is very legible, except for some pages where ink from one side of a page bled through the paper to the other side. The whole document is intact.

There are 106 households (*fuochi*) listed in the registry that show an average of 7.3 people living in each, a majority representing extended family members of grandparents, aunts, uncles, and other relatives. Mr. Giovanni Di Marco should be given a trophy for having the most people (nineteen) under his roof. The total number of individuals living in these households is 774, with only two elders living in their eighties, the eldest being eighty-five years old. Most of the heads of the households were in their forties. Their labor centered on working with grain (*graniale*), making flour in mills, farming, and animal husbandry, especially with cows and sheep. Almost all had one or more vegetable gardens.

When the registry was completed, it was signed by Mayor Fabrizio (first name illegible), Vice Mayor Antonio Iacobozzi, and other village representatives. Looking at the family names of the heads of the 106 households, Scalzitti had the most common with ten, followed by Di Marco with seven, Orlando with six, and Baltasarro [spelling uncertain], Di Luca, Fabrizio, Richiuto, and Ziroli each at four.

◀ Cover page of the *Catasto Onciario*.
State Archives of Naples.

The following list of family names shows those that could be read clearly, while there are certainly others that have questionable spellings, such as Baltasarro, Ialotta, Monocchio, and Di Manon.

Altobelli	Di Marco	Gonella	Pede
Bonaminio	Di Martino	Iacobozzi	Persogna
Cacchione	Di Nicola	Mannarelli	Pietrocerro
Calvano	Di Ninno	Martino	Ricchiuto
Caserta	Donatone	Milò	Sansone
Danese	Donatucci	Miraldi	Scalzitti
Del Forno	D' Onofrio	Narducci	Villeo
Di Filippo	Fabrizio	Orlando	Ziroli
Di Fiore	Gasbarro	Pallotto	
Di Luca	Gigliotti	Palmiero	

▼ Detail of a sample page from the 1753 *Contasto Onciario* listing the names, ages, and occupations of nineteen people living in the home of Giovanni Di Marco. State Archives of Naples.

San Clemente

Patron Saint of Montenero

The most important festival to take place in Montenero every year is held in celebration of its patron saint, San Clemente. The day is marked by a procession in and around the village, headed by the parish priest, an entourage carrying a statue of the saint, and a stream of locals and foreign visitors who have roots in Montenero. Even in foreign countries, those with ties to Montenero recognize the saint with celebrations in cities including Lorain and Chicago (United States), Toronto (Canada), and Mulhouse (France). But ask for some details about San Clemente, and most can only say that he was a martyr whose body was transported from Rome to Montenero. According to Vincent Caserta (Erie, Pennsylvania), there are two stories about the saint. Presented here are versions I adapted from translations Mr. Caserta made from Italian into English.

Saint Clemente's real name, as well as his dates of birth and death, are unknown. He was born into a rich Roman family at the end of the first century. After some schooling during his youth, he joined the Roman Legion and was promoted to the rank of officer. He was soon held in high esteem by military leaders, who made him commander of a legion.

During this period, Caligula, the emperor of Rome from 37 to 41 CE, pronounced a law that stated, "Whoever is affiliated with the Christian religion will be killed and given as a meal to the lions." In order to find out what the new religion was all about, "Clemente" dressed up as a commoner to attend a meeting featuring a Christian orator. The orator and other Christians would gather in the catacombs of Rome in order to avoid the police or legions, and to attend masses.

After having attended many gatherings in the catacombs, Clemente converted to Catholicism and began helping the Christians with financial donations and by giving advice on how they could elude authorities. Eventually someone accused him of being a Christian, and he was condemned to death by Emperor Caligula. He was put to death, but he was not given to the lions because he was Roman.

D ivi Clementis Martyris vera Icon,
cuyus ossa jacent Montenigro Vallis Cocchiariæ e Roma illuc translata anno salut
et ejus festivitas solemniter celebratur MDCCLXXVI *magno Populi concursu in Dominica 2ª*

▲ Etching of the martyr San Clemente as he rests in his casket.
Roman numerals show the year his relics arrived in Montenero: 1776.

Clemente's family reclaimed his body, embalmed it, and laid in it a crypt. After the passing of centuries, Pope Pius VI (1717–1799) proclaimed him a saint and martyr because his body was miraculously preserved and because of the assistance he provided to Christians. The sanctification probably took place in early 1776. Pope Pius VI gave him the name Clemente.

In the mid-eighteenth century, the Montenerese were intensely faithful. They greatly desired to bring a saint's body to the village, as relics were believed to possess divine powers for protecting them from any potential disasters, large and small. In order to obtain a saint who would inspire the village, a request was sent to the Vatican, and days were spent waiting for a reply. Pope Pius VI honored the request, and the body of Saint Clemente was schedule to be transferred to Montenero.

It is at this point the saint's story diverges. In one version, Saint Clemente's family planned to take his body for burial in his hometown. They laid his body on a cart pulled by a mule and started the trip. Along the way, the mule stopped and would not go any farther. Believing the mule was tired, they stopped overnight to rest. The next day, the well-rested mule still refused to move. Bending to the wishes of the mule, the family came to an agreement with the locals to leave San Clemente there. The village where they had spent the night was Montenero.

The preceding version should be recognized as an entertaining fable. There are similar tales of saints and mules that became a standard stock of folktales. One example is found in a story about another martyr. Saint Stephen was stoned to death in 36 CE. While his body was being transported from Jerusalem to Rome in the fifteenth century, the donkeys pulling the cart refused to move farther. After being beaten, a donkey began to speak, saying: "Why do you strike us with those whips? Stephen should be buried here."[14] This story is beautifully presented in a tapestry (c. 1500) in the Musee de Cluny in Paris.

Any relic would have been transported with utmost respect and caution—and delivered according to strict regulations between the Vatican and the intended destination. Records show that San Clemente's body was removed from the catacombs of San Callisto, near the Appian Way. It was among the largest and most important of the Roman catacombs, being the official cemetery of the Church of Rome. It is large enough to hold nearly a half million bodies, including the remains of sixteen popes and over fifty martyrs. The catacomb was named after the deacon Callixtus (later Pope Callixtus I) who was appointed by Pope Zephyrinus as the cemetery's administrator. Eventually the popes ordered the removal of sacred relics to the city churches. They did this for security reasons, fearing that Arabs would attack the city, desecrate the catacomb, and steal the holy relics.

There is no doubt that the body of San Clemente arrived in Montenero as planned. In 1765 an altar was gifted by G. Mannarelli, perhaps in anticipation of the saint's arrival. The village's new patron saint arrived on 6 June 1776, to the welcome of hundreds of inhabitants, as well as religious and civil authorities. The parish priest at the time was Arch-priest Severio Orlando. A great celebration was held in the parochial church of Santa Maria di Loreto. Although the church went through a reconstruction in 1744, the marble altar on which the saint's body now rests was completed in 1777, nearly a year after the saint's arrival. Since then, there has been an annual "Festa di San Clemente Martire."

In 1976 there was a special bicentennial anniversary celebration in honor of the saint's arrival in the village. Don Pasquale Maria Di Filippo (1911–1995), who served as the parish priest of Montenero Val Cocchiara from 1942 to 1992, was the main organizer of this holy event. The martyr's body had rested in a special polychrome marble altar in the Church of Santa Maria di Loreto. It was decided that he would be encased in a new casket made of metal and glass.

As a final note regarding San Clemente, we should be aware that the Montenerese of the eighteenth and nineteenth centuries had very different feelings for him than do those living in modern times. As a patron and protector of Montenero, San Clemente's presence gave spiritual and psychological support to the people of the village, helping ease their way through daily struggles. The reality was harsh. For example, in the years of 1763 and 1764, a famine devastated south Italy, bringing starvation and disease that killed two hundred thousand in the kingdom. Italy's first cemeteries came into being at this time. A devastating earthquake in Calabria occurred in 1783. It seems that the people of the south were consistently facing natural and man-made disasters. San Clemente was the one villagers could go to when no one else would help: when the nobles abused their positions, when bandits raided, when an epidemic struck or an earthquake occurred. In the earlier times, praying to the martyr came from the depths of the heart and soul.

Until the first half of the seventeenth century, the population of Montenero remained under five hundred inhabitants. The village experienced a significant growth in population in the latter half of the eighteenth century. In 1780, four years after the arrival of San Clemente, there were 1,285 inhabitants in the village. The prosperity of the village was, perhaps, a result of blessings from the saint. For sure we know it reflects some of the administrative decisions made in Naples during this period, such as building a convenient vehicular road between Naples and Isernia that was completed in 1780.

◀ June 2, 1951, celebrating the 175th Anniversary of the transportation of Saint Clemente's body from Rome. Don Pasquale Di Filippo accompanied by Don Vincenzo Rapa Di Villa from Sconctrone. *Courtesy of the Montenero V. parish.*

▲ Procession of San Clemente in 1948. Oddly enough, the priest did not participate. *Montenero V. Archive.*

▶ Pasquale Di Filippo's Communion. *Courtesy of Dominic Orlando.* Father Di Filippo, the village's spiritual leader for fifty years. *Montenero V. Archive.*

▼ Jubilee of the Children, June 2, 1951, at the foot of Mount Calvary. *Courtesy of the Montenero V. parish.*

• An annual festival for Montenero's patron saint includes a procession from the Church of S. Maria di Loreto, up and around the village to the Court, and then to the Monumentino Mariano at the base of the village. Statues of San Clemente, the Madonna of Mount Carmel, and S. Margaret —three protectors of Montenero— are featured. *Photographs by M. DeMarco, 2017.*

Photographs by M. DiMarco, 2017.

FINAL FLOURISHING OF THE SPANISH BOURBONS

Under the ruling periods of both Charles VII and his son Ferdinand IV, the Kingdom of Naples blossomed. One of the most notable achievements was the building of the Royal Palace of Caserta, with the foundation stone being laid by King Charles himself on his birthday, 20 January 1752. As a royal residence for the Bourbon kings, Caserta is close to Naples. One of the most luxurious palaces in all of Europe, it also proves to be the largest royal palace on the planet. More than four hundred slaves worked to construct the royal palace.[15] Because Caserta is a common family surname in Montenero, it is highly probable that it was adopted from the name of this location.

123

Other construction projects include the Palace of Portici (today a botanic garden of the University of Naples), the Theatre of San Carlo, and the Palace of Capodimonte (now housing one of the largest art museums in Italy). One of the oldest art schools in Italy is the Naples Academy of Fine Arts, built in 1752. The Capodimonte Porcelain Factory, built by King Charles and his wife, shows a refined taste for fine art. On a very practical level, King Charles nourished the work of skilled craftsmen, bringing work to a segment of the kingdom that was suffering from imports. In addition to the arts, other important areas were developed.

The Bourbon kings looked to the past and to the future. They started the Herculaneum Academy and began excavations at this archeological site as well as at Pompeii and Paestum. The National Archaeological Museum was constructed to house collections from these rich sites. It came to include Greek and Roman items, and more. Many find peculiar entertainment when viewing the "Secret Room," a private museum arranged by the Bourbon Monarchy to house a collection of erotic items. The majority of the artifacts were excatated from Pompeii and Herculaneum.

There was a buildup of military power when a royal naval academy was founded, supported with the establishment of an artillery factory. The study of engineering flourished and helped Naples build as a city and become recognized for its status as the vital center of the kingdom. The very first national bank was opened there in 1794. Outside the city, provinces benefited from the government's eliminating of regulations on provisioning and trade in 1788, as well as forbidding the private enterprise of charging street tolls.[16] Such changes had good effect on the small villages throughout the kingdom.

Other areas of study were flourishing too, such as medicine, law, and philosophy. Certainly rational and practical thinking was needed to solve the pressing problems of the southern peninsula. The Bourbons supported scholarship and nourished intellectual development. The best-known philosopher of the period was Giambattista Vico (1668–1744), whose writings are valuable to this day for the understanding of southern Italy. He approached history in an encompassing, organic way. His focus on the social sciences was a welcome glimpse from the feudal age into a more humanistic world. An example of this move toward humanism is the law of 1789 that abolished torture. In Naples, philosophers of the period were living in the eye of a storm that consisted of squalls of opinions about the southern Italian mentality. The words of Antonio Genovesi (1712–1769) strike to the heart of the matter:

[Reason] truly is always beautiful, but where she is not active she is yet unripe and can, if you wish, adorn men, but not be of use to them. . . . Reason is not useful until she has become practice and reality, nor can she be such until she has so spread in customs and crafts that we employ her as our sovereign rule, almost without realizing it. . . . [We Neapolitans] still love disputing more than doing. . . . A certain vanity of mind still attaches us to things more specious than useful, we still believe ourselves greater when we are admired as incomprehensible than when we are held as useful.[17]

Charles VII should be given much credit for putting pragmatic philosophy into practice. Regarding his kingship in Spain, American historian Stephen Payne wrote that Charles "was probably the most successful European ruler of his generation. He had provided firm, consistent, intelligent leadership. He had chosen capable ministers. . . [and his] personal life had won the respect of the people."[18] His talent and wisdom as a ruler were also profoundly apparent in the Kingdom of Naples. He forged a "Neapolitan nation" by building a well-organized administrative foundation, conducive to a social order rarely enjoyed under previous governing leadership.

During much of the 1740s, many European powers in the north were participating in the War of the Austrian Succession. The Spanish had been at war on a number of fronts, but their presence in northern Italy was set to remove the Austrians from dominating the area. Worried that the Austrians would overpower the Spanish and move farther south, Charles decided to send a force of Neapolitans to join the Spanish and French to help push out the Austrians. They met at the Battle of Velletri on 12 August 1744. The united forces were victorious. In part, their success should be credited to the participation of many commoners from the Kingdom of Naples. An influential intellectual, Gaetano Filangieri (b. 1752), wrote that in the war, "those who held out most courageously against the enemy . . . were from the provincial regiments, made up of peasants called only a few weeks earlier from their plows and led by Neapolitan nobles."[19]

In 1758 Charles VII departed Naples in order to succeed his brother as king of Spain. Charles abdicated his Neapolitan and Sicilian titles and put his infant son Ferdinand IV on the throne in Naples. Because Ferdinand had not reached the age of majority, a council of regency was set up with Bernardo Tanucci as Minister. Tanucci tried to bend the government according to his personal ambitions. He deliberately chose to stunt Ferdinand's talents, encouraging the boy to play sports and fritter away time rather than providing him with a good education. Ferdinand's minority ended in 1767, and Ferdinand IV took over the reign in Naples and managed to continue the work of his father.

The Kingdom of Naples was threatened by wars in the north involving the French, Austrians, Spanish, and others. There was also the French Revolution (1789–1799), which overthrew the monarchy and established a republican government. The political and social changes in France inspired movements toward dissolving absolute monarchies in favor of republics and representative democracies. It was a natural outcome that feudalism was abolished in France.

▲ Ferdinand IV on a Neapolitan silver coin (*piastra*) dated 1805.

Ferdinand was persuaded to go to war with France with hopes to reinstall the papal government in Rome. In 1798 he put together a Neapolitan army of seventy thousand men and sent them to face the French near Rome. The number of soldiers was bolstered by the conscription of peasants and criminals. Because the French counterattack was so forceful, Ferdinand and troops retreated to Naples with French forces in hot pursuit. He escaped to Sicily on a British ship. A satirist wrote of the king, "He came, he saw, he fled."[20]

Ferdinand's ship was escorted by Francesco Caracciolo, an officer of the Bourbon navy. In the face of chaos in Naples, Prince Francesco Pignatelli held the city together while in negotiations with the French. Ettore Carafa, whose mother was Margherita Pignatelli, defended Pescara for the republic. The Caracciolos, Pignatellis, and Carafas, we remember, were Neapolitan noble family names with connections to Montenero. Pignatelli signed a treaty giving the kingdom to the French. Although the people of Naples put up great resistance, the French abolished the Kingdom of Naples by proclaiming it their own Parthenopean Republic in January 1799.

Once in power, the Parthenopean Republic found itself financially weak and militarily feeble for providing any long-term government stability. As they were trying to organize their house, the Cardinal Fabrizio Ruffo arrived from Sicily to raise a counterrevolution—an "Army of the Holy Faith" formed from the peasantry, starting in Calabria. With some support by Russian and Turkish ships, Ruffo's troops united much of the land, then finally subdued Pescara and Naples, the last two Republican holdouts. In July 1799, King Ferdinand returned to Naples to reestablish his kingdom.

Because of great hostilities against anyone siding with the republic, Pignatelli had to flee to Sicily. Earlier Caracciolo had joined others in praise of the French revolutionary ideals and found work as commander of the Republican fleet. As a result, he too fell under the anti-Republican net and was put to death by hanging after a court-martial by Royalist officers. Ettor Carafa was likewise executed for defending Pescara, one of the last Republican strongholds. In the aftermath, the Kingdom of Naples was choked by oppressive measures taken to suppress any signs of rebelliousness.

By the start of the nineteenth century, France had become the dominant power on the Italian peninsula. A coalition of countries was organized to thwart the French expansion in Europe, and Ferdinand joined the group. Over the following months, French forces had victory after victory against their adversaries. General Napoleon Bonaparte had a growing reputation because of his successful campaigns. At the start of 1806, Napoleon called for an invasion of the Kingdom of Naples. Within a few months, the Neapolitan army withered away, and Ferdinand was on a ship scurrying to Sicily. Shortly thereafter, on 30 March 1806, Napoleon placed his brother Joseph Bonaparte on the throne.

AGAINST THE CURRENT

The Bourbon government had made good progress in making structural and institutional reforms. Spreading across Europe, the wave of intellectual enlightenment had reached the south. The French Revolution of 1789 proved to have a two-sided effect. Rather than keep the flow of progress, court officials in Naples became fearful of new ideas and unknown consequences. Reform work ceased and problems remained.

As mentioned earlier, the Parthenopean Republic found itself financially weak and militarily feeble; therefore, what it did accomplish in Naples did not extend far beyond the city. In 1792 Ferdinand IV established a department for the administration of communes, but it did not have enough time to produce the desired effects. The main problem was "the failure to link republican interests in the capital with provincial concerns" in time to secure the republic.[21] The government never gained control of the provinces, and the decay of the republic soon came from familiar quarters: the barons and peasantry.

The contrast between life in the capitol and life in the provinces was all too apparent. Naples was a hot spot of European tourism. Why? There was an abundance of exquisite art and architecture, the romantic bay, and the spectacular opera house. Plus the added spice to life that brought Naples fame: a lifestyle of uninhibited vulgarity, gambling, and prostitution. "Naples dominated the impressions of foreigners; until mid-century, very few dared visit the provinces, where bandits, bad

▲Giambattista Vico. ▲Antonio Genovesi. ▲Gaetano Filangieri.

roads, and few decent accommodations awaited."[22]

Any foreigner who ventured outside Naples was stunned by the poverty and backwardness of the common people. Rumor spread of the dangers of traveling in the countryside populated by savages. Small villages in the high Abruzzo-Molise certainly weren't on tourist itineraries. At this time, most villages in the southern peninsula didn't have paved roads. It was mainly the nobles who made their presence known in the countryside. They had reason to make the effort.

A large number of nobles still had their grip on lands and people. "The wealthiest ninety barons still lorded over about two million vassals, a total feudal income in the kingdom was about the same as the entire royal revenue."[23] Montenero was still subject to the political strings pulled by nobles. Following a clash between the count of Forlì and the Marquis of Acquaviva in 1795, for example, the Carafa of Traetto took over ownership of Montenero. Under such conditions, the peasantry was kept uneducated, poor, and unable to do much beyond work on their allotted lands. The reality of their life was a contrasting disparity with life in the northern peninsula. "Persistent feudal power, weak manufacturing and trade, and the dreadful poverty of many southern peasants helped to shape northern Italian views of the South."[24]

Astarita notes that the "crisis of feudal authority opened the way to the expression of violent rural animosities."[25] Peasants with the support of nobles rose up against the republic, and conspiracies festered. Even pirate raids continued throughout the south, with people either being murdered or taken captive to be rowers on ship galleys—or slaves in foreign lands such as Constantinople or numerous cities in North Africa. A contemporary living at the end of the eighteenth century witnessed that, "the populace is evermore insolent and unchecked, thieving and murderous."[26]

Impotent to solve problems in the provinces, the Republican elites feared mostly for their own safety. They feared not only rebellion but also the thoughts that would instigate any type of protest or revolt. There was the deep chasm between the peasantry and the intellectuals, and it was predictable that any subversive ideas would be quashed. There was a massive undertaking by the government to extinguish any idea or person who would threaten the republic. As noted by Professor Astarita:[27]

> Thousands of people were jailed, including 132 ecclesiastics. Thousands fled or were exiled, many were summarily killed. One hundred and twenty people were executed in Naples and 50 more in the provinces. The 120 included 13 nobles, 26 lawyers and jurists, 10 priests, 1 bishop, 6 other clerics, 16 university professors, 17 military officers, but only 7 artisans and 1 farmer.

Thus with the martyrs of 1799, a "generation of the intellectual elites was decimated."[28] In defeating the republic, the violence by those in the counterrevolution removed the very people that could have built the nation—the people Benedetto Croce called "the intellectual and spiritual flower of the country."[29]

The Dandy King

chapter 9

The French Return and the Spanish Follow

The bloody anti-French counterrevolution, assisted by the papal army and an English fleet, allowed Ferdinand IV's return to power in 1802. The French, of course, were highly agitated by this. They were also inflamed with a desire for vengeance because Ferdinand had joined England, Russia, and Austria in a coalition against France. However, when Napoleon emerged with a great victory at the Battle of Austerlitz in 1805, Austria and Russia withdrew from the coalition. The Kingdom of Naples was basically left defenseless. Ferdinand claimed neutrality only to double-cross Napoleon by allowing the British and Russian expeditionary forces to land in his kingdom.

Napoleon Bonaparte and his forces had already invaded north Italy in 1796. They forced the Austrians out of Milan and had instituted a modern political system there. Napoleon carved out the Kingdom of Italy in the northern peninsula and declared himself king. While he was off leading campaigns in Egypt and Syria, he plotted revenge against Ferdinand. In February 1806, Napoleon sent an invasion force of forty thousand under his brother Joseph. They headed south, through the Abruzzi via L'Aquila, with slight resistance. Joseph arrived in Naples and found no resistance. Instead, he was welcomed as a liberator. Ferdinand fled to Sicily along with money and valuables of the state and bank. Joseph was appointed king of Naples on 30 March 1806. After ruling for a couple of years, he was enthroned as king of Spain and therefore turned the Kingdom of Naples over to his brother-in-law, Joachim Murat (r. 1808–1815).

◄ King of Naples, known in Italian as Gioacchino Murat (1767–1815). Oil painting by François Pascal Simon Gérard, circa 1812. Private collection.

In the meantime, Napoleon was trying to consolidate areas on the northern peninsula, annexing Marche and Tuscany to the Kingdom of Italy in 1808 and occupying Rome a year later. Some priceless artifacts from the Papal States found their way into the Louvre Museum. However, tides were changing in the north. By forging a new alliance with the major partners that included Austria, Prussia, and Sweden, Russia defeated Napoleon at the Battle of Leipzig. Napoleon was forced into exile on Elba in 1814. His Kingdom of Italy was dismantled with sections going to Austria and other minor states. This was most unfortunate for Murat, whose position relied on French strength.

In 1805 Isernia was split in half by a devastating earthquake.[1] The city was built on the ridge of a hill. One side of the city crumbled from tremors. In a way, this was symbolic of Ferdinand's fall from power and the arrival of Joseph Bonaparte and Joachim Murat in 1806. French influence over the next ten years was substantial, largely in response to public protests, including demonstrations in Calabria and Abruzzo for a constitution. Such pressures succeeded in creating new institutions to give people in the kingdom ways to participate in government with greater representation. The Napoleonic Code, which was a highly organized set of laws, replaced the former chaotic system. "The French Decennio (decade) transformed administration, justice, and social and economic structures in the South."[2] Murat made many changes that affected all in the kingdom.

The major change was the ending of feudalism after its being infused in south Italian culture for seven centuries. In 1806 the kingdom was reorganized into fifteen provinces, with Molise becoming an autonomous province. Professor Astarita highlights the change: "Old feudal domains, which in many villages were open to partial use by villages as pastures, woods, or meadows, were now divided up and distributed among village residents," while "the hereditary nobility remained a prominent social group and continued . . . to occupy most leadership positions in the armed forces and in provincial administration."[3]

The reorganization affected everyone. For example, when a national military force was created, urban and provincial militias were formed to assist in maintaining domestic order and to be mobilized for national defense if necessary. To pay for the military and other expenses, a steady stream of income was assured by a uniform tax on real estate. Royal monopolies on salt and tobacco played a substantial role in providing income to the government coffers.

After making a tour of inspection in the Abruzzi region in 1807, Joseph Bonaparte reported that it was "a savage mountainous country unsuitable for agriculture, icy cold in winter and torrid in summer, populated by a people as savage in character as the landscape which surrounded them."[4] Obviously, conditions had to change. Councils and mayors now came to manage even the smallest villages. Elementary schools were created in the communes and high schools in every province, although the primary schools in communes usually included only male students.

The 1809 endeavors inspired scholarly works that were supported by the new government. Scientific research flourished in geographic studies, which helped improve mining projects. The government offices also became important for archiving data on births, marriages, and deaths—useful today for genealogical research. In summary, much was accomplished in the short time of the French Decade, particularly under Murat. "He suppressed feudalism, dissolved the all-too-powerful convents, sold crown lands, began to organize primary schools, founded universities, [and] divided the kingdom into provinces administered on similar lines to those of French departments."[5]

In reference to the Napoleonic Code of laws put in effect in 1805, we see a ramification in Montenero just five years later. In a legal document dated 12 April 1810, the municipality of "Montenero Vallecocchiara" pushed to clarify the rights of citizens to lands and water rights previously controlled by the former feudal lord, the Duke of Traetto. Even land use for grazing and the collection of dead wood was debated. In addition, annual fees paid previously to the former baron were to be terminated. To top it off, the baron was required to pay for his own use of water on his lands at "the mouth of the Pantano and Fonte di S. Sisto" to hydrate his flocks.[6] His lands were limited to what the feudal lord bought in 1685.

▶ Napoleon I writing the Napoleonic Code while being crowned by the personification of time. In terms of both law and philosophy, the influence of his code bears international significance. Painting by Jean-Baptiste Mauzaisse (1748–1844). Oil on canvas. Musee Nat. du Chateau de Malmaison, Rueil-Malmaison, France.

According to the new laws, "The location known as Vallecocchiara is a feudal domain, on which the inhabitants of the fief, without paying any fee, compete full civic uses also for reasons of trade between them. . . . The law has declared the pasture as properties of the settlers. . . . The naturally flowing water is common for everyone."[7] The above shows some of the significant changes brought about in Montenero during the French Decade. A great symbol of the social and political change is the purchase of the fief of Vallecocchiara on 6 July 1830 by three local families, Fabrizio, Gigliotti, and Martino.

THE NEOPOLITAN WAR OF 1815

After Napoleon escaped from exile on Elba and returned to France, Murat declared war on Austria on 15 March 1815. Murat established a military headquarters at Ancona with about fifty thousand soldiers with hopes that others would join his cause. They did not. The Austrians had a force of 120,000. Murat had some success until his forces met the main bulk of the Austrians just southwest of Venice. Step by step, encounter after encounter, the Neapolitan forces retreated. A turning point was at the Battle at Tolentino on 2 May 1815. To make matters worse, a British fleet was on way to Italy following their declaration of war on the Neapolitans. Murat's forces crumbled, and their morale bottomed out.

Because Napoleon returned to Paris, most of the Austrian forces were diverted for a planned invasion in France, leaving only thirty-five thousand remaining in Italy. Murat's main army retreated south, while the 4th Division, commanded by General Pignatelli-Cerchiara, had veered off in a different direction. General Frederick Bianchi, with his Austrian force of one thousand infantrymen and one thousand cavalrymen, chased Pignatelli's Neapolitan unit into the Abruzzo cities of L'Aquila, then to Popoli, Sulmona, and Roccaraso. The Neapolitan force consisted of 1,900 infantrymen. After hours of walking, Pignatelli's army finally reached Castel di Sangro and Rionero Sannitico on May 12. The next day, the two armies met near Castel di Sangro, the town where just months earlier Murat had ordered that a civil hospital be built.[8]

The best reference regarding this battle is *Castel di Sangro, 13 May: A Forgotten Battle*, by Alessandro Teti (2015), who was born in the city. His research indicates that the Neapolitan army in the field was under the command of General Michele Carascosa. For the Austrians, Matthias von Gavenda was in command on the field. They clashed in the area locals refer to as the "bridge for sheep crossings" or the "railway tollgate."[9] Today, this is just north of the junction where State Roads 17 and 83 meet. Carascosa's troops were organized in five groups. His line was north of the

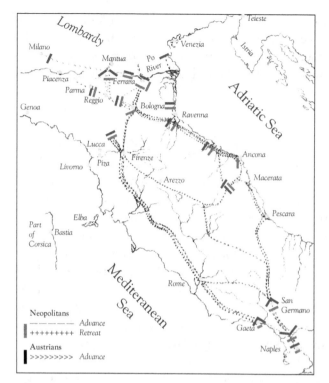

Invasion
of Italy
by Murat
May 1815

Based on an
original map of
the Neapolitan War
from *An Historical
Sketch of the
Campaign of 1815*
published in 1820.

bridge over the Zittola River (sheep crossing). Another line was located near what today is Orsini Supermarket. Three more were aligned with one just west of the Montenero railroad station, another near the Sangro River, and the last group was located just on the plain below the village of Scontrone.

The results of the battle show that the Neapolitan soldiers where overwhelmed. While it is estimated that only fifteen Austrians were killed or wounded, perhaps four hundred of the Neapolitan infantry were killed or wounded and 206 captured. The remaining Neapolitan soldiers scattered to the southwest.

As Austrian generals led their troops south, Murat was forced to flee on a Danish ship, eventually landing in Cannes, France. After planning a strategy to reclaim his kingdom, he took a ship to Calabria and landed in October. Bourbon troops caught and executed him by firing squad, putting an end to the Neapolitan War.

While Murat was in power between 1808 and 1815, he transformed the Kingdom of Naples, primarily by implementing the Napoleonic Code. The code ended feudalism and eliminated privileges of the churches and barons. He also managed to balance the budget. In Europe, as in the United States, political and social ideals were evolving, becoming more humane and egalitarian. A key to this was through education, and schools were opened for the general population. As these programs were implemented throughout Sicily and the Italian peninsula, some common threads were sewn into the minds of people, ideas that came to inspire the thoughts of a unified nation.

SPANISH BOURBON RESTORATION

After the Austrians pushed Murat out of the Kingdom of Naples, a congress was held in Vienna to formulate a peace plan out of the bloodshed associated with the French Revolution and the Napoleonic Wars. For our area of interest, Ferdinand IV was restored to power in Naples. The king was persuaded by Austrian officials to allow the Austrian military to enter the capital for security and stability. Ferdinand had the opportunity to merge the kingdoms of Naples and Sicily into the Kingdom of Two Sicilies, a reversion to political boundaries from medieval times. The two had been ruled under a common king since 1735, and in 1816 the official union materialized. Parallel to the merging of kingdoms, the individual known as King Ferdinand IV of Naples, as well as Ferdinand III of Sicily, became the sole King Ferdinand I, king of the Two Sicilies. Although he was said to rule from 1816 to 1825, it was the Austrian ambassador who was responsible for much of the administration of the kingdom. He was the figurehead of Austrian dominance.

The standards of living in the Two Sicilies suffered greatly due to disruptions brought about by wars and chronic corruption. Predictably, the discontent of the populace emerged in a series of revolts against Bourbon rule, as well as Austrian meddling. From 1800 to 1831, secret societies clustered under the revolutionary theme. Their main goal was to forge either a constitutional monarchy or a republic. A revolt in 1820 prompted King Ferdinand I to agree to write a new constitution and to establish a parliament. Although there was a growing sense that unity may be possible for the Italian peninsula and Sicily, Ferdinand did not embrace the idea. In part, he is responsible for the south's lack of participation in the vision, planning, and founding of the future united Italy.

There were notable achievements made during the mid-nineteenth century under Bourbon rule; however, these were largely due to Murat's foresight in developing educational and scientific academies. Examples include the first iron suspension bridge (1832), the first railway (1839), and the first overland telegraph cable. Naples, the second-largest European city by population, utilized gaslit lamps on the main streets (1839). The Kingdom of Two Sicilies also had the largest merchant fleet in the Mediterranean. Another praiseworthy accomplishment was that

◀ A reproduction of the inaugural train that ran on the first Italian railway section. The king opened the first 4.5 miles of the line on 3 October 1839. By the end of 1839 it had carried 131,116 passengers. Pietrarsa Museum.

the administration employed many who obtained their positions by merit.

Ferdinand I was briefly succeeded by his son, Francis I. In 1830, the grandson, Ferdinand II, filled in the royal seat. He was destined to be the last King of Naples. In the summer of 1830, groups in the northern peninsula revolted against the Austrians. Between 1848 and 1849, revolts in Sicily against the Bourbons brought the people close to independence, but in the end the Bourbon army won out. Europe was in social and political turmoil with tremors in the Italian peninsula and Sicily. Such times of turmoil are conducive to thought, and the Age of Enlightenment of the eighteenth century did serve as a directing beacon for the early nineteenth century. And with this, new leadership appeared on the Italian peninsula. Professor Frederick Artz, who specialized in philosophy from the Middle Ages to modern times, wrote:

> For nearly two decades the Italians had the excellent codes of law, a fair system of taxation, a better economic situation, and more religious and intellectual toleration than they had known for centuries. . . . Everywhere old physical, economic, and intellectual barriers had been thrown down and the Italians had begun to be aware of a common nationality.[10]

▲ Giuseppe Garabaldi visiting Alessandro Manzoni on 15 March 1862.
Painting by Sebastiano de Albertis. Civico Museo del Risorgimento, Milano.

FORGING UNITY OUT OF DIVERSITY

Before the nineteenth century, those living on the Italian peninsula, Sicily, and Sardinia had been accustomed to seeing the historical and cultural differences among themselves. Small city-states had common traits that formed bonds between the inhabitants while creating boundaries of separation from others. Each individual state had to fight for its own survival, sometimes in alliance with other states and foreign powers. Usually, when opportunities arose, those bonds would be broken in order to form alliances with others.

In the south during the Kingdom of Two Sicilies, a sound philo-sophical base was formulated for dealing with the most serious problems. One of the bright thinkers of the Neapolitan Enlightenment was Gaetano Filangieri (1752–1788), known for the masterwork *The Science of Legislation*, published in 1780. Critical of the social and political situation of the time, his book was banned. Over the centuries, the politicians in Naples had inadvertently placed a veil over the eyes of the southern population, the effect being that what people believed their social reality was proved incomplete at best—or severely distorted at worst. In understanding this haze as the true plague of south Italy, Filangieri wrote:

Man becomes used to anything. An unjust government familiarizes the spirit of its subjects with injustice, and gradually leads them to regard it without horror. Without a long habit of being oppressed, we would shudder at the sight of the evils that surround us, of the violence that overcomes us from all sides, of the dangers to which our innocence is exposed. We would try to put an end to our woes.[11]

We have looked at the many changes in the southern peninsula over hundreds of years. Usually, there is a rise to power through military might, followed by an attempt to organize an administration to establish a functioning state. When one ruling government fails, another takes its place. What is the underlying cause for reoccurring failure? Enrico Cenni (1825–1903) sensed something more fundamental than the ebb and flow of political groups. As he writes, "this history unrolls in all its essential breadth below the political catastrophes visible to the eye."[12]

Another light in the fields of philosophy and economy was Antonio Genovesi (1713–1769). He struck at the root of the southern problem, writing:

My only wish is to be able to leave my Italians a little more enlightened . . . a little more addicted to virtue, since this alone is the true mother of well-being. It is useless to think of art, trade, and government without attending first to a reform of morals. As long as men find it advantageous to be rogues, there is little to be expected from hard work.[13]

To date, it seems this aspect of life in the southern peninsula has not been given serious attention. The result is stagnation. As Benedetto Croce wrote: "We have here a history that is no history, a development that does not develop."[14] The south produced some of the best minds in Europe, but too often the great philosophers were silenced by imprisonment, sent into exile, or killed. Their words went unheeded. "But," Croce continues, "one fact must be noticed . . . that while the first germs of political virtue in our age . . . sprang up in the soil of Naples, merit has always been treated there as a crime, and fame as infamy; and this injustice has been more frequently the act of their own countrymen than of foreign enemies."[15]

From the Alps to Sicily and Sardinia, urgency called for a solution to the ongoing social and political problems. The lead toward finding a solution was taken in the north.

Risorgimento: To rise again. In the nineteenth century, a smoldering idea took light: a united Italy could rise again to the splendorous heights

▲ Alessandro Manzoni
(1785–1873).

▲ Giuseppe Mazzini
(1805–1872).

▲ Benedetto Croce (1866–1952)
was born in Pescasseroli, about
twenty-seven miles from Montenero.

once exemplified by magnificent Rome. The idea had been around for centuries, but the time seemed right when the Italian peninsula and Sicily were emerging from foreign domination and eyes were set on the future. The basic goal was to consolidate the various states into one political entity, a singular Kingdom of Italy. But how to do this? Bringing about political unity asks for social harmony as well.

By the nineteenth century, it became obvious to some that, in order to survive, it would be necessary that small states join forces with others. City-states had formed confederations. Elsewhere, confederations were fused into nations. France was the leading example of sociopolitical change, influencing all of Europe. Italian intellectuals took heed, creating a literary movement that pressed for a new ideology for freedom from foreign domination and achieving political unity.

Several key thinkers tried to broaden the consciousness and vision of the masses, encouraging the people beyond their parochial views to embrace nationhood. The initial push for a Risorgimento is usually credited to King Vittorio Emanuele of Piedmont-Sardinia and to General Giuseppe Garibaldi. They may reflect the political and military reasons for unification. Should a united Italy come under the dominant political power in the area, or under the moral guidance of the Pope, or perhaps form a democracy? Although many wanted unity, there were certainly conflicting proposals to consider.

Alessandro Manzoni's *The Betrothed* became the most celebrated literary work promoting nationalism. Other politicians and intellectuals fueled the fire of the Risorgimento, including Carlo Alberto, Camillo Benso (Cavour), Francesco Crispi, Giuseppe Manzini, Carlo Cattaneo, Nicola Fabrizi, and Benedetto Croce. They gave much for the cause, some publishing periodicals and writing books. Some were members of such secret societies as the Beams of Light (*I Raggi*) and the Carboneria, and others were forced into exile. The combined and consistent efforts put forth by those seeking unity came to fruition in 1861.

chapter 10

Quasi-Unification, Social Unrest, Emigration

THE KINGDOM OF ITALY (1861–1946)

As the Kingdom of Two Sicilies wrestled for control of itself, insurrections were occurring in leading cities in the north. There were eight states in the peninsula in 1830, each with its own unique history, dialect, and cultural tradition. By 1848, the states in the north bonded by their anti-Austrian sentiment—a factor that for prominent writers, such as Alessandro Manzoni, inspired the idea of a united Italy. A series of rebellions marked the nineteenth century in much of Europe, with the French rebellion of 1848 offering inspiration on the Italian peninsula and Sicily. In the south, first in Sicily then in Naples, tides turned against the Bourbons. In the north, Tuscany, Milan, and Venice erupted against the Austrians. This was an opportune time for the Kingdom of Piedmont-Sardinia to join the cause against Austria.

Born in Turin, Carlo Alberto was king of Piedmont-Sardinia from 1831 to 1849. He legally forged together various states in the Piedmont area with a constitution and Turin serving as the capital. He declared war on Austria, starting the First Italian War for Independence (1848–1849). His troops were supported with volunteers from the Papal Army and other northern states. Ferdinand II promised to send twenty-five thousand troops from the Kingdom of Two Sicilies. He sent a corps of only eleven thousand that arrived late. When they were crossing the Po River, they were recalled to Naples. For some unknown reason, one unit of the Bourbon military did join the Piedmont troops. They were the 10th Regiment, known as "Abruzzo."

◀ Episode from the Five Days in Piazza Sant' Alessandro (1898).
Painting by Carlo Stragliati. Museum of the Risorgimento, Milan.

The combined forces of King Alberto were formidable and brave, but they lacked any organizing ideology or military directive. Austrian forces were massive and disciplined. After many battles, the Austrians emerged victorious. King Alberto and his prime minister returned to the drawing board to plan another war with Austria. This time they found a valuable ally in France. Camillo Benso, who was the count of Cavour and usually referred to simply as Cavour, was serving as the prime minister of the Kingdom of Piedmont-Sardinia. Cavour negotiated with Napoleon III, who became a firm supporter of the independence movement in northern Italy. Along with an allied group of central states (Duchy of Parma, Duchy of Modena, Grand Duchy of Tuscany, and the Papal States), the Second Italian War of Independence was fought in 1859.

The progression of the war was going in favor of Piedmont-Sardinia. To the dismay of Piedmont-Sardinia, an early settlement was privately agreed upon by the French and Austrians. They did so because the French feared that the German state of Prussia would intervene. They signed an agreement in 1860. Excluding Venetia, much of the land previously claimed by Austria in the northern peninsula eventually went to Piedmont-Sardinia in exchange for Nice and Savoy being transferred to France. In addition, the central states (Parma, Tuscany, Modena, and Romagna) voted to join the Kingdom of Sardinia.

The dust from two wars for independence had not yet settled. One of the generals from these wars was Giuseppe Garibaldi (1807–1882). This colorful personality gained fame in wars for independence in South America and Europe. In 1849 he had moved to Rome in support of the Papal States, but he was forced out by French troops. Garibaldi's driving force was his vision of a united Italy. He was greatly disappointed when Nice was given to France for its help in the Second War for Independence. This went against his goal for unification and, because he was born in Nice, was also a sorrowful personal loss.

Where would Garibaldi volunteer to serve next? In early 1860 there were uprisings in Sicily against Bourbon rule, which had returned to power with the help of the Austrians. The Kingdom of the Two Sicilies was ripe for Garibaldi to bring it into the process of Italian unity. He set sail with only about one thousand volunteers. He landed in Marsala in May, and soon his troops swelled with local rebels. After he overcame pockets of resistance and Sicily was subdued, Garibaldi moved on to Naples, arriving in September, and King Francis II gave up his crown.

General Garibaldi was welcomed in Naples but had to face the army of the Kingdom of Two Sicilies in a number of battles occurring around the River Volturno, near Capua. The Bourbon troops achieved a narrow victory, but Piedmont forces arrived to defeat them. King Francis II had to flee. Garibaldi had faith in Vittorio Emanuele to be king of a unified Italy, so he gave Emanuele the lands he had conquered. Then Garibaldi temporarily retired to the island of Caprera.

On 17 March 1861, a newly formed Sardinian Parliament elected Vittorio Emanuele the first king of Italy, with Turin as its capital. The kingdom's administrative and legal system replaced those of the absorbed regions, bringing uniformity to all. As the capital, Turin became the center of power in the kingdom, and Piedmont became the wealthiest region in Italy. Piedmont took advantage of unification to its own benefit. Simultaneously, Naples went into decline.

▲ Giuseppe Garibaldi in Naples, 1861. *Library of Congress. CC BY 4.0*

The next target for Italian unification was the Papal States, a geopolitical entity that had existed since the eighth century with Rome as its capital. The French military stationed in Rome was instructed to maintain the independence of the Papal States from being absorbed by the Kingdom of Sardinia. There was a stalemate because Vittorio Emanuele was cautious of any possible repercussions that may have resulted from encroaching on the Papal States. His hesitation exasperated Garibaldi, who could no longer remain planting vegetables in his garden on an island. In 1862 he raised a group of volunteers, but the Italian army prevented him from going to Rome. They shot him in the foot and put him in jail.

It wasn't until 1866, when war broke out between the Austrians and Prussians, that Garibaldi returned to the field. He assisted the Italian government in its alliance with Prussia. The goal was to take Venetia from Austria in the Third Italian War of Independence. Austria lost the war, and Venetia was relinquished to Italy. The remaining objective for Italian unity became Rome itself.

In 1867 Garibaldi again attempted to conquer Rome. This time his voluntary force was overpowered by Papal and French forces. Garibaldi suffered another gunshot wound in the leg and spent some time in prison. The capture of Rome came after war started between France and Prussia in July 1870. France had to transfer its garrison from Rome to fight the Prussians. The Piedmontese army had already taken over much of the Papal States territory during the Second Italian War of Independence. Although the Kingdom of Italy claimed Rome as the new capital, it did not yet control the land. In October the Italian army entered the city and with little resistance annexed Rome and Latium to the Kingdom of Italy. Rome officially became the capital in July 1871.

TERRA INCOGNITA: "HERE ARE LIONS"

Vittorio Emanuele, the first king of Italy, was born in Turin, the son of northern royalty. On paper, the Kingdom of Two Sicilies became the Kingdom of Italy's southern region. Unfortunately, political unification does not equal social unification. It didn't take long for the new administration to realize that the plan to hold the south in its grip was like holding a hive of furious bees with one's bare hands.

In the annexed states in northern and central Italy, brigandage was extremely rare. Not so in the south. For centuries, the south had regularly experienced rebellions against governments, and brigands were especially active in forests and mountainous areas. When the Kingdom of Italy was proclaimed in 1861, the economic conditions went from bad to worse, especially for the south. The new government allowed wealthy individuals to use public lands and lands that were procured from the church. The poor were forbidden to use these lands, even when they regularly had in past centuries. They had no right to vote, as there were restrictions set by age, literacy, and income. That left only 2 percent of the population on the voting roster. Taxes were raised to help pay government debts. Plus, there was compulsory military service, which removed productive men from families and villages. The overall situation certainly contributed to lawlessness.

A hundred years earlier General Pietro Colletta reported: "In the city of Naples alone, the judicial census numbered thirty thousand thieves. Homicides, inroads of banditti, and violent acts of robbery, were frequent in the provinces; and there were so many cases of poisoning in the city, that the king instituted a . . . [Junta of Poisons], to discover and punish the delinquents. This crime was especially prevalent among women," since it was easily administered by the weak, "while the strong are more tempted to deeds of open violence."[1] By the mid-nineteenth century, brigandage and political protests reached new levels of violence.

Violent acts were committed by an assortment of individuals, including common robbers, ex-soldiers and loyalists of the Bourbons, resentful nobles, and the lazzari—the poorest of the poor. The objects of the brutality were not limited to political figures and upper-class elites. Commoners of cities and little farming villages were beaten, killed, and robbed. Disregard for the law was total. Without bounds, a single criminal act was often followed by other illegal acts. These included acts of rape, the burning of buildings and crops, extortions, and kidnappings. Brigands even attacked rival brigands.

Authorities of the Kingdom of Italy decided to take effective measures to harness the chronic brigandage in the "infected provinces." A common view held by northerners of the southerners was in line with the theories presented by Cesare Lombroso (1835–1909). He was an Italian criminologist and physician who believed that southern Italians were subhumans with inherent criminal traits. Minister Luigi Carlo Farini (1812–1866) was given the task of subduing the bandits of the south. Upon returning from Campobasso, he made the following report to Camillo Benso: "What are these countries of Molise and working land? This is Africa. The Bedouins, compared to these peasants, are flowers of civil virtue."[2]

Such negative views as expressed by Lombroso and Farini played largely into conquering the south in a brutal war. For example, southern "criminals," could have been placed in prison, as an unknown number were put into the huge Fenestrelle Fort in Piedmont, which some now call a concentration camp.

The Pica Laws of 1863 made it so anyone who gave any assistance to a brigand could be arrested. This included relatives. Because police forces in the south were totally inadequate, more than one hundred thousand soldiers were sent to bring order out of the southern chaos. Nobody will know the true totals, but thousands were arrested or killed as reported in many narratives.

Between 1861 and 1872 a number of 266,370 people including "brigands" and opponents of the regime, died as well as 23,013 Italian soldiers. 51 villages were destroyed. The new Italian State deployed against the "brigands" a number of 120,000 soldiers (a half of the whole Italian army); 7,489 carabineers, 83,927 soldiers of the National Guard, a total of 211,416 men against 135,000 "brigands" divided into 488 bands. The figures are terrific.[3]

According to Meffei, the Duke of Savoy's viceroy of Sicily, the total number of brigand groups in the Neapolitan provinces was 410.[4] Perhaps he didn't count the smallest groups, but even a small group could cause much damage. An example of the collision of forces took place in Benevento Province when thirteen brigands were executed and, in retaliation, forty-five Italian soldiers were murdered by locals. The same strong-armed repression was carried out in Sicily. One example is the manner in which forty thousand Italian soldiers quelled the Seven and a Half Days Revolt in Palermo in 1866.

There were many famous brigand leaders, both male and female. One of the noted leaders was Carmine Crocco (1830–1905). Previously he fought with Garibaldi but later turned against the new government for its failure to fulfill promises to the south. Crocco soon raised an army of two thousand volunteers and conquered lands in the south while promoting a return to the Kingdom of Two Sicilies. He blackmailed or killed a number of wealthy politicians and landowners. He took money from them and municipal treasuries only to distribute it to the poor. Some of his raids went into Molise.

Many feared brigands, and with good reason. One brigand leader, Ninco Nanco (1833–1864), was known for cutting out hearts from soldiers he captured. In his four years as a brigand, Giuseppe Carusco (1820–1892) killed 124 people. Later he switched sides, working with authorities to repress brigandage. Molise-born Michele Carusco (1837–1863) killed over a hundred soldiers, national guards, and citizens in his home province. He was caught and shot.

Brigand groups sometimes were headed by brothers and sometimes by husband and wife. Marianna Olivierio (1840–1864), who killed her own sister by hacking her forty-eight times with an ax, was a partner in arms with Pietro Monaco. Brigantese Filomena De Marco (known as Pennacchio because she wore feathers in her hat, 1841–1915) killed her husband by sticking a silver needle in his throat. She not only loved being a brigantese, but she was also a lover of brigand leaders Giuseppe Caruso, Giuseppe Schiavone, and the top brigand, Carmine Crocco. "The Lioness of the South," Michelina De Cesare (1841–1868), joined up with Francesco Guerra. She was known for her leadership skill and practical tactics utilized against the occupation forces. When finally caught, Michelina's group was massacred by soldiers. She was interrogated under torture, raped by the soldiers, and then killed at age twenty-seven.

It is undeniable that many disgusting atrocities were committed by the kingdom's soldiers as well as by the brigands of the south. The most infamous acts of the Italian soldiers are massacres in the towns of

Pontelandolfo and Casalduni. About a thousand soldiers under Colonel Pier Eleonoro Negri (1818–1887) descended on the towns, killing, looting, and burning homes to the ground. Elsewhere, a number of other villages suffered the same fate. Colonel Negri, serving under General Enrico Cialdini, was occupied executing brigands in Abruzzo-Molise. In 1861, there were about fifty-four bands in the Abruzzo-Molise area for a total of 216 men.

If we focus on the Molise area, we read in a journal that the Italian army plundered and burned a number of towns, including the following, with the number of dead in parentheses: Guaricia (1,322), Campochiaro (979), Casalduni (3,032), and Pontelandolfo (3,917).

While the army tried to systematically extinguish brigands, innocent people often got caught in the crossfire. As we know, some brigands sought refuge in "the woods of the province of Molise, where the brigands could safely conceal themselves, and baffle every effort of their pursuers."[5] A brigand leader named Giorgi was active in Abruzzo-Molise, close to Montenero. The army tracked him down in Isernia. "The sanguinary deeds of Isernia consisted of fierce conflicts between the soldiers and the lower class. The bands of Giorgi . . . were composed of the most rapacious adventurers."[5]

Montenero's population of 1,794 in 1859 was not left untouched by brigands. People of the village were in constant vigilance. At night, homes were secured. Many homes still retain heavy metal bolts, bars, and grilles for their doors and windows. The De Arcangelis home displays a superb example of what preparations were made for security. A thick oak beam was placed across the inside of the front doorway to reinforce it from any attempt to push or ram in the door. When looking toward the home from the outside, above and to the left side of this doorway there appears a small angular passage directed from inside the home toward the outside. The placement of the channel through the wall allows for positioning a rifle to defend against anyone attempting to enter through the door. Landowners could afford such security measures. Others could only resort to their hunting rifles, pitchforks, sickles, or knives.

The term "brigand" has been used to describe people acting with a variety of objectives. We must keep in mind that many were motivated by the desire for a return to the Kingdom of Two Sicilies. Others, however, were not much more than robbers and thieves. Imagine the sentiments aroused in local inhabitants when Piedmont troops arrived in Castel di Sangro, escorting King Vittorio Emanuele II on 21 October 1860, at 4:00 p.m. The king was on way to Isernia, traveling through an area noted

▲ Portrait of Vittorio Emanuele II by Giuseppe Ugolini. Museo del Risorgimento Museo del Tricolore.

for its anti-unification stance. Only one month before, Italian soldiers put down a rebellion in the area. However, the king was received with hospitality and stayed the night in "the palace of the Fiocca brothers, who were then contractors of the postal service between Pescara and Naples."[6]

Early the next day, 22 October, the king departed Castel di Sangro. A farewell gathering was organized at the bridge over the Zittola River with many attending from villages within a day's ride by horseback. Of course, leading officials, national guards, and prominent families attended. A priest from Montenero, Don Clemente Orlando, recited a sonnet suitable for the political setting. It pleased the king, who asked for a copy.

A French publication of 1902 mentions that some of the citizens of Montenero provided hay for transporting the Italian troops. In the report, Vito Di Filippo divulged that after "a few months the Piedmontese sent the money for the purchase of hay to the Municipality of Montenero, but the suppliers did not receive a lira."[7]

While King Vittorio Emanuele was escorted through Molise by the military, there were at least a dozen arrests in Montenero. Most of the arrests involved were related to activities that were pro-Bourbon or against the Kingdom of Italy. There were charges of conspiracy, murder, vandalism, theft, and threats on lives. These arrests are presented in the following list, as translated from the original documents stored in Montenero's Municipal Archive. Individuals were charged over political differences, and their cases illustrate great tensions among the citizens of Montenero.

ARRESTED
BY ORDER OF THE JUDGE OF FORLI AT THE END OF OCTOBER 1860[8]

1) **Erechia Del Forno:** charged for conversing with reactionaries from whom he received an order to be always present at the arrival of the mail courier to

prevent the Mayor from concealing the provisions of the Bourbon King, who hoped to receive something any day. When the Bourbons arrived in Isernia, he said that at least five people had to take off to Montenero. He incited the reactionaries to face the Garibaldi forces if they would enter Montenero or Castel di Sangro, showing ideas contrary to the Italian cause. He daringly called the invading General Garibaldi a thief.

2) **Pasquale Danese:** charged for conspiring with reactionaries. He was absent while participating in opposition activities. Upon return, he put the Bourbon star back on the privileged store with a picture of Francis II and burnt candles on it, animating devotion and loyalty to the Bourbons. He frequented the reactionaries and especially the Tornincasa group with whom he joined the morning proclaiming insurgencies and the killing of the Mayor and the Commander of the National Guard. On October 3, he left for Castel di Sangro to catch up with the reactionaries. While in Montenero he announced that Bourbon orders had been received to bring into force the City Guard. In fact, shortly thereafter he had a call from the deputy of Forli Sg. Rotelli who gave him the title of Urban Chief, and so he gained more influence over the plebs. He formed lists of individuals (sic) attached to the Italian cause and sent them to Germano Clemente and to Majors Liguori and Sardis in Isernia. After Garibaldini forces arrived in Rionero, he hid the Bourbon busts but assured the plebs that Francis II would always be the King.

3) **Clemente Cacchione:** charged for being armed. He was guilty of vandalism and burglaries with threats of life, especially committed in the house of Del Forno.

4) **Fedele D'Onofrio:** charged for continuing to propagate alarming news; committing thefts during the night causing damage in the homes of citizens; instigating the reactionaries to physically attack those who had been denied to deliver money due. He received the stolen objects in his own home, and tried to hide them in the house of Leonardo D'Onofrio, who, though an honest man, could not deny it for fear.

5) **Clemente Ricchiuto:** charged for being adverse to Italian principles. He plotted against the National Guard Fiorenzo Di Martino.

6) **Nicola De Nicola** and

7) **Giovanni Di Fiore di Crescenzo:** guilty of vandalism and thefts committed in the Del Forno house.

8) **Giuseppe Fabrizio:** he was among the first to promote rebellion; guilty of disarming workers; being armed and threatening the lives of people, including the National Guard Fiorenzo Di Martino. He took the Mayor inside the church, disarmed him and forced him to shave his beard.

9) **Vincenzo Di Mares:** guilty of having armed himself and of vandalism and thefts in the house of Del Forno.

10) **Nicolangelo Mannarelli:** because he strongly supported the rebellion. He committed theft and more than others threatened people with life. He was among the first of those who cried "Viva Francesco II" and animated the reestablishment of the Bourbon coats of arms. Armed, he entered the church in search of Don Beniamino Mannarelli. At night, he severely beat Martiniano Fabrizio and stole some documents.

11) **Pietro Bonaminio:** he armed himself and went with others to various homes during the night to threaten their lives. He resisted the National Guard by giving the [illegible] to the National Guard Raffaele Mannarelli, Teodoro Di Marco, and Ferdinando Mannarelli. Also at night and armed with a *scardalana* [a wood/iron comb used for separating wool] he attacked Nicolangelo Forlì in his home.

12) **Sebastiano Tornincasa:** he joined his father and was the principal author of the rebellion, proceeded with others to disarm the owners and the Guard Corps. He threatened people with their lives and beat the Rural Guard, Ascenzo Iacobozzi. In the house of Don Andrea Del Forno he stole what was said to be a silver candlestick. He also was present during the theft of the stores of Ascenzo Mannarelli. He spread news unfavorable to the Italian cause and stirred up turmoil and sought private revenge. He promoted hostilities against Vittorio Emanuele II and the Nation, extolling Francis II with the coat of arms of the Bourbons. He voiced: "My dear people of Montenero. Hurray to Francesco the King of the Two Sicilies and put down Vittorio Emanuele and the Nation."

Funeral services occurred in greater frequency in Montenero at this time. Ringing church bells announce each new death. In 1863, a new bell tower replaced the older tower originally built in 1570. No need to ask for whom the bell tolls. Death came not only to those involved in the political struggle, but also from cholera that spread when a passenger arrived in the city of Ancona on a steamship in 1865. This was part of an epidemic around the Mediterranean spread by pilgrims returning from Mecca. Montenero suffered thirty-three deaths. A few years later, more deaths came as a result of starvation.

> In 1869 there was a famine throughout the region with intermittent rains throughout the year and abundant snow in the winter months. It was a year without true seasons and without crops. Old and young died of hunger and many women aborted. In that year, taxes began to be paid to the government to rehabilitate the state budget. For the first time, the King sent free seeds (bought in America) to the peasants.[9]

▲ Cycles of Life—1932 funeral for Montenero's pharmacist Gaetano De Arcangelis. Thirty-one people in this photo, including Tommaso Procario in the center holding his hat. *Photograph courtesy of Renata Procario Hunter.*

During these periods of cholera and famine, there were still episodes of brigandage. One that touched the core of Montenero occurred in Venafro on 8 December 1870, following the Concetta Fair. Because Montenero was known for its special breed of Pentro horses, three young men—all in their thirties—took some young horses to sell at the fair. These men were Giovanni Felice, the father of Callisto Gigliotti, and an employee of the Gigliotti family. After making their sales, they started their twenty-eight-mile trek back to Montenero in the early morning. That afternoon they stopped to eat at a home owned by a friend's acquaintance. After food, drink, and chatting, the owner invited them to stay the night to have a fresh start the next morning.

They didn't get far on departure day. It seems brigands knew the three men had sold horses and had cash on hand, so they trailed them. Along the road, rifle shots killed the three Montenerese, and the brigands made off with all their valuables. This is a clear case of brigands committing murder and robbery. Perhaps brigands inspired by political motives are more honorable.

On top of a remote mountain about seventy-five miles north of Montenero there is a cluster of limestone rock slabs known as the Brigands' Table (*La Tavola dei Briganti*). It is located between the Orfento and Selvaromana Valleys in Abruzzo. Brigands and shepherds took shelter there. Some engraved their names and ideas into the stone. At the mountain refuge, isolated in an existential atmosphere, a man writes in despair on a stone table:

In 1820 was born Vittorio Emanuele II, the King of Italy.
First was the Kingdom of Flowers.
Now it is the Kingdom of Misery.

Brigandage faded, in part because of the suppressive measures taken by the Piedmont army, and in part simply because there were signs of improvement in the lives of those in southern Italy. A major development was the introduction of a railway system in the south. According to Montenero's 2018 *Festa del Ricordo*: "The results already produced by railways amply confirm all the views that had been formed of the salutary influence which they would exercise on the material as well as the moral condition of the population. . . . [T]he people have had before their eyes an obvious proof of the power of civilization."[10]

1879 EARTHQUAKE IN BOVINO

Some disasters result from human blunders. Other tragedies result by nature's fury, as shown when sixteen Montenerese died as a result of an earthquake on 25 November 1879. They had gone south for work during the winter period (November through March). Their trip was one of the annual transhumance—the shepherds' drive of sheep, cows, and donkeys to southern lands for grazing and sales. Foggia was a main destination for the trails (tratturi), but the men were staying in the village of Bovino, about eighteen miles southwest of Foggia. The city's name, Bovino, is derived from Latin *bovinus*, relating to cattle.

The men were staying at a two-story farmhouse. They were just finishing dinner and resting as the earthquake occurred. The building collapsed. Nazzaro Fabrizio, who was nearly ten years old at the time, was close to his father Nicola as the earthquake struck and remembered to have heard him gasp before he died.

An original document, dated 31 December 1879, is preserved in the parish archives of Montenero. It gives a report on this tragedy. The document was handwritten by sixty-one-year-old Archpriest Pietro Mannarelli. He recorded the names and ages of those who died, plus their parents' names. I have noted the few instances where the archpriest's writing is difficult to discern.

1) **Benedetto Scalzitti** (24 years 8 months 3 days)
   son of Domenico and Angela Maria Presogna.
2) **Biase Cacchione** (22 years 9 months 28 days)
   son of Vincenzo and Anna Laura Di Fiore.

3) **Clement Tetuan** (19 years 8 months 9 days) son of unknown father and Vincenza Di Nicola.

4) **Domenico Scalzitti** (60 years 3 months 16 days) son of Giuseppe and Barbara Gasbarro; widower of Angela Maria Presogna.

5) **Desiderio Di Marco** (57 years 8 months 16 days) son of Michele and Maria Bonaminio; husband of Speranza [spelling uncertain].

6) **Felice Pede** (48 years 8 months 23 days) son of Evangelista and Margarita Di Filippo; husband of Carmela Miraldi.

7) **Felice** [surname illegible] (24 years 1 month 14 days) son of an unknown father and Angela Presogna.

8) **Giovanni Scalzitti** (58 years 5 months 4 days) son of Giuseppe and Barbara Gasbarro; husband of Pasqua Palmieri, his second wife.

9) **Gregorio Bonaminio** (57 years 1 day) son of Lorenzo and Chiara Fabrizio; husband of Giuseppa Di Filippo, his second wife.

10) **Michele Scalzitti** (21 years 6 months 1 day) son of Giovanni and Margarita D'Onofrio.

11) **Modesto Gasbarro** (20 years 6 months 2 days) son of Giovanni and Angela Maria Riotta.

12) **Nicola Fabrizio** (22 years 1 month 2 days) son of Berardino and Angela Scalzitti; husband of Rachele Del Forno.

13) **Nicola Scalzitti** (45 years 3 months) son of Pietro and Pulcheria Iacobozzi; husband of Giovanna Fabrizio.

14) **Pietro Palmieri** (45 years 3 months 2 days) son of Valentino and Serafina Di Fiore; husband of Clementina Manocchio.

15) **Pietro Pallotto** (36 years 5 months 1 day) son of Antonino and Cristina D'Onofrio; husband of Marta Di Marco.

16) **Vincenzo Orlando** (19 years 7 months) son of Carmine and Donata Donatucci.

Main Shephard Trails

— L'Aquila – Foggia

— Centurelle – Montesecco

— Celano – Foggia

— Pescasseroli – Candela

— Castel di Sangro – Lucera

Archpriest Pietro Mannarelli notes that he had proposed having a Holy Mass, parade and funeral for the departed on December 10, 1879. It was "unanimously accepted by all the priests of the clergy and welcomed by the citizens."

Many in southern Italy suffered from periodic earthquakes, epidemics, and famines, in addition to the arrival of Piedmont soldiers. In 1884, a few years after the earthquake tragedy in Bovina, another serious cholera epidemic hit Naples and spread to Molise. In Montenero there were fifty-eight victims. Their ordeals were not the result of just one cause, but they were brought about by the volatile synergy of factors. The most reasonable and rapid solution for delivering people from the hardships of the south was emigration.

EMIGRATION

After unification, life became unbearable for most in southern Italy. If one looked around, it was as if being in a house that was burning down on all sides. There was only one reaction: flee if possible. From 1880 to 1915, an estimated thirteen million Italians migrated out of Italy, making Italy the scene of the largest voluntary emigration in recorded world history. Four million made the long trip by boat to the United States. To alleviate some of the economic pressures in the south, the Italian government encouraged emigration, with about 85 percent of the emigrants leaving from the south. The year 1913 recorded the strongest emigration with 560,000 southerners leaving Italy for the United States and another 313,000 going to northern European countries.

The earliest emigrants helped pave the way for others to follow. They helped each other find work and a place to live, and to adapt to a new location, be it in north Italy or in a new country. Montenerese found solace in Italian communities around the world, including Erie, Pennsylvania; Chicago, Illinois; Cleveland and Lorain, Ohio; and New York. Italians also relocated en masse to Toronto, Canada; Mulhouse and Paris, France; Lörrach, Germany; Buenos Aires, Argentina; Santiago, Chile; Caracas, Venezuela; and Belgium. Decades later, the children, grandchildren, and great-grandchildren spread out to other cities and countries. Communication with those in Montenero became easier when a government telegraph office became available in August 1905.

The individual stories of every emigrant from Montenero are fascinating, filled with adventures, struggles, and successes. For many decades there were strong ties between the Old Country and the new. Many sent money and goods to relatives in Italy. Almost half of those who lived abroad worked to save money so they could return to their place of birth. Separation of relatives brought awareness of a daily longing for loved ones and, for the emigrant, thoughts of familiar sights and sounds of the village.

Born in Montenero in 1883, Marco Tenne had a unique story to tell his children. His son Roland Tenne (1930–2017) was also born in

▲ Certificate of Citizenship for my Grandmother, Lucia (Caserta) DiMarco dated 1939. She always respected her tutor for the citizenship examination. Because she never attended school, she was very proud of her accomplishment.

Montenero but moved to Chicago in 1935 with his mother Emerinziana and siblings Asunta and Emilio. Roland recounted the story of a stranger from north Italy who came to Montenero in 1835. Why or for what reason he came to the village has been forgotten—or not discussed with others. We do know that he was a doctor who took up with one of the local girls (we don't know her name), and she became pregnant. She kept it a secret. Marco explained that it would have been easy to conceal a pregnancy, as the clothing style for women in those days was wide and loose fitting.

A baby boy was born. That night, just after the birth, the young lady walked north to the top of a hill above the village. She found an ideal spot at the side of the road to leave the baby. The placement would surely be in clear view of anyone passing by on the way to work the fields in the morning. As expected, the baby was found and taken to the municipal office and, for registration purposes, was given the name of Marco Tenne. The road where the baby was found has since been known as La Via del Tenne.

Marco Tenne (b. 1835) marks the first of the surname Tenne in Montenero. Twenty-four years later he had a son Francesco (b. 1859), who had a son twenty-four years later named Marco (b. 1883). Today, there are many related to Marco Tenne I. From Montenero roots, the Tenne name can be found in Chicago, Boise, and Seattle. From those decades of hardship in the village, we see an example of one family that prospered in a new country, inspired by their Italian roots.

▲ Tenne memorial in a Boise, Idaho, cemetery, includes Montenero's village emblem.
Inspired by his roots, the Roland Tenne Family knows the value of
"love, loyalty, and friendship." *Courtesy of the R. Tenne Family.*

BATTLES NEAR AND FAR

The effects of quasi-unification, social unrest, and emigration could be seen and felt in Montenero. So dysfunctional had the village become that on 16 July 1886 the Provincial Committee of Campobasso passed a resolution to disestablish the "Congregation of Charity of the Municipality of Montenero Valcocchiaro following serious irregularities and abuses found in its administration; Considered that, depending on such abuses, criminal proceedings were started against some of the administrators of said Congregation."[11]

By 5 September, an Extraordinary Delegate was selected by the province prefect to manage Montenero on a temporary basis. Did all run smoothly ever after? Not quite.

Over twenty years later, Montenero's management was still not managing. In early 1909 investigations were carried out to discern the problems and provide solutions. The report would be comical if not for the fact that it was dealing with real human events of the village. The report notes

the persistence of a serious disorder to all branches of the civic company. The municipal office, which has also been left without a secretary for many months, works irregularly, both due to the lack of all the most important registers prescribed by the current regulatory provisions, and to the state of true confusion in which the archive is located.

In the performance of public services, especially those pertaining to the urban police, serious shortcomings occur: thus the cleanliness of the inhabited area is extremely deficient, so as to compromise the hygiene and health of the inhabitants; the road network is in very difficult conditions due to lack of maintenance and there is no public lighting service.

The treasury service proceeds without observance of the most elementary accounting rules and without any control for the Administration, so that all accounting management closed with significant debts of the treasurers, totaling a considerable sum overall; nor has the Municipality so far effectively used to obtain payment. Likewise, it did not care to demand other minor claims that it has against its own employees.

This very regrettable negligence has seriously affected the financial situation, to which the abuses that occurred in the management of the consumption duty, and above all the negligence of the Administration regarding the protection of the municipal patrimony have also been damaged. It has in fact been ascertained that the woods owned by the municipality are in a process of deterioration, and their income is very scarce even for the abuses to which the sale system of the wood obtained from them is given. The income of other goods also appears to be very scarce, and this is due to the usual negligence in collecting the roles of pasture and hay.

It should be added that the negligence of the administrators has then made possible frequent usurpations of state-owned land, facilitated moreover by the absolute lack of the prescribed inventories of the goods. To remedy a state of disorder that seriously affects the interests of that civic company, it is convenient to resort to the dissolution of the City Council, just as even the Council of State held in the current meeting of March 7th.[12]

159

▲ There is beauty here at the crossroads of Via La Nostra Signors Lourdes and Via Fonte in Montenero. In the layered history of this stone wall are signs of repair from damage done by weather, earthquakes, rebellions, and wars. Repairs and regular maintenance are necessary to keep buildings functional. Another destructive element seen in the village history stems from abuses, negligence, and general dysfunction of village government. This too requires constant vigilance and rectification. Kudos to anyone in Montenero's municipal office who has served with integrity for the well-being of the village, its inhabitants, and visitors. *Photograph by M. DiMarco.*

Following the proposal of the minister, secretary of state for internal affairs, and president of the Council of Ministers, the Municipal Council of Montenero Valcocchiara was dissolved on 9 March 1913. Most likely by reason of sanity, Giovanni Corradi refused the appointment as royal commissioner. However, Alceste Marzari assumed the position from March to the end of November in that year. Due to the extreme dysfunction of the village, the powers of the royal commissioner were extended on 5 June 1913. The request for the extension was made because

> a complex work is needed, for which the normal period . . . of extraordinary management is not sufficient. In fact . . . it is necessary to carry out the deeds for ascertaining the heritage of the Municipality, especially the forest, for the formation of inventories, and to define the accounting, also through the settlement of the active and passive residues, ascertaining any responsibilities of the Ceased Administrations.
>
> . . . It is also necessary to establish the conditions for the organization of finance and for an effective and lasting settlement of offices and public services, to promote the improvement of the hygienic conditions of the town and to take care of the execution of the necessary public works.[13]

The proposal passed, giving Royal Commissioner Alceste Marzari three additional months to bring some degree of functionality to Montenero's municipal office. What lessons were learned? How were improvements made? Are there any perceivable effects in Montenero today, one hundred years later? How many other south Italian villages suffered the type of dysfunction illustrated here? The status of Italian villages at this time became an important indicator of the nation's integrity. It determined how Italy would develop politically, economically, and socially.

The Inferno

Michele DiMarco
in a formal photograph
taken before leaving
for the front lines.

chapter 11

Political Undercurrents and the Advent of World War One

Those leading the Kingdom of Italy were attempting to build a country on a foundation that was more fluid than solid. Millions were emigrating. Violent protests were common. The economy was crippled. Just as in previous centuries, the population remained sharply divided between the rich and very poor, especially in the south. Of course tremendous hatred festered between the landowners and working peasants. In 1887 tariffs boosted the sales of northern grain while drastically stunting grain production in the south by 42 percent. By 1899 the workforce in southern Italy was half of what it was just fifty years prior. Many were jobless or worked part-time wherever they could find work. For decades, some intellectuals and politicians had been focusing their efforts on the socioeconomic conditions of the south. However, their progress had little impact on life in the area.

The difficulties of the time did forge family bonds. Peasant family members couldn't expect much help from others besides their own relatives and close confidants. As a result, local groups devised ways to function beyond the reach of powers of the central government, giving south Italy an opaque way of doing business that continues today. Villages were given the duties of administrating themselves in matters such as public works, hygiene, finances, and law enforcement. Agostino Depretis, who was prime minister from 1881 to 1887, did make some important reforms. Previously, anyone who failed to pay taxes or debts could be thrown in jail and have his property and land confiscated. Depretis abolished this practice. He also made elementary education compulsory and free, and made religious instruction optional. These certainly brought benefits to Montenero, where the population peaked in 1901 with 2,089 inhabitants. Thus the tax base grew while the standard of living slightly rose too.

This internal flux was compounded by external changes occurring on the international political and military chessboard. Imperial powers were trying to extend their influence with many countries trying to acquire lands for their own benefit. The ability to obtain the desired results rested largely upon political alliances. When Francesco Crispi was prime minister during the late 1880s and late 1890s, the Italian government started to follow the great powers of the time, which were expanding their influence by establishing colonies in foreign lands. For example, Britain, Germany, France, Belgium, Portugal, and Spain had colonies in Africa. Italy started acquiring land in the African countries of Eritrea and Ethiopia. However, Prime Minister Crispi realized that it was more important to attend to the political situation with Austria, seeking secure borders for northern Italy.

Whenever we look at a map of Europe, we notice how the Alps form a natural border for northern Italy. Austria had controlled lands from Venice to Trieste, and along the Adriatic Sea. Because Prussia had been in conflict with Austria over their mutual borders, it formed an alliance with Italy for added support. After Prussia defeated Austria in wars along their borders in 1866, the Prussians allowed Italy to annex Venice. Austria remained in control of the area from Trieste and along the Adriatic Sea. With hopes that Austria would not venture farther south, Italy signed a secret agreement with Austria and Germany in 1882 called the Triple Alliance. They agreed to support each other and that none would make any move to extend its influence in the Balkans without consulting the others. Austria annexed Bosnia-Herzegovina in 1908, taking it over without letting the Italians know beforehand. Geographically, Austria-Hungary was the second-largest country in Europe. The Russian Empire was the largest.

Austria-Hungary encompassed a large variety of cultures with different languages, religions, and political views. Frustrations led to protests against the ruling Habsburgs in Vienna, much like the anti-Habsburg sentiments stewing in Italy. Archduke Franz Ferdinand, the heir presumptive to the Habsburg throne, went with his wife to Sarajevo, the capital of Bosnia and Herzegovina, which was then part of the Austria-Hungarian empire. Both were assassinated on 28 June 1914, following a plot organized by a group of Serbian revolutionaries who wanted independence for Bosnia and Herzegovina. Although the assassination of the archduke didn't cause much concern for many in Austria, it gave the Austrians pretext to declare war on the Kingdom of Serbia on 28 July 1914. In view of the major problems in Europe at this time, the assassination was relatively insignificant. However, it had a domino effect, increasing international tensions that burst into the Great War in August 1914. In

Europe it seemed inevitable that the Triple Alliance (Germany, Austria-Hungary, and Italy) would contend with the Triple Entente (Britain, France, and Russia).

Italy declared neutrality at the start of World War I. Its leaders had time to observe and assess the unfolding of warfare between the power players, particularly of Germany and Austria. As the war in Europe progressed, the British asked Italy to join the Triple Entente. If Italy would join, its presence would occupy a portion of German and Austrian forces on a battlefront that could otherwise be used against the British, French, and Russians. For its participation, Italy was offered extensive territory along the Adriatic Sea. On 26 April 1915, Italy switched alliances, signed a secret treaty with the Triple Entente, and joined the war against Germany and Austria.

The breakout of war took place in an atmosphere of great rivalry spurred on by advancements in communications, transportation, and manufacturing. The mentality that drove empire-building countries led to the exploitation of many through their quest for land and wealth. Relationships between the countries involved were marked by insecurity and mistrust. All the parts in this complex political arena were interrelated. What one country did had an effect on other countries.

ITALY AT ARMS

Why did Italy enter the war? Italian diplomats had no explicit goals, except the desire to take over lands in the Italian-speaking areas under Austria-Hungary. In a secret treaty made with the Triple Entente, the Italian government explicitly requested lands stretching from the modern province of Trentino north to the Brenner Pass, east to Trieste, and south along the Adriatic coastline.[1] As the British military historian John Keegan states: "Territorial avarice and strategic calculation prodded Italy towards a declaration of war through March and April."[2] On 23 May 1915, Italy declared war on Austria.

Italy had been on relatively good terms with Austria when the countries were allies in the Triple Alliance. Then it changed sides to ally itself with the Triple Entente. "Alone among the major Allies, Italy claimed no defensive reasons for fighting. It was an open aggressor, intervening for territory and status."[3]

The Italian military was now formed of soldiers from the north and south. The northern soldiers were more professional, having more experience and education—plus they had more reasons for being patriotic. The southern soldiers often felt subservient as a conquered population. Mainly from peasant stock, they had a low military reputation. Keegan states that the Italian army "grafted the remnants of the papal and Bourbon armies of the south, toy armies without loyalty to their dynastic rulers or any sense of military purpose."[4] Officials scrambled to mobilize 1.2 million men to bear against the Austrian front, but the troops were certainly not properly prepared for the large-scale attack they planned. They were undertrained and ill equipped.

The methods of warfare had changed greatly by 1915. The Italian-Austrian front zigzagged for over four hundred miles. What began with hopes for a quick victory led to years of war, mainly stuck in trenches along the eastern Alps. There were eleven battles along the Dantian River, followed by the Asagio Offensive, in which the Austrians tried to reach the Po Valley. The Italians held their ground, but other battles followed. At the Battle of Capporetto (October to November 1917), the twelfth battle of the Dantian, German troops arrived to help the Austrians. The German use of poison gas contributed to the Italian defeat, with ten thousand killed, thirty thousand wounded, and 265,000 taken prisoner.[5]

After the devastating loss at Capporetto, the Italian army retreated to the Piave River and prepared for another battle. There the Austrians attacked only to suffer a big defeat and plummeting morale. Rather than a quick follow-up to bring the Austrians to full surrender, the Italians waited for reinforcements to arrive. On 24 October 1918, they mounted an offensive at Vittorio Veneto, pitting 1.4 million Italian soldiers against 1.8 million Austrian. The battle ended with 40,378 casualties for Italy versus 528,000 for Austria. This decisive battle contributed to the end of World War I, one week later.

Perceptions about warfare can often be limited to a study of statistics. This view may limit the real significance of the profound effects that rumble through survivors and their ancestors. Rather than focus on cold facts and physical reconstruction, the following pages bring attention to the psychological wounds that result during times of war. The inflicted emotional damage not only affects those directly involved in war but also extends to the immediate family members and others. Greater empathy for the people and countries recovering from any war can perhaps be obtained by giving attention to actual experiences shared by individuals through reports, including oral histories.

EXPERIENCING THE ART OF WAR

All wars are horrible, violent encounters, bringing pain and suffering far beyond the actual killing fields. Some battlefronts are worse than others. *Smithsonian Magazine* published a special issue dealing with World War I. One article highlights the Italian front. The title is "The Most

Treacherous Battle of World War I Took Place in the Italian Mountains."[6] An estimated one million people died on the Italian front.

What made the area so perilous? Rifles, machine guns, mortars, hand grenades, flamethrowers, artillery, tanks, and aircraft were all the common weapons of the time. The Alpine heights and extreme winters are what made the Italian front more hazardous than elsewhere. For example, in two days, nearly ten thousand Italian and Austrian soldiers were buried by avalanches and died. Frostbite, malnutrition, and diseases took life and limb. Many injuries and deaths were caused by rock fragments, secondary projectiles resulting from explosions. Austrian forces used a mix of phosgene chlorine gas for the first time on 29 June 1916, attacking the Italian lines on Monte San Michele. Soldiers died when their lungs and throats swelled, cutting off their oxygen.

For much of the time, the Austrians held positions on top of mountains. A relatively small number of machine-gun positions could easily stop thousands of Italian soldiers, who tried to advance up the steep inclines. As recorded in Professor Mark Thompson's book,[7] an Austrian captain yelled to his gunners, "What do you want, to kill them all? Let them be." And the gunners shouted to the Italian soldiers: "Stop, go back! We won't shoot any more. Do you want everyone to die?"

Being shot at. Carrying equipment. Italian soldiers, when trying to get up the steep inclines, were often also hindered by rows of barbed wire. Barbed wire, invented in the 1870s by American cattle ranchers as a cheap way to fence in cattle, was now used to deter human movement. Many Italian soldiers, hindered or caught in the wire, were easy targets. They would run from their trenches time and time again, trying to advance uphill against machine-gun fire, over fallen comrades. The routine would go on for months because opposing forces were often held in stalemate. Trenches were open-pit latrines where there were more rats than soldiers.

Under such conditions, a charge was almost certain suicide. A thousand men would be massacred; then another charge would be ordered with the same result. Of course any sane soldier could refuse to charge, but the general chief of staff of the Italian army, General Luigi Cadorna, used his position to convince his soldiers to press forward. Cadorna "exercised that authority with a brutality not shown by any other general in the First World War." He "ordered the summary shooting of officers of retreating units with pitiless inflexibility."[8] The year 1917 became known as the "year of decimation."

An example of the harsh measures taken to force soldiers to fight is seen in an incident involving the Abruzzi Brigade (3rd Battalion of the 58th Infantry), deployed on Mount San Gabriele.

One night, a five-man patrol moved around no-man's land, hoping to take prisoners who would spill details about the Austrian's rumored offensive. When the patrol returned empty-handed, the battalion commander tore into them: "So they thought they could save their skins by hiding in a crater, did they?" . . . [T]he major ordered two of them to be shot at once. Other men were present, and someone shot the major. The divisional commander moved the regiment several kilometers behind the lines where 14 men were chosen by lot from the 3rd Battalion, and executed.[9]

RESULTS AT WAR'S END

World War I ended on 11 November 1918. During the first two years of the war, Italian troops only reached ten miles inside Austrian territory. The total number of military and civilian casualties on all fronts was around twenty million deaths and nearly twenty-one million wounded. The number of Italian war casualties varies according to sources. One study based on official government data published by Yale University Press[10] lists the following:

Total Italian military deaths: 651,000
- killed in action or died of wounds: 378,000
- died of disease: 186,000
- deaths of invalids due to war related injuries (1918–1920): 87,000

Total Italian civilian deaths: 1,021,000
- caused by food shortages: 589,000
- caused by Spanish Flu: 432,000
- civilian deaths due to military action: 3,400

Prisoners on both sides also suffered, and many died in captivity. About one hundred thousand Italian prisoners died in Austrian and German camps. Of survivors, 950,000 were wounded and 250,000 were crippled for life.

The above certainly does not fully describe all the horrors the Italians faced on the front. The brief overview indicates how Italian soldiers—including men from Montenero—spent years on the Italian front and perhaps in captivity. Because they were on the winning side with the Triple Entente, their sacrifices resulted in the Italian government's receiving much of the land it sought upon entering the war. These gains are recognized in the Treaty of Versailles.

Because able-bodied men had been required to leave Montenero to serve in the war, only women, children, and the elderly remained in the village. Without the men to work the fields, basic food necessities became scarce. Plus, we need to take into account other factors affecting life in the village, such as the 1915 earthquake in Abruzzo that caused about thirty thousand deaths. The government spent more money on World War I than it had spent over the previous fifty years. Taxes were raised to go toward the cost of the war. There was less income during a time when inflation doubled the cost of living. The war took a heavy toll on the soldiers and civilians of Italy, and more so in the south. Certainly the people of Montenero bore physical and mental scars for years to come.

For World War I, soldiers enlisted in the regions where they lived. Following the draft, men from Montenero were usually registered under the Military District of Campobasso. It is logical that many from Montenero fought in the Campobasso Brigade, in either the 229th or 230th Regiment. Following a series of Italian losses on the Isonzo front and a great drop in morale, one victory stands out. The Campobasso Brigade took Mount Santo, the "Holy Mountain," famous for its medieval monastery that dates to the 1540s. Italian forces "by evening took the convent therein."[11] The mount overlooked the lower Isonzo and was an important observation post for the Austrians who were entrenched there. During the ninth campaign in October and November 1916, Italian artillery and airstrikes pounded the site, killing an estimated five hundred.

◄ Mannarelli brothers, World War I soldiers: Giuseppe, Domenico, and Antonio, 1915.

By May 1917, the Tenth Battle of the Isonzo was underway, and Mount Santo was a prime target. In a brilliant book on the Isonzo, Professor John Schindler writes the following:

> Under the protection of a deadly barrage, a wall of steel, the 10th Division's Campobasso Brigade advanced up the steep slopes of the 2,250-foot high "Holy Mountain." The shell-scarred summit was held by a battalion of the 25th Hungarian Militia Regiment, a Croatian outfit. The unfortunate militiamen were pounded relentlessly by VI Corps artillery; the barrage was so strong that it literally blew many defenders off the mountain. The Campobasso Brigade's regiments approached Mt. Santo carefully, hiding when possible in the underbrush on the west face, overlooking the Isonzo. When the fanti [infantry] charged the summit, they surprised the Croatian defenders and captured many of them. The summit, with its ruined monastery, was in Italian hands. Elation spread through the VI Corps and then the whole Army of Gorizia. . . . The joyous news was read to the Parliament in Rome, bringing spontaneous and unrestrained applause. Monte Santo, the unattainable objective, had fallen at last.[12]

In Montenero's municipal square is a plaque placed to honor the fallen soldiers from the Great War. It reads

> Animated from the most holy enthusiasm, with perpetual faith in the victory for the conquest of the natural borders of the homeland, and for the liberation of irredenta brothers, with Italian courageous struggle in the conclusive war of national redemption and fallen heroes.

CITIZENS
PROUDLY HOLD IN PERMANENT MEMORY
Montenero V. September 6, 1919

• Marcello Bonaminio	• Biase Cacchione	• Erminio Del Sangro
• Isidori Di Filippo	• Alfonso Di Fiore	• Cosmo Di Luca
• Achille Di Nicola	• Gregorio Di Nicola	• Alessandro Fioritti
• Giulio Freda	• Giulio Gigliotti	• Nicola Mannarelli
• Giovanni Micigan	• Emidio Orlando	• Giuseppe Procario
• Romeo Procario		

Most of the people listed here lived in Montenero, but not all. Biase Cacchione and Giulio Freda, for example, lived in the United States and fought with the United States Army. Julius Tornincasa, who settled in Chicago, received his United States citizenship by volunteering to serve in the US Army. Others with Montenero roots lived in other countries and served in World War I.

▲ Giuseppe Bonaminio. *Courtesy of R. P. Hunter.*

▲ Michele Miraldi (8 maggio 1915).

▲ Luca Di Fiori. *Courtesy of Sandra Di Fiore.*

Romeo Procario, died in WWI. *Courtesy of R. P. Hunter.*

ORAL HISTORY:
MONTENERESE IN WORLD WAR I

PAOLO BONAMINIO (1892–1974)

Luciano Bonaminio shared a story about his grandfather, Paolo Bonaminio, who fought on the Carso plateau during the Sixth Battle of the Isonzo. This arid area is a nearly barren limestone plateau southeast of Gorizia. Some said the Carso was a howling wilderness of stones sharp as knives. A primary target here was Mount San Michele, defended in August of 1916 by Hungarian forces. The use of poison gas was substantial in the conflict. With great effort and losses, the Italian forces took the mount with fierce hand-to-hand fighting.

◀ Paolo Bonaminio.
Courtesy of Montenero Municipal Office.

Luciano recounted his grandfather's story, which took place in a Carso trench:

While my grandfather was in the trenches on the Carso, he had a dream. St. Antonio appeared to him and told him to cover his eyes with both hands. Then the saint asked, "Paolo, what can you see?" My grandfather of course replied, "Nothing!"

Then St. Antonio told him to remove a hand from his left eye but to leave the right eye covered. He repeated the question again, "Now, what do you see?" Grandfather responded, "Now I can see a little, but not very well." St. Antonio told him, "Well then, you should be content." After the dream ended, my grandfather immediately woke up.

The next day, in combat, an Austrian soldier caught grandfather's right eye with a bayonet. Because of the dream, my grandfather was convinced that St. Antonio had saved his other eye. After my grandfather returned to Montenero, he bore a son and named him Antonio (1925–1978) in honor of the saint. He also built a small altar with a statue in his bedroom. My grandfather never missed a day to light a candle in front of the statue.

Paolo Bonaminio was one of many soldiers who returned home from the war with crippling injuries. After the war, the government did not provide pensions in such cases, but it did make a few jobs available so former soldiers could make a living. Since Paolo was able bodied, he got the position of guard for the municipal office. Crippled soldiers also had the option to run a government-sponsored store, called Salt and Tobacco. These stores sold government-controlled salt, tobacco, snuff, stamps, postcards, state document paper (*carta bollata*), school notebooks, and pencils. Paolo and his family operated the second store to open in Montenero, the Sali e Tabacci Store #2. The family eventually turned it into a grocery store and has been serving locals ever since. Today you can find Sergio Bonaminio at the storefront, a hundred years after his grandfather opened the doors.

ERNESTO MIRALDI (1893–1929)

Ernesto Miraldi's story is similar to Paolo Bonaminio's. Both served on the Italian front in World War I and lost an eye in battle. Ernesto was a marksman (*bersagliere*) in the infantry corps. In addition to the loss of an eye, he lost a leg due to severe wounds. In order for him and his family to make a living, they were given permission to start Salt and Tobacco Store #1. Ernesto was unable to handle all the duties associated with the store because of pain and mobility issues. Eventually Ernesto went to a military hospital in Naples to treat the infections to which he succumbed. His father Matia Miraldi ran the store until he also passed. Ernesto's wife, Domenica Tenne, then ran the store for many years.

Ernesto and Domenica had four children, two dying at childbirth or soon after. His son Tommaso served in World War II and unfortunately passed away from cancer at age twenty-eight. His daughter Lucia Elia Miraldi (1913–2003) fell in line to run the store, which she did until 1957. Elia married Oreste Caserta (1910–1981), whose father Vincenzo Caserta (1859–1935) went to Erie in 1900 to prepare for his family to emigrate to the United States. Upon arrival at Ellis Island he had $12 in his pocket. After Elia moved to Erie, her daughter Clara took over the store. Clara started to stock grocery products in the store too, such as pastas and canned food. In the early 1960s she moved to Erie with her husband, Clemente Pede (1928–2017). Clemente's sister Eva Pede then took over the store with her husband, Getulio Di Nicola, until they moved to Canada. Finally, Eva's sister-in-law Santa Di Nicola was the last owner. Store #1 closed its doors in 2015.

Originally, the Salt and Tobacco Store #1 sold the same government products as the Bonaminio. Vincent Caserta (b. 1935), son of Elia

and Oreste, recounts interesting details about how the store was run. Four of the children worked there, including Vince, Clara, Antoinette, and Ernesto. Bruno and Enio were too young to work. The store took up one floor of their home at Via Giuseppe Mazzini #15. Living quarters were on the floor above, and animals occupied the lowest level.

Vincent clearly remembers how the products were displayed, how a scale was on a counter to weigh items, and how sales were recorded in a register book using a pencil. There were no scheduled work hours, but usually customers came from early morning until about 9:00 in the evening. Supplies for the store had to be picked up from a state supply outlet (*magazzine*) in Castel di Sangro. It carried supplies for a large area of Abruzzo-Molise. Vince would usually drive a cart pulled by a donkey if there were many items to get, or he would bicycle the 12.5 miles round trip to fetch a light load. When bus service was initiated, that became the regular transport until the early 1960s, when the car made the trip much easier.

Of course salt and tobacco were in demand. The store had hundred-pound bags of salt from which customers could purchase small amounts for home use. The minimum age to purchase cigarettes was eighteen. A customer would usually purchase one to six cigarettes or some tobacco for pipes. Surprisingly, it seems a good amount of snuff was sold to women. Upon purchase, they would say, "Don't tell anyone!" They found it useful to clear a stuffy nose when one had a cold.

Because many would arrive in the evening after work to have a cigarette or two, the store served as a gathering spot for socializing. Conversations in the smoke-filled room gave Vince special insight into the life of all in Montenero. Their topics were serious or humorous. They often joked about friends or about each other. They talked about crops, farming, and animals. Some chat turned to politics, the past, and the future. Perhaps they'd discuss their hardships, a vacation, or ideas of immigrating. In all, it was interesting and entertaining for Vincent. How much of these conversations echo in the collective memories of Montenerese today?

OTHER STORES AND BUSINESSES

After World War I the number of stores, cantinas, and restaurants increased. There were five or six cantinas where customers usually played cards while drinking some wine with food. Giovanni Orlando ran one of the early cantinas. Matilde Procario served food and drink at her cantina at the intersection of Corso Vittorio Emanuele III and Via Cerreto. Also on Corso Vittorio Emanuele III there was a grocery store owned by Pasquale Pede. This was across from where his grandson Giani Pede recently established the Casa Nuova restaurant pizzeria, which many frequent today. Terenza "Buccuche" Scalzitti's cantina also had a room to rent on Via Roma. Quintino Zuchegna operated a grocery store close to the piazza, while Chiara's cantina and grocery store was in the piazza. Near the church, Florideo Iacabozzi had a store called the "Piccizeria" because a number of items were spicy (*picante*). His son Erolo ran it before moving to France. Rinaldo Freda (1911–1991) ran an "after work" (*doppo lavoro*) where people could purchase some grocery items as well as enjoy an evening of drink and cards. These and other establishments were convenient for the postwar population, primarily for the hardworking, hard-drinking men.

MICHELE DI MARCO (1893–1975)

▲ Michele DiMarco.

I was named after my grandfather, Michele DiMarco, and lived in the same house in Erie, Pennsylvania, during my early years. He and my grandmother Lucia Caserta lived on the first floor, while my parents, sister, and I lived on the second floor. I'd spend most of the daytime hours with my grandparents.

It seems I'd often follow my grandfather around like a puppy—to the kitchen for lunch, to the living room to watch TV, to the garden to pick some vegetables. One of our pastimes was playing checkers. He'd sit in his favorite chair, I'd sit on the floor, and the checkerboard would be between us on a footstool. From that angle, I noticed an ace bandage wrapped around my grandfather's leg, showing slightly between his sock and pant leg. As I have written, this is when he talked about his experience as a soldier. He pointed to his lower leg where he was shot, then to his thigh, then to the other leg, then to his arm. I lost count of all the places he pointed. He explained that he was a machine-gunner, and that the enemy would target machine-gunners before soldiers who had single-shot rifles.

I was too young to know what World War I was about, or to comprehend the places my grandfather mentioned. All I knew was that he fought in northeast Italy. Somewhere on that front, all in his platoon were killed, except for him and one other man. They became prisoners of war, kept in a cave where they ate only grass. Gramp mentioned the Carpathian Mountains. It seems he was transferred there, probably to a prisoner-of-war camp. He was moved to other locations at least a few times, picking up some basic German language during his internment. In one of the camps, the diary he kept was confiscated. I wonder if it has been preserved in a museum or is in someone's collection of antique war memorabilia.

Given that one hundred thousand Italian prisoners died in Austrian and German camps, how did my grandfather survive? I asked him and he shared details about his long escape road from prison camp back to Montenero.

According to a document from the military office in Campobasso, my grandfather served from December 1913 to December 1919. Six years total in the army. I was surprised to learn that Gramp had gone to the United States before the war, in 1910, to immigrate. Before he could settle, he received notice from the Italian Consulate in Philadelphia dated 24 August 1913: war was imminent, and he was being drafted. Three months later he returned to Italy, was enlisted, and had basic training in Perugia. It took nearly seven and a half years and a world war before he could return to the United States.

Gramp departed Montenero on a train to embark from Naples on 11 August 1921. On 26 August 1921, he arrived at Ellis Island on a ship called S.S. San Giovanni. He was twenty-seven years old. His brother Pasquale (1891–1985) and sister Elvira (1896–2006) were already settled in the United States. Two other brothers, Carmine and Giuseppe, emigrated to Argentina. We can only imagine how heartbreaking it must have been for Gramp to leave his parents Serafino (1860–1942) and Antonia (1865–1926), ten-year-old brother Berardino (1910–1995), and five-year-old brother Clemente (1915–1991), never to see each other again. Gramp married the young Lucia Caserta (1898–1983) 17 September 1925, at St. Paul's Church. Together they raised three boys.

Gramp kept a few mementos from the war: paper money from Austria-Hungary, Romania, Russia, Bulgaria, and Germany. The latter was a German five-pfennig note, equal to about five cents. This was not ordinary paper money. In 2016, one hundred years after my grandfather got this note, I translated the fine print on the currency: *Prisoners Camp—Zossen Half Moon Camp Coupon. Vouchers, which are presented by other persons as prisoners of war for payment or exchange, are not recognized. It is forbidden for the prisoners of war to receive cash or German paper money for this voucher.*

The Half Moon Camp was a prisoner-of-war camp in Wünsdorf (a district of Zossen), Germany. It is less than thirty miles south of Berlin. It housed nearly five thousand Muslims, whom the Germans tried to persuade to wage jihad against the United Kingdom and France. Without success in this project, many prisoners were transferred to Romania to work on farms. If my grandfather didn't go to the Half Moon Camp, he certainly was in Romania and perhaps got the note from someone in a camp there.

About fifty years after the war, my grandfather received a package from Italy containing three medals and a small check—tokens for his part in the war:

- **50th Anniversary of the Victory 1916–1966**
  Commemorative medal for the 50th anniversary of the victory in WW1.
  18K/Ar750 gold; red, green, and white ribbon.

- **Great War for Civilization 1914–1918:**
  To the Combatants of the Allied and Associated Nations
  Campaign medal of bronze with multicolor ribbon.

- **Knight of the Order of Vittorio Veneto**
  Order of Knighthood medal. Black metal with multicolor ribbon.

When I visited the archives in the basement of Montenero's municipal building in 2016, I saw a few World War I medals on a shelf. Nearly hidden among stacks of papers, they are easily overlooked. Unfortunately, like the medals, many of the Montenero men who fought in the war have been set aside, out of sight and out of mind.

"Threshing in Abruzzo"
Oil painting by Peder Severin Kroyer. Statens Museum of Art.

chapter 12

Back to Work: Tools, Land, and Home

TOOLS OF THE TRADE

For many centuries, life in the villages in the upper Volturno revolved around agriculture and animal husbandry. People would produce almost all of what they needed on their own lands. In these mountainous areas, production seems to fall short considering the great effort invested. The daily activities in Montenero centered on working the fields, taking care of the animals, and the regular tasks at home and in other trades. Men, women, and often children, had a work schedule that usually ran from dusk to dawn. They knew when quitting time came by holding two fingers at arm's length horizontal to the mountain ridges where the sun set. When the sun appeared to touch the top finger, they had enough time to walk home before dark.

All the tools used by the Montenerese are fascinating from the point of agricultural history. They are much more significant when one knows how they were used, the human energy utilized, and the effects the work had on their bodies and minds from the long hours of toil and sweat. This certainly made holidays and holy days welcome respites from the labor.

The able-bodied men who returned to Montenero after the war came back to neglected agricultural lands. They went straight to work, utilizing many methods virtually unchanged since medieval times. Cultivating land required special tools. The plow was essential. It was drawn by horses or donkeys, and later by tractors. A variety of hoes, spades, and rakes could be used to refine the soil where needed for planting and tending what was being grown.

Farmers reap what they sow, and tools were designed specifically for harvesting. A scythe's blade is over five feet long and used to cut grass and reap crops. The smaller sickle was also used for harvesting and cutting succulent forage for feeding animals. Whetstones were usually carried to keep these tools razor sharp. To the people who lived in those days, the rhythmic sliding of sharpening stones along the blades created a sweet-sounding melodious resonance that colored the air.

Horses and donkeys pulled large stones over the wheat for hours in a threshing process that separated the wheat grains from the straw on the ground. In order to fully separate these, men and women would use wooden pitchforks to throw the mixture high up into the breeze. Special winnowing baskets were also used. The straw was blown to the side, leaving the wheat grains to fall to the ground or in the basket. The people hoped to gather enough grain to last for the year.

After the threshing and winnowing work is done, the next step is milling grains into flour, with wheat being the most important. Wheat is the staple of the European diet. Bread is the primary product made from flour, but other products such as pastas and pastries can be made. Bread has been so vital to the lives of Italians that it was often the focus of political and economic development. A number of rebellions were ignited when the price of a loaf of bread rose. In 1647, for example, there was the famous Masaniello's Revolt in Naples, brought about by bread shortages. When the wheat harvest in Italy fell in 1897, a riot broke out in Milan that was put down in a massacre.

So vital for any village, mills were of major importance for the local and national economy. Owners had to be authorized to run the mills, and they were obligated to collect fees and pay annual fees. An example of this is found in the *Collection of Royal Laws and Decrees of the Kingdom of the Two Sicilies*, where the municipality of Montenero was advised by the government on 18 July 1832 to require Fortunato Ricciuto of the strict responsibilities in building and operating a mill.[1]

There were seven mills in Montenero, according to Daniela Ricci, who renovated one of the old mills into the fully functional Mulino Museum (MOMU), inaugurated in 2015. The other mills were beyond repair, in part from years of neglect and, in larger part, from the destruction caused by bombings during World War II. The MOMU was originally built in a very suitable location adjacent to a stream with a strong water flow to drive horizontal paddles. Today you can see how all the parts of the mill function, including the grinding of grain by two original millstones. There is no need to grind large quantities of wheat as done in days past, but vast amounts of flour would fall into a wooden dumpster, later to be put into bags made of hemp or cotton.

The two-story mill made of stone with thick wooden floors was probably constructed before World War I, when Italy was making strides in productive capacity. Thanks to Miss Ricci, Montenero's water mill serves as a learning center. It shows how a functional mill operated and is furnished with artifacts of daily life, rural tools, ancient crafts, and related technologies. It is an ideal setting where Miss Ricci also sponsors contemporary art exhibitions that are linked to natural themes, gastronomic events, and cultural activities.

Sometimes we forget or are unaware of work-related dangers present in village work. In a mill, the flour dust would float thickly in the air. It is flammable! In fear of fatal explosions, all were careful to not light candles or lamps inside the room during milling. Of course injuries could result from using the variety of tools utilized in the village. In addition, farmers could be stung by scorpions, bees, wasps, and hornets, or bitten by snakes. When heavy machinery came into use, injuries were common and sometimes lethal. Almost any agricultural labor called for long hours of repetitive work, which would cause chronic muscle and joint pain.

In addition to the tools used for sowing, reaping, and milling grain, there were numerous tools used in the other trades and in the home. Stonemasons worked with an array of chisels and hammers to turn hard stone into millstones and marble into ornamental pieces for churches and buildings. Cobblers, with strips of leather, pitch, nails, and resin, kept shoes in repair. Tailors, including my great-uncle Clemente Di Marco, relied on sewing machines, pins, scissors, chalk, thimbles, and needles. They often adapted hand-me-down clothes for a new owner. It has been said that, during the beginning of the nineteenth century and earlier, villagers were so poor that, "Often, on the deathbed, they wore the same suit of the marriage day."

Since the time when people first built small one-room huts along the pantano, this marshland area became noted for its abundant animals and fish. Hunting and fishing made it possible to add a variety of food on the table. Rifles were necessary for game such as wild boar and bear. Shotguns made it easier to bag a variety of birds. Before the Zittola River became polluted, one could grab a fish or eel out of the water by hand.

Shepherds had the lonely task of tending their sheep day and night. To pass the time, they often carved wooden items. Shearing done with manual clippers is hot, dirty, and time-consuming work—but it is usually done only once a year. Other large animals, including the horse, cow, and pig, required their own tending.

Others cut hair, worked iron, or made utensils. Some work and crafts were part-time. My grandmother, Lucia Caserta, sat on her balcony, facing the warm sun over the pantano, while she crocheted or knitted. Many household chores were done by hand or with a diverse collection of tools. Of course, preparing meals was of great importance. All the homes had a mortar and pestle. Baking bread usually took place late at night to eat the following day. In addition to the standard pots, pans, and tableware came the specialized containers and instruments for food preparation and preservation.

The above is a simple, brief overview of how work was done in Montenero, especially before the 1960s. The pantano was a blessing, providing grains and grazing grounds for horses and cows, and the Zittola River offered water and fish. Anyone born in Montenero has intense sentiments for the pantano and its beautiful surroundings. Loved ones have been born and died in the pantano. When his mother had sudden labor pains while working in the fields, Giuseppe Calvano (1894–1981) was born! Isidoro Caserta died shortly after being gored by a bull there. Any mention of the pantano evokes a spectrum of thoughts and feelings for those who have roots in Montenero.

THE PEAT REBELLION OF 1917 & 1918[2]

A river runs through it. The majestic pantano is nourished by the waters of the Zittola River. For centuries it has mainly been used as pasture land and a key to Montenero's economy and social life. The pantano was a unique blessing for the village—until it turned into a curse just after World War I. According to Guido Martino, the librarian for Montenero's municipal library, a couple of business groups wanted to purchase the land. They must have known of the report by an engineer to the Office of the Ministry of Agriculture and Commerce. Dated 14 May 1896, the report states the peat (*torba*) deposit would reach "several meters thick, especially in the middle of the valley." A typescript kept in the municipal library provides additional details:

> The engineer added that he had not been able to cover the ground in all its extension but to estimate its length at 5 kilometers and 7–800 meters as the average width. By means of calculations based on this estimate of the area and on its presumed depth, it assessed the possible return of the fund in "over 250 million tons of peat in the natural state." Following this report, the Ministry of Agriculture and Commerce and the Civil Engineering Office of Campobasso, planned to drain the quagmire to extract its peat, but the idea was not put into effect for technical reasons underlined by the Real Body of Mines.[3]

There was a coal shortage after World War I, so one company wanted to turn the pantano into a hydroelectric basin while the other company wanted to sell the peat as fuel. Locals became upset when they discovered the village administrators were seriously considering selling it. In protest of the potential sale of this state property, villagers attacked members of the Municipal Council on 22 July 1917, causing some injuries.

Municipal Board Members	Age
Casto Danese, son of Clemente	55
Francesco Ricchiuti, son of Felice	58
Eliodoro Iacobozzi, son of Ferdinando	59
Marco Gonnella, son of Matteo	39
Ferdinando Fabrizio, son of Evangelista	45
Giovanni Di Nicola, son of Pietro	69
Giovanni Di Procario, son of Nicola	52

Although a trial was scheduled, the mayor called the police and had it cancelled. The arrested were released, except for the following individuals, who waited six months behind bars before being freed and pardoned:

Pietro Di Marco	Elisa Miraldi	Angela Maria Presogna
Carmelitana D'Onofrio	Maria Miraldi	Francesco Ricchiuti
Clorindo Iacobozzi	Nicolina Miraldi	Filomena Ziroli

Then, on 17 January 1918, during the festival of San Antun', hell broke loose. Pent-up anger burst into a violent attack directed toward the town hall, where police (*Carabinieri*) stood guard with rifles affixed with bayonets.[3] From the archway above Portanuova, women hurled stones toward the town-hall doors. Police fired their guns to try to scare off the crowd. Sixty-six-year-old Francesca Di Marco, wife of Antonio Scalzitti, was stabbed in the stomach by a bayonet and died.[4]

The next day, soldiers arrived from Sulmona and camped in the square. They were sent because some officials thought the revolt in Montenero was political. Because the protests were over the topic of peat and the marshland, the soldiers remained passive. However, the police were active, trying to arrest those involved in the Peat Revolt. Unfortunately, a youth of surnamed Scalzitti, who was only eleven or twelve years old, was struck on the head and died.[5] Some escaped. In the end, 123 people were arrested, forced into a large truck in front of the Palazzo De Arcangelis, and jailed in the district prison in Forlì del Sannio. Most spent a month incarcerated, but others were jailed for six months. The arrested are listed here with surname first, as recorded in the original document.

Accused on January 17, 1918

1. Ricchiuti Francesco, son of Felice
2. Milò Berardino, son of Teodoro
3. Pede Giuliano, son of Michele
4. Gonnella Michele, son of Clemente
5. Iacobozzi Clorindo, son of Ferdinando
6. Pallotto Isidoro, son of Donato
7. Tornincasa Luigi, son of Domenico
8. Iacobozzi Eliodoro, son of Ferdinando
9. Di Marco Pietro, son of Michele
10. Di Fiore Nicola, daughter of Angelo
11. Di Nicola Giulio, son of Luca
12. Orlando Giuseppe, son of Carlo
13. Calvano Pasquale, son of Antonio
14. Di Marco Nicola, daughter of Camillo
15. Di Marco Annibale, son of Achille
16. Di Nicola Luca, son of Giulio
17. Milò Nicola, son of Teodoro
18. Di Marco Raffaele, son of Achille
19. Di Marco Serafino, son of Filippo
20. Orlando Giuseppe, son of Vincenzo
21. Miraldi Maria, daughter of Giovanni
22. Orlando Maria, daughter of Gerardo
23. Pallotto Filomena, daughter of Domenico
24. Miraldi Nicolina, daughter of Francesco
25. Gonnella Palma, daughter of Clemente
26. Ziroli Filomena, daughter of Donato
27. D'Onofrio Carmelitana, daughter of Vincenzo
28. Presogna Angela Maria, daughter of Giovanni
29. Miraldi Elisa, daughter of Francesco
30. Scalzitti Lucia, daughter of Pasquale
31. Fabrizio Innocenza, daughter of Nicola
32. Tornincasa Amalia, daughter of Luigi
33. Tornincasa Cornelia, daughter of Luigi
34. Romagnoli Guglielmo – police sergeant
35. Passariello Lazzaro – police officer
36. Pettinicchio Michele – police officer
37. Pitone Luigi – police officer
38. Iacobozzi Pio, son of Giuseppe
39. Pallotto Nicola, son of Donato
40. Danese Casto, son of Clemente
41. Di Marco Pietro, son of Michele
42. Di Marco Liborio, son of Giacomo
43. Di Marco Giacomo, son of Liborio
44. Di Marco Emilio, son of Giovanni
45. Di Marco Maria Teresa, daughter of Giulio
46. Fabrizio Clemente, son of Evangelista
47. Mannarelli Felice, son of Pasquale
48. Narcucci Filippo, son of Vincenzo
49. Narducci Angelo, son of Filippo
50. Di Filippo Domenico, son of Angelo
51. Caprorio Giulia, daughter of Ignoti
52. Bonaminio Donato, son of Agostino
53. Procario Rodolfo, son of Giovanni
54. Domodossola Pasquale, son of Domenico
55. Scalzitti Francesco, son of Felice
56. Scalzitti Vincenzo, son of Francesco
57. Iacobozzi Agnese, daughter of Crescenzo
58. Di Marco Giovanni, son of Angelo
59. Orlando Francesco, son of Rocco
60. Scalzitti Vincenzo, son of Antonio
61. Miraldi Mattia, son of Giacinto
62. Di Nicola Giovanni, son of Pietro
63. Danese Concetta, daughter of Casto
64. Iacobozzi Filiberto, son of Ferdinando
65. Miraldi Domenicangelo, son of Giacinto
66. Scalzitti Sabina, daughter of Domenico
67. Iole Maria Carmela, daughter of Tommaso
68. Bonaminio Domenica, daughter of Giuseppe
69. Bonaminio Costantino, son of Agostino
70. D'Onofrio Margherita, daughter of Nicola
71. Danese Angelina, daughter of Casto
72. Di Marco Lucia, daughter of Pietro

73. Di Marco Irma, daughter of Pietro

74. Narducci Carmina, daughter of Angelo

75. Scalzitti Pietro, son of Vincenzo

76. Domodossola Florina, daughter of Domenico

77. Di Marco Filomena, daughter of Domenico

78. Iacobucci Donato, son of Donato

79. D'Onofrio Elisabetta

80. D'Onofrio Palma, daughter of Vincenzo

81. Ziroli Anna, daughter of Giuseppe

82. Ziroli Palma, daughter of Giuseppe

83. Miraldi Emerenziana, daughter of Francesco

84. Tenne Grazia, daughter of Marco

85. Di Filippo Alfonsina, daughter of Domenico

86. Di Filippo Candida, daughter of Domenico

87. Di Nicola Maria, daughter of Nicola

88. Di Nicola Tommasina, daughter of Ignoti

89. Di Marco Quintino, son of Angelo

90. Ziroli Romualdo, son of Carmine

91. Tornincasa Elisabetta, daughter of Sebastiano

92. Altobelli Anna Teresa, daughter of Domenico

93. Di Marco Antonio, son of Giovanni

94. Di Marco Maria, daughter of Concetta

95. Gallo Cherubina, daughter of Filippo

96. Mannarelli Angelantonio, son of Francesco

97. Calvano Emilia, daughter of Pasquale

98. Del Sangro Angelo, son of Giuseppe

99. Scalzitti Pietro, son of Domenico

100. Ricchiuti Angelina, daughter of Domenico

101. Ricchiuti Cecilia, daughter of Luigi

102. Danese Sofia, daughter of Clemente

103. Colonna Amalia, daughter of Giovanni

104. Fabrizio Francesco, son of Gennaro

105. Di Fiore Berardino, son of Crescenzo

106. Iacobozzi Marco, son of Giovanni

107. Ricchiuti Manfredo, son of Nicola

108. Donatucci Carlo, son of Pietro

109. Di Marco Giuseppe, son of Vincenzo

110 Bonaminio, Domenica, daughter of Giuseppe

111. Iacobozzi Ernesta, daughter of Romualdo

112. Pallotto Anna, daughter of Domenico

113. Orlando Clementina, daughter of Benedetto

114. Santucci Emiddio Torinto, son of Pietro

115. Santucci Giuseppantonio, son of Pietro

116. Pede Callisto, son of Michele

117. Pede Stanislao, son of Evangelista

118. Pede Angela, daughter of Evangelista

119. Iacobozzi Biase, son of Lorenzo

120. Tornincasa Pietro Nicola, son of Giacomo

121. Di Marco Domenico, son of Innocenzo

122. Di Marco Innocenzo, son of Domenico

123. Iacobozzi Berardino, son of Tommaso

In the above list, four of the men (numbers 34 through 37) were police, questioned about the killing of the woman and child, but it could not be proven who was responsible. From numbers 1 to 33 and 38 to 120 are those accused of crimes of violence and threat against the royal police. The first thirty-three were arrested on 18 January 1918, and were detained in Isernia. Those numbered 9 to 16 were accused of complicity in crime or personal injury to the royal police. Pietro Di Marco (9) unsuccessfully attacked Brigadier Romagnoli with a weapon. About a month later, 114 detainees were released. The remaining nine were held for about six months. All were eventually pardoned, and all cases were closed on 7 April 1920.

■ Visiting the Mulino Museum and stepping back in time to experience daily life in Montenero. In addition to the functional mill, many tools are displayed relating to farming and other occupations. *Top photo courtesy of D. Ricci; bottom by M. DiMarco.*

▲ Mulino Museum: At the mill's grinding stones. ▼ Variety of tools.
Photographs by M. DiMarco.

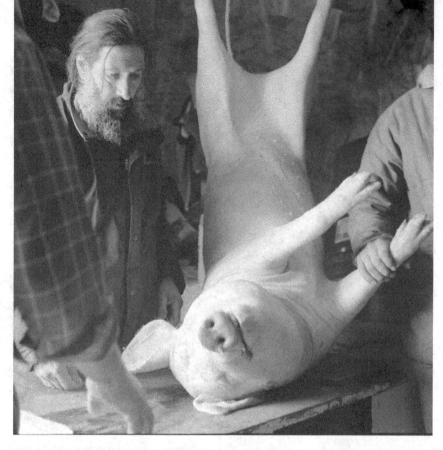

▲ For centuries, the ritual of killing full-grown pigs was an annual occurrence in Montenero and elsewhere in Italian villages. Pigs were killed during the cold winter months when the moon was in descent—la mancanza. It took a special knowledge to know how to kill and fully utilize the pig for the kitchen. As John Caserta witnessed: "The pig is led out onto the snow, where its throat is cut open, and then it bleeds to death. Then, they take the intestines and various other parts out of the animal and set them aside. They let the carcass hang like this for two days. All the blood drips out and, since it's freezing outside, the meat cools and dries out."[2] Along with the quest to modernize and comply with government sanitary standards, this old tradition was pronounced illegal. Laws state that all pigs be sent to a government-sanctioned butcher. *Photograph courtesy of John Caserta.*

WHAT'S BREWING?

There was much brewing in the 1920s, in part because of the Sulmona–Isernia railway line that came into service in 1897. The Montenero Val Cocchiara train station was one stop on the line. A small two-story building, the passenger station had only the basic services: a waiting room and ticket office. Senator Giuseppe Andrea Angeloni, who was born in Roccaraso, did much to promote the line. Tourists could now visit the area in addition to railroad cars geared to moving soldiers

188

to military camps, and the transporting of cattle and sheep so vital to the local economy. Today, anyone can enjoy the diesel-driven Italian version of the Trans-Siberian Railway for its spectacular views of land and mountainside villages. The Rivisondoli–Pescocostanzo station sits at 4,160 feet (1,268 m) above sea level, second only to the Brenner Pass station. What business would be ideal to build near the railroad line?

A group of wealthy men from Castel di Sangro and nearby villages gathered to discuss business opportunities. What seemed to have great potential was a brewery. Although there were 140 breweries on the Italian peninsula before World War I, by 1920 there were only fifty-eight. Considering the railroad for transportation, the pure waters of the Sangro River, and peat from Montenero's pantano, the decision was made to start a brewery named Birra d'Abruzzo (Beer of Abruzzo) in 1921. Although its administrative office was in Milan, a large production facility and water well were located near the Montenero train station.[6] The brewery employed about one hundred people from Castel di Sangro, Montenero, Scontrone, and other villages.

The company was immediately successful. Production went from fifty thousand gallons per year in the early years to over 160,000 gallons per year in the latter half of the 1920s. There were strong sales in Abruzzo-Molise, but also in Campania and Marche, reached by train. In addition to the beer sales, the company resold caramelized barley to the local farmers for animal feed.

Men used shovels to extract the peat from Montenero's pantano. It was used as a fuel for the brewery because coal was scarce due to its demand for military industries. A facility was specifically built to process the peat. After being extracted, it was refined by chopping to make it easier to dry, and then transported by railway carts to the factory. Those doing this work came from Castel di Sangro, Villa Scontrone, Scontrone, Montenero, and Rionero. After a few years, when coal became available from Germany and proved more economical to use as fuel, peat was no longer required.

Birra d'Abruzzo's distribution cut deeply into the profits of the Peroni company, the major Italian brewery. In 1930 the Peroni company became a majority shareholder in Birra d'Abruzzo. Then, somehow, Birra d'Abruzzo fizzled out. The best guess is that the shareholders unaffiliated with Peroni were bought out. The board of directors decided to close the brewery, and on 19 September 1936, it was legally dissolved. The building and the machinery were sold.

Color of Magenta

chapter 13

Modern Black Shirts: Dressing for World War Two

With the close of World War I, people in the Kingdom of Italy could focus their attention more closely on the internal conditions of their state. Since the birth of the kingdom, Italy had been trying to mold a national identity. The vision was quite blurry. In the ideal state, what lands should be included? How could the various regions be social equals under one government? And what steps should be taken in order to establish a modern Italy that would be respected among leading nations of the world?

A whole slew of philosophies bubbled up to the surface with theoretical schemes that promised to solve all of Italy's problems. These strands of thought covered an intellectual spectrum with much disagreement between each. Such chaos can only lead to stagnation or further disintegration until a group emerges to dominate. In this case, during the following decades, the strong arm of fascism came to the forefront.

The philosopher Giovanni Gentile (1875–1944) is credited with formulating the concepts of Italian Fascism, but Benito Mussolini is the man who implemented it throughout Italy. Both men wrote the influential essay *The Doctrine of Fascism*, published in 1932. When Mussolini organized a mass demonstration in Rome in 1922, he brought the National Fascist Party to the helm of Italian politics. Rather than let Mussolini force his way into power, King Vittorio Emanuele III made him prime minister.

◀ *The Red Bull in the Winter Line*.
Painting by Donna Neary.

When Mussolini came into power, he was faced with a crippled economy that was further hampered by mass strikes. At the start, his regime swiftly and competently dealt with any problem, be it labor unrest, race struggles, or organized crime. His totalitarian method was supported by a new Voluntary Militia for National Security, better known as the Blackshirts. They were inspired by the Arditi, the Italian elite military special forces, or shock troops, that were formed during World War I. Many of the Blackshirts were former soldiers. Under Mussolini, order was restored and corruption was curtailed. The Italian economy and foreign policy were left to professionals who were mainly non-Fascist.

According to an oft-quoted line of John Acton (whose grandfather was prime minister of Naples under Ferdinand IV)—"Power tends to corrupt, and absolute power corrupts absolutely." By 1925, Mussolini had created a one-party dictatorship. Although in the past decade progress had been made in areas such as curbing abuses in the tax system and trimming government spending, Mussolini pushed for alternate policies. Because Italy lacked many important natural resources, new programs sought to develop domestic production where possible and to look abroad for strategic materials not readily available. The solution for the latter was to make trade deals for specific raw materials and through colonization. Russia became a major trading partner. This economic development contributed to polarization between capitalist and Marxist thought within Italy. Regarding colonization, Italy invaded Ethiopia in 1935, adding it to the previously annexed areas known as Italian East Africa. My great-uncle Berardino Di Marco (1910–1995) was drafted into military service from Montenero to fight in Ethiopia.

In the quest to modernize, the Fascists had expanded trade, formed colonies, and nationalized important banks and industries. Great spending went into social welfare programs and public works. Historian Hibbert lists some of the Fascist accomplishments: "Bridges, canals and roads were built, hospitals and schools, railway stations and orphanages; swamps were drained and land reclaimed, forests were planted and universities were endowed."[1] Great progress resulted, but with each passing year, Italy went deeper and deeper in debt.

The Fascist movement affected all aspects of Italian life, be it through the industrial or agricultural sector. By 1939, the Italian state "controlled over four-fifths of Italy's shipping and shipbuilding, three-quarters of its pig-iron production and almost half that of steel."[2] The impact here was mostly in the industrialized north. In the south, the hand of Fascism also took a toll. In trying to direct agricultural usage, the Fascists pushed wheat production, which caused a number of more suitable crops to be neglected.

"The regime's emphasis on Italy's self-sufficiency in grain production forced southern production away from more lucrative crops, thus increasing rural poverty in the South."[3] Through the 1930s, the per capita income in the south was about 40 percent below that of the north. Southern Italy was hard hit by domestic policies as well as a worldwide economic depression in this decade.

Mussolini believed that Italy was heir to ancient Rome's legacy, the empire that once ruled the "known world," and was once again destined to become economically rich and militarily powerful. Fascism was an addictive philosophy that drew both politicians and the populace into dangerously overstepping the limitations of the kingdom and beyond moral restraints. Although Benedetto Croce (1866–1952) stood out as Italy's leading intellectual, his sound criticism of the Fascist government was muffled by the roars of those who believed Mussolini's propaganda. This current took Italy into World War II.

WORLD WAR II ENTANGLEMENT

Early on, Mussolini had encouraged Germany to absorb Austria, Italy's longstanding nemesis. Mussolini and Adolf Hitler shared some common traits, with similar temperaments and ambitions. Since World War I, Germany harbored resentment over territorial losses, such as the area of Alsace-Lorraine, where many from Montenero later immigrated. This is one of the main reasons Germany started annexing German-speaking areas, including Austria. Another reason for growing aggression was the dire economy in Germany.

When German intentions became known, a series of alliances were made. First came the alliance between Germany and Italy in October 1936. Then Japan joined to form the Axis powers, with the three countries forming a military alliance in 1940. As a counterbalance, France, Poland, and the United Kingdom, plus their dependent states, formed the Allied group, which was formalized by the United Nations.

Hitler ordered the invasion of Czechoslovakia in March of 1939. The invasion of Poland followed on 1 September of that year. Two days later, Britain and France declared war on Germany but were reserved in any military action. Then came the German blitzkrieg of 1940—the "lightning war" when they quickly invaded and occupied Denmark, Norway, Holland, and Belgium. After this blitzkrieg, other countries became alarmed and joined the Allied group. These included Canada, Russia, the United States, and China. When Winston Churchill became prime minister and the head of a wartime coalition government, there was a concerted Allied effort to stop Axis aggression.

France could not maintain the front against the German army and eventually had to sign an armistice. With France occupied by German forces, Hitler started the Battle of Britain. Here the British successfully held off a German invasion. A week later, on 11 June 1940, Italy entered the war. Realistically, Italy was not prepared in any way to go to war. However, Mussolini saw an opportunity to expand Italian influence with luck and the support of Germany.

Although the Italians were routed from North Africa by British forces in December 1940, by early 1941 they joined German forces to attack Yugoslavia, Greece, and the island of Crete. While the Axis forces were on fronts in the west and south, Hitler sent an army of three million into Russia on 22 June 1941. This came as a shock for the Russians, who had signed a treaty with Germany back in 1939. Now Germany also had an eastern front.

Allied powers faced an unprecedented task of shrinking the Nazi and Fascist expansion on all fronts. The British held firm despite German bombings of their major cities, and Russian armies were successfully holding on their front, in part because German troops were overextended and immobilized by harsh winter weather. After six months of horrific fighting, the Battle of Stalingrad ended with the first major German defeat in February of 1943. By May, Axis powers were pushed out of North Africa by British and American forces. In addition, Italian forces were badly defeated on the Russian front and in Greece.

In July 1943, British, Canadian, and American forces invaded Sicily by sea and air to fight against Italian and German troops. About six weeks later, the island was in Allied hands. During the engagements in Sicily, there was a meeting of the Grand Council of Fascism that voted to remove Mussolini as leader of the Fascist party. King Vittorio Emanuele III immediately replaced him with Pietro Badoglio as prime minister. To top it off, the king had Mussolini arrested. Much of the political and civilian population in Italy had turned against Mussolini and the German presence on the peninsula.

There was fear that the Germans may try to get Mussolini back into power, so in late August he was secretly transported to Campo Imperatore in the Abruzzo mountain wilderness. During Benito's imprisonment, Prime Minister Badoglio took steps to quietly dissolve relations with Germany. He terminated the Fascist party. On 3 September 1943 there was formal recognition that the Kingdom of Italy surrendered to the Allies. The German attitude toward the Italians turned very hostile because of this.

With the loss of North Africa and Sicily, Germany prepared for

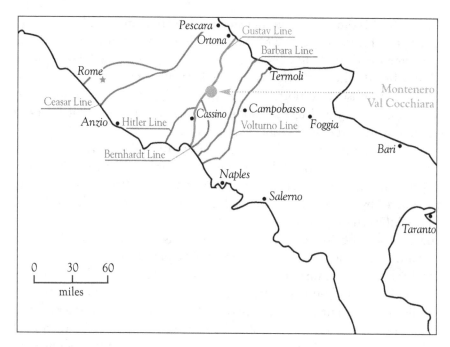

▲ German lines of defense.

an Allied invasion on the Italian peninsula. Where to draw the battle line? Of course the Germans wanted to keep Allied forces at a distance from their homeland. Symbolically, it would be beneficial to keep control of Rome, the Eternal City. Hitler drew three defensive lines across the boot, just south of Rome: the Volturno, the Barbara, and the Gustav Lines. There were some German troops patrolling farther south as well.

On 3 September, British forces landed at Taranto by ship. With little resistance, they moved north and eventually captured important airfields near the city of Foggia. Two infantry divisions soon arrived as reinforcements. Also on 3 September, British and Canadian forces landed on the west coast at Messina. German forces retreated but slowed Allied progress by demolishing transportation routes.

A major Allied thrust in Italy came on 9 September 1943. American and British forces landed at Salerno against heavy German opposition. Each Allied division fought its way to specified beach locations and made gains inland. Salerno was captured, but Allied forces became bogged down. By 12 September, the Allies had lost momentum, and they went on the defensive. German counterattacks caused heavy casualties. Allied strength in the air and sea turned the tide again on the 14th, and the commander of the German forces, General Kesselring, ordered a withdrawal.

At this time, glider aircraft silently brought German troops to Gran Sasso in Abruzzo to retrieve Mussolini. Not a shot was fired, which defies the propaganda that elite forces rescued him in a daring raid. Hitler made Mussolini the head of the Italian Socialist Republic, a puppet Fascist regime established in north Italy with few supporters. There were two governments now in Italy: Mussolini's in the north and the Allied-backed government in the south under Pietro Badoglio.

The Allies continued to advance. With the Salerno area secure, the next objective for the Allied forces was Naples. Fighting their way northward, the Allied entrance into Naples on 1 October was greatly facilitated by an uprising among the local population against the Germans. The Allies then pushed on toward the Volturno Line, the first line of defense specifically designed by the Germans. This extended from the mouth of the Volturno River just north of Naples through central Molise to Termoli on the Adriatic coast. In the area of Castel San Vincenzo, for example, mopping-up operations were carried out by Canadian troops, while observing enemy movements and defending against counterattacks.

By 6 October, the British 8th Army on the Adriatic side forced German troops to retreat to the Barbara Line, their next line of prepared defenses on the Trigno River. Five days later, the U.S. Fifth Army broke through the Volturno Line, forcing German troops to the Barbara Line, less than ten miles from the Volturno Line. Given the challenges of transporting military equipment and supplies over difficult terrain, the Allied divisions took a few weeks to regroup. Italian resistance fighters had been assisting the Allies, as they did in the uprising in Naples. On 13 October 1943, Italy declared war on Germany and became a member of the Allied side.

Allied fighting commenced on 3 November 1943 and finally, on 9 November, the forward units stood face to face with German forces on the Gustav Line. This was the most formidable defensive line to be drawn south of Rome. It ran along natural river courses. On the western side of the peninsula are the Gargiliano and Rapido Rivers. The latter river reaches Monte Cassino, the site of a famed Benedictine Abbey originating in the sixth century. Because Monte Cassino was in the most strategic position, it was the main German stronghold on the Gustav Line. On the other side of the peninsula, the Sangro River marked the western portion of the Gustav Line, ending about fourteen miles north of Vasto.

In the fall of 1943, fifteen German divisions were stationed along the Gustav. Along the line were soldiers with their portable firearms, machine-gun emplacements, pillboxes, and artillery placements. Minefields and barbed wire were carefully placed to obstruct expected Allied charges.

Adding the troops that retreated from the Barbara Line, the total of German divisions on the Gustav Line increased to twenty-three. This made a formidable force of 215,000 troops who were in the best positions along the line to defend against an oncoming Allied force that nearly tripled the number of German troops.

▼ Polish military map showing positions of Allied and German divisions along the Gustav Line. *Courtesy of Miroslaw Kucharski.*

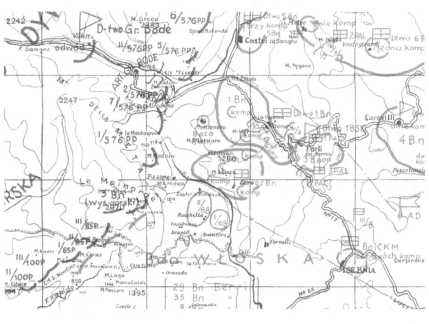

• A Universal Carrier with machine gun guarding the entrance to Montenero, 2 March 1944. 3rd Carrier Platoon, 3rd. Battalion. Signal Corps photo #MM-5-44-2044. *Courtesy of Dave Kerr. National archives, photo no. SC-187829.*

Montenero sits on the Gustav Line point between the German forces and the Allies, on the border between Abruzzo and Molise, in the Apennine mountains about sixty miles from the Adriatic coast and sixty miles from the Tyrrhenian coast. Its location placed it between the U.S. 5th Army and the British 8th Army.

As early as 2 November, before Allied forces actually reached Montenero, the British 1st London Irish Rifles were positioned on high ground south of the Sangro River covering the road from the village. More forces were on the way. On 4 November, a British infantry unit entered deserted Isernia. Five days later, Forlì del Sannio was taken. General Miles Dempsey ordered the British 5th Division to advance toward Alfedena and Castel di Sangro. Heavily defended, Alfedena was a strategic point along highway 83, and the route through Montenero "was the only route to the inner line of enemy defences" that the Germans deployed there.[4]

The British planned a major attack along the east coast. In hopes of distracting the Germans and thinning their defense in that area, they planned to feint a major attack toward the Alfedena/Castel di Sango area.

> On 14 November Headquarters . . . defined the leading role assigned to the 3rd Canadian Brigade in the deception plan. The 5th Division, simulating an attempt to link up with the American Fifth Army, was to cut the lateral road between Castel di Sangro and Alfedena.[5]
> . . . [P]lanners devised an elaborate scheme to create the impression that the assault would be made by Dempsey's Corps through the mountains, rather than by the 5th Corps along the coast. This meant concealing the concentration on the right and, before the main assault was launched, presenting a strong threat by the 13th Corps against Castel di Sangro and Alfedena—two towns on the upper reaches of the River Sangro commanding the roads which led northwestward to Avezzano.[6]

According to Kemp, Montenero was still in German hands on 22 November, but the Germans chose to retreat while Allied troops moved in. "The night of November 22/23 was one of incessant rain. Battalion Headquarters moved into Montenero and set up there with the ammunition point, while Royal Engineers were employed in removing German mines in the dark."[7] On the same day, the 8th British Army began an offensive on the Sangro River. The British 5th Division reached

Alfedena, a seven-mile walk north of Montenero, and found that German troops had withdrawn. With the assistance of American support artillery, a Canadian platoon captured Castel San Vincenzo, about a ten-mile walk south of Montenero. By early December, the Canadians made their move from Isernia toward Castel di Sangro via Rionero. Their adventure is captured by David Cole's firsthand experience, which is worth quoting in detail:

> After a bone-shaking lorry ride along mountain roads we were dumped in the one-mule town of Rionero. From there on, as frequent signboards and the evidence of burned trucks warned us, the road forward was under enemy observation and shellfire the whole way.
>
> Rionero was a dreadful place, its buildings largely destroyed by German demolitions and shelling; its roads and fields awash with mud; rats, understandably disenchanted with their accommodations, scurrying from ruin to ruin; and low cloud casting a damp mist over everything. While we were there a number of huge German shells burst in the mud and rubble around us, reminding us that it no longer mattered how many shopping days there were to Christmas.[8]

Anyone who has visited Montenero knows well the road to Castel di Sangro, where State Highways 17 and 83 meet near the Zittola River bridge. Arriving at the crossroads from Rionero, there is a sharp right turn to Castel di Sangro. As Cole narrates:

> Here, at a T-junction, we turned right and, inviting decimation, hurried down a straight, flat road [SS 17] leading under the eyes of the Germans, towards Castel di Sangro. The river, running parallel to the road, was so close in places that we could hear the roar of its torrent and glimpse the moonlight glinting on its ripples. On the far side we could see the railway line winding around the foot of the mountains and, beyond that, the wooden slopes from which the vast mass of the ridge rose steeply unto the sky. It was an eerie and rather frightening walk. Only the river separated us from the Germans and indeed their patrols, as we knew, regularly crossed it to lay mines or ambushes along the road.[9]

Even by November, it was evident that whenever German soldiers withdrew from a town or village, they destroyed everything and anything that could be useful to the Allies. This scorched-earth policy included the buildings. In some cases, this might have been done in revenge for Italy becoming an Allied member. Locals would read an evacuation notice to leave and know their homes would be destroyed on a specified day. "With typical thoroughness the Germans had seized all food stocks and cattle, evicted the unfortunate inhabitants and then demolished and burned their homes."[10] We see this in the firsthand observation recorded in a war diary: "Castel del Giudice visibly burning. . . S. Pietro flattened, also burning. Ateleta observed burning. Caprocotta burning."[11] Many were left homeless.

For Montenero, 6 November was the unlucky day. The Germans announced that they would destroy the village and all should leave. The family of Oreste and Elia Caserta and others went to Cupone, near Cerro al Volturno, where American troops were stationed. Some went to other villages or into the countryside. The bombing left almost no home untouched. Even the gems of Montenero architecture were destroyed or damaged. For example, two beautiful homes owned by Filippo Procario were leveled. They once stood near where the small sacred shrine, "the Monumentino," stands today.

Numerous villages suffered the same consequences. When the 3rd Canadian Infantry Brigade and the West Nova Scotia Regiment arrived in Castel di Sangro, they found it wasn't spared. A soldier reported: "The town was in ruins. So exposed were we that any movement made without the cover of walls or vegetation would attract an immediate hail of shells, mortar bombs or machine-gun bullets."[12] The source of the most deadly fire came from Point 1009, the steep hill that towers over the city. The B Company of the West Nova Scotia Regiment attacked it on 23 November, but the Canadians were driven back with casualties: four killed, ten wounded, and sixteen captured.

The following day, artillery pounded Point 1009. Within thirty minutes, five thousand rounds were discharged. The bombardment was followed with A Company charging the hill, while C Company provided fire cover. When troops reached the summit, the Germans had already withdrawn. Point 1009 was a prize, as it provided excellent observation of the Sangro River Valley. Most of the buildings in Castel di Sangro were destroyed. "There were, by mistake, a few buildings left intact."[13] Advanced Battalion Headquarters moved into one. Locals started to return to the city from hiding in the mountains, but they found no homes to enter.

Nearly all of the area between Alfedena to the Adriatic was now void of German forces. However, they had placed battalions of the 305th Division on the high ground just up the road from Alfedena toward Barrea to defend the mountain passes. Another regiment of the 305th was near Pizzone. About ten miles north of Castel di Sangro, in Rocca Cinquemiglia, the German 1st Parachute Division was given the task of breaking communications and harassing the Allies. German artillery was positioned on Mount Arazecca, just west of Rocca Cinquemiglia and overlooking the road running between Castel di Sangro and Roccaraso. The area was relatively quiet for the following week.

As German forces withdrew to the fortified Gustav Line, Allied forces approached to feel out the terrain and define enemy positions. During the cold months of November and December, Montenero felt the impact of the weather as well as troop movements along the line. In November, troops were arriving in and around Montenero. Those under the British 8th Army consisted of a mix of Scottish, Irish, British, Belgian, and Polish. The 2nd Battalion Wiltshire Regiment included the Irish 2nd Royal Inniskilling Fusiliers and the 2nd Cameronians Scottish Rifles. Belgian and Polish troops were under the British 8th Army. Their prime duty was reconnaissance.

Action could be fierce. Some troops were sent on leave to Campobasso to refresh. Others were moved to other battle sectors. Colonel J. Kemp gives a good description of the conditions of one such troop transfer that serves as an example of other transfers yet to come:

> On the afternoon of November 26 the 2nd Seaforth [Highlanders] arrived from Brigade reserve to replace the Fusiliers. The German shellfire was increasing in intensity, and the tracks leading off the road from Rionero to Montenero by which the relief was being undertaken were under heavy fire, causing dispersions and delays. However the relief was completed by 4 a.m. on November 27, and the Fusiliers were carried back to San Angelo in the transport which had brought the Seaforth forward. The total casualties of the Battalion in this operation were four killed, 25 wounded and 11 missing.[14]

In recounting his experience with the 5th Battalion, The Northamptonshire Regiment, Ivor Cutler wrote the following:

> Reconnaissance parties under the Commanding Officer went to the area of Montenero and on the night of 10th December . . . we relieved 2 Battalion Wiltshire Regiment (5 Division). The ground was very rugged and mountainous, heights ranging from 3000 to 5000 feet and it was necessary to employ mules to transport rations, ammunition and other supplies to the forward Companies.
> The mule track was over a difficult mountain track, and it took about an hour to accomplish the journey. Two platoons, 75

mules in each, were stationed in the village at the disposal of the [battalion].[15]

Cutler continues, explaining the battalion's activities:

Our patrols were busy, mainly to prevent infiltration of enemy patrols, to find out the enemy's intentions, not let him break contact, and to find suitable river crossings. The enemy were occupying the high ground immediately on the other side of the river and we found their patrols were enterprising. Two parties of enemy were seen to be wearing white cloaks as camouflage, blending with the snow.[16]

Germans shelled strategic points in and around Montenero, and British troops hit targets with rounds of artillery and heavy 4.2 mortars. There were deaths and some soldiers captured. The Allied presence in Montenero was bolstered when four South African officers arrived on 22 December, and two days later another officer and eighty-six soldiers join the roster.

The troops would never forget celebrating Christmas in Montenero. They divided duty and leisure, with roughly half the troops celebrating on the 25th and the other half on the 27th. As Cutler recounts:

A carol service followed by Communion was held in the village the following morning and then the men had a wonderful Christmas dinner. [Battalion] funds had bought turkey, Christmas pudding, oranges, tangerines, figs, nuts and mincemeat. The [Navy, Army, and Air Force Institutes] issue of wine, beer, whiskey, chocolate and cigarettes, as well as an issue of pork, ensured that there was nothing lacking. Indeed it was wonderful.[17]

The company positioned nearest to the enemy could hear the carol "Silent Night" being sung in German,[18] as originally written by a Roman Catholic priest in Austria. The silence those soldiers enjoyed became a memory, as many stationed in and around Montenero would soon be transferred to the western sector to partake in the battle for Cassino.

ENTER THE COMMANDOS

Earlier in December, the 3rd Canadian Division moved from Rionero to meet up with British troops in Castel di Sangro. Other troops soon arrived in the area to provide support. Under the British 8th Army was the special British No. 10 (Inter-Allied) Commando Unit. It consisted of eight troops,

▲ A Universal Carrier of the 3rd Carpathian Rifle Division
advances near Montenero in March 1944.

mainly composed of foreigners. Three of the units were positioned in the
Montenero area, including the exiled commandos from Belgium (Number
4 Troop) and Poland (Number 6 Troop).

Van der Bijl notes: "On 13 December they joined 56th [London
Infantry Division] and were placed under command of its 56th Reconnais-
sance [Regiment], whose tactical frontage extended from Villa Santa Maria
to Castel di Sangro, facing the centre of the German defenses known as the
Gustav Line."[19] It is interesting how peoples forced into exile in northern
Europe by German invasion came to Italy to fight against the Germans.
The Belgian and Polish troops were supported by Number 3 Troop, a group
also known as X Troop, largely composed of German and Austrian Jews.

The primary mission of the Polish 6th Troop was to patrol the area
and attack or disrupt the enemy where possible. Likewise, another Polish
group, the independent 3rd Carpathian Rifle Division under Major
General B. B. Duch, conducted reconnaissance along nearly twenty-five
miles of the Gustav Line. The principle objective was "the reconnaissance of the strategic high ground of Montenero, with the aim of denying
this terrain to the Germans who would then have threatened the eastern
flank of the Eighth Army."[20]

They were successful in attacking the railroad station in Alfedena,
and they weakened German defenses in the area south to Pizzone. The 3rd
Carpathian Rifle Division held its ground and provided safe travel over
the roads connecting Alfedena, Castel San Vincenzo, and Rionero,
including the intersection at the Zittola River. The roads were important
to keep open for the transport of supplies. Soldiers patrolled in armored
cars in Montenero and hiked to nearby hilltops—Il Calvario, Colle

Gallina, and Monte Sitacciaro—toward Alfedena on reconnaissance missions. They likewise scouted from key points of elevation, such as Mount Miglio, Mount Pagano, Montagnola, Mount Morrone, and Mount Curvale. The enemy was near. On several occasions German troops sneaked into Montenero and were repulsed by Polish troops.

▲ 4th Belgian Troop, 10th Commando in Montenero. They arrived in December 1943 to carry out patrols and raids.

▶ One of the smocks from Montenero, now in the Museum of Belgium Commandos.

The Belgian 4th Troop participated alongside the Poles, conducting reconnaissance and dealing with the enemy. This group of commandos was composed of over one hundred men under the direction of Captain George Danloy. One of the officers who helped form the unit was Lieutenant Albert Deton. While leading a night patrol on a hill near Montenero on 3 January 1944, Deton was shot and killed. His name is immortalized on a plaque on a monument in the piazza of San Pietro Avellana, about seventeen miles from Montenero. Corporal Marcel Mairesse's name is on the same plaque. He was mortally wounded during a night patrol behind enemy lines near this commune. To help the Belgian commandos blend in with the snow-covered terrain, the parish priest in Montenero provided white smocks that worked as camouflage. One of the smocks is exhibited in the Museum of Belgian Commandos, located in Flawinne, just south of Brussels.

As noted in the Polish diaries, "[T]he most important direction of the reconnaissance was the area of Montenero."[21] For the 17 February operation called "Foxtrot," troops went through Colle Alto and Il Calvario "towards the Alfedena railway station, where they prepared an ambush and destroyed German defenses and the enemy took significant losses."[21] Similar actions were taken on 20 February in Operation Orzel and 3 and 4 March in the area of Colle Gallina.

The Belgian and Polish troops welcomed the London Irish Rifles 2nd Battalion, which arrived in Montenero at 7:00 p.m. from Campobasso, via State Road 17 passing Rionero:

> On December 27 they started a move which eventually brought them into the line again in the hills near Montenero. New Year's Eve came, and with it a blizzard which those who experienced it will never forget. The snow fell all day, gradually getting thicker and thicker. At 1600 hours G Company came across a German patrol, some forty strong, and a sharp encounter ensued. But visibility was so bad that little could be seen of the effect of the fire or of casualties to the enemy. They eventually retired and disappeared into the blizzard. At night the snow was three to four feet deep, and the next morning permission was given to withdraw the forward companies to Montenero.[22]

On 30 December the London Irish Rifles, together with the Belgian troop, attacked the Germans around Montenero. Such skirmishes with German troops occurred regularly. Fortunately, security around Montenero would be strengthened when the Northamptonshire Regiment was relieved and the London Irish Rifles took over the headquarters in the village on 31 December. Troops were organized into companies and a battalion in and around the village with Major-General Keightley as divisional commander:

Company/Battalion	Location
F Company: Alto 0447	above SS 158 N of MV
E Company: Colle Calvario 0346	above SS 158 W of MV
G Company: Il Monte 0342	above SS 158 SW of MV
H Company and Battalion HQs	in Montenero 035829

Company Quartermaster Sergeant Edmund O'Sullivan wrote of the London Irish Rifles' arrival in Montenero with five hundred men. Three hundred were posted on surrounding hills, but about two hundred stayed in the village. "This meant that much of the local population had been displaced. The story was repeated across Italy. A populous and overcrowded state had two vast armies that took over nearly all the limited accommodations and were at the same time destroying most of the country's facilities."[23]

In the early months of 1944, there were numerous encounters between the German and Allied forces along the Gustav Line in the Montenero sector. As the day dawned on 19 January, two platoons of E Company were positioned in the snowy woods on Mt. Calvario near Alfedena. They were hit with twenty shells, one being a direct hit on platoon headquarters. Only the commander was left uninjured. Troops jumped into their trenches for protection. Soon after the initial shelling, both platoons "were rushed at short range, each by a party of about twenty Germans who used Schmeissers, rifle and stick grenades and the bayonet."[24] Members of one platoon composed of thirteen men were killed or captured. Five men from the other platoon escaped.

Other troops of E Company were called in, and they counterattacked with British artillery support, causing the enemy to retreat toward Barrea. The Germans had taken some prisoners. Following a shootout, the British prisoners were rescued. In all, the Allied troops had suffered six killed, fourteen wounded, and nineteen prisoners. The Germans had six killed, one wounded, and one taken prisoner, with others who retreated possibly wounded.

A few times the Germans actually entered Montenero, as on 7 March, but were soon repulsed. Between 19 March and 20 April, they lost Montenero and also Alfedena to Allied powers.

War Diaries

War diaries for the London Irish Rifles, Polish 6th Commando Troop, and the 2nd Cameronians Scottish Rifles provide detailed day-by-day accounts of what transpired in Montenero from November 1943 to June 1944. We get the feel for constant flux as German and Allied troops adjusted their battle lines. Patrols probing for any sign of change and gathering intelligence gave snapshots of enemy positions, artillery placement, and use of mines.

The daily reports detail any casualty, killed or wounded, resulting from small-arms fire to aerial bombing. This includes notes on both the Allied side and the German side, in addition to statistics on prisoners. Day and night, homes and bridges were bombed. Military activities depended greatly upon the weather, and precise measurements were taken even for river depth and snow cover. During the winter months, supplies often could not be delivered by motor vehicle. Many times supplies came on the backs of mules. Ski patrols were practical in the terrain, as the Belgian troops were noted for their experience. The state of communications—or lack of communications—was monitored as the vital link between Allied troops. There was constant maintenance and work to keep up with the changing front. The intensity of military duty found some relief with periods of rest and leave, usually to Campobasso.

War diaries also include notes on the activities of civilians, some of whom acted as informants, and who were trying to adapt to war conditions. Church functions and parades bolstered morale. For all the details recorded in war diaries, the most profound aspects of facing life in Montenero during this time can only be found through personal stories provided by those who survived the war. Their firsthand experiences are often so painful that they are not easily shared.

PERSONAL ACCOUNTS

"*Mano a borsa.*" Everyone is familiar with the hand gesture—all fingers and thumb tips meet, and the hand is moved back and forth toward one's mouth—used when questioning just about anything. A big question requires both hands in gesture. Some say the hand posture is the same used when people ate using their hands without any utensils. People simply picked up food with their fingers and placed it into their mouths. But what happens when there is no food to eat? The hand is empty. It is a big problem: how can one eat? This problem occurred often through Italian history, and in Montenero during World War II, civilians often went to sleep hungry.

War disrupted farming and the activities associated with food production. Mills, barns, and homes, for instance, were totally destroyed in Montenero from German bombing. During and after the war, children often went through the debris of such buildings in search of food or any other item that may be useful, including tools and clothing.

Before Italy changed sides by declaring war on Germany, relations between the German soldiers and the Italians were bearable. When the soldiers occupied the village, the locals hid food and even animals when possible; otherwise, the goods would be confiscated. Children were brave enough to steal cigarettes out of the soldiers' backpacks without worry of drastic consequences. Civilians obeyed rules and regulations demanded by the military officials. But the German-Italian relationship changed after Italy joined the Allies. The word "atrocity" entered conversations of German activities throughout Italy.

GERMAN OCCUPATION OF MONTENERO

Thousands of stories could be recounted about the personal experiences that occurred when Montenero was occupied by German troops. Feelings of horror and disgrace keep many memories from surfacing. We do know about the scorched-earth policy that resulted in the destruction of so many homes in Montenero. One could hear the whistles caused by the fins of falling bombs, which gave some seconds for people to run out of the house or to safer areas. Children would squat down in the open fields or roads with hands on top of their heads. Homes were leveled from the top of the village to the bottom. Near the intersection of Via Nostra Signora Lourdes and Via Immacolata, Filippo Procario had two beautiful homes destroyed. Today there is empty space where a house once stood in the Corte district in upper Montenero. As mentioned earlier, only rubble remains of the home of Serifino (1860–1942) and Angela Di Marco (1865–1926), my great-grandparents. However, the loss of material things is only part of what affects the innermost being of people.

When German troops first arrived in Montenero, some took over the best homes to live in. As months passed, the relationships soured, particularly after Italy had joined the Allies. It was a time of war. German troops kept order through intimidation at the point of their gun barrels. Curfew was in effect. The best observation post over the village was the church bell tower. A German machine-gunner who was placed there saw a man walking toward the pantano. The gunner shouted a warning, but the man didn't flinch and kept walking. The German fired, and the man was killed. This man was Pietro Iacobozzi, brother of my great-grandmother Filomena Iacobozzi Caserta. He was a senior citizen, nearly deaf. He never heard the warning.

Another relative, Mariano Di Marco, was among those lined up to face a firing squad near the archway Portanova at the start of the street with the same name. Two men, Mariano and Alfredo Tornincasa, bolted for their lives. Mariano was shot in the back. His death left behind a widow to care for three boys and a girl. Alfredo Tornincasa suffered injuries and recovered. In the scuffle, the others were fortunate to escape.

Whenever a soldier is far from home and knows he may die any day, normal moral restraints can easily be lost. Villagers were abused in ways that were often too painful for them to describe. Germans cut off women's breasts. Italian women were often targets for rape. In Montenero, some hid in their homes, trembling as German soldiers paused on their doorsteps to smoke. They prayed the soldiers would continue walking after finishing their cigarettes. In one incident, soldiers approached a young lady, and her mother stepped in to try to protect her daughter. Both were killed for resisting.

After living under such tyranny and seeing horrific acts of crime committed regularly, many locals left Montenero seeking safety. After Mussolini was arrested, Italian soldiers were unsure which political side to support. One's fate hung in the balance. Amelio Procario, a Montenerese soldier stationed in Rome, thought of a way where he didn't need to decide: he disguised himself as a woman and, with his purse under arm, made his way to Greece. Many chose to stay in other villages or hide in the mountains. Near Montenero's pantano, there is a cave where many hid while German soldiers were staying in the village. During the night, villagers would sneak back to their homes and to secret hiding places to retrieve food. Today, the entrance to that cave can barely be seen through the overgrowth, and the interior has since crumbled. It was more spacious in the 1940s; however, the best comfort was having some straw on which to sleep. Under such tensions and conditions, it is not surprising that a young pregnant woman lost her baby while in the cave. Shielded by the night's darkness, in order to avoid being shot by the Germans, her courageous husband and his friend took the infant's swaddled body to the cemetery church to be left on the altar. It was all they could do.

As the Germans were preparing to retreat from Montenero, they rounded up whoever they could from the village to transport them to camps, such as one in Pescocostanzo. While Aristide Di Marco was being ported away by truck, he noticed thick brush by the roadside and jumped off the truck into it. Perfect timing kept his escape from being noticed, and he lived to tell the story. He eventually raised a family. While in custody, he had prayed to the Madonna, promising that if he escaped, he would name a child Maria in gratitude. He kept his promise.

Aristide's mother, Rosa Di Nicola, was a petite elderly woman at this time. Her family members, along with members of the Pede family, were contemplating how to break free from the Germans. Rosa put her life on the line by offering a guard food and begging him to let the two families escape. Pasquale Pede sent his young son Clemente to their barn in the San Sisto area of the pantano to save their horse. He slipped away and stayed in the shelter for three days, alone and terrified, waiting for the others to join him. They arrived at the barn, as did a few other Montenerese. From the barn, all could watch as the village was engulfed in flames.

Even after the Germans left and Allied forces were in the village, dangers lurked. One day an explosion suddenly broke the relative calm. As soon as the blast was heard, my great-aunt Ernesta Caserta (Gonella/Mazzocco) ran to an open window screaming. It seems she instinctively knew that her son Antonio Mazzocco was killed. He and four other children were collecting metals and other items they could sell. They found a grenade, dropped it, and it detonated in Piazza Gigliotti near the present location of the Monumentino. The location has also been referred to as the Piazza of the Five Martyrs. The same happened to other youngsters on Via Roma.

While children were playing soccer, they noticed a man approaching. He was holding a grenade he had just found. When the ball was kicked, young Ludovico Di Fiore ran a distance to retrieve it. As he picked up the ball he heard an explosion that killed his childhood friends, including his cousin Guerino Tornincasa. The boys were cut down in the flowering of their youth.

A seven-year-old boy found a grenade in the yard next to his home. He was little Ernesto Caserta (1937–2010), son of Oreste and Elia Miraldi. The grenade exploded in his hand, and he lost a few fingers. The Allies took him to Rionero, where he was treated in an American medical unit. To prevent any complications, the doctors decided to remove Ernesto's hand. A few months later he returned home, accompanied by a lady named Bonaminio, who was treated for a leg wound. Ernesto would not be able to do much of the work associated with village life, so his parents sent him to Naples at the age of twelve to attend school. He graduated from Antonio Genovesi State High School in 1957 and continued to pursue his passion for academics.

After the Caserta family immigrated to Erie, Pennsylvania, Ernesto kept up his studies and received a doctorate degree from Harvard University. He taught Italian language and literature at Boston University from 1967 to 1970 and at Duke University from 1970 to 2001. Professor Caserta was the author of numerous books and articles published in Italy and America, notably on the philosopher and literary critic Benedetto Croce, and nineteenth-century writers Alessandro Manzoni and Giacomo Leopardi. He inspired many worldwide in the study and appreciation of Italian history and culture. In large part, this book would not have been written without his thoughtful encouragement and exemplary role.

All in Montenero who were on the Gustav Line, from newborn to elderly, suffered physical and mental scars from the war. The above accounts provide only a glimpse into the hardships faced during that period. The survivors persevered, some more successfully than others. Visions and memories of the horrors of war are often overbearing and can crush the human spirit. Or, the experience can serve to inspire others to live their lives with purpose. The sacrifices of those who came before us offer better lives to those who follow.

Since World War II, there have been pending legal cases concerning German atrocities in Italy. There were many incidents against civilians that occurred as German troops retreated from the Gustav Line northward. Concerning Nazi war crimes, records claim that close to fourteen thousand Italian civilians died in more than 5,300 individual cases involving many children, women, and elderly. These numbers do not include cases involving Jews. One of the most infamous incidents took place in a Tuscan hill village. "As the Nazis retreated in northern Italy in August 1944, the SS 16th Division murdered 560 civilians, including more than 130 children at Sant'Anna di Stazzema in the Tuscan hills."[25] Less than fifteen miles from Montenero the Pietransieri massacre occurred when Nazi soldiers killed 128 civilians on 21 November 1943. The legal case for Pietransieri, often associated with Rocarasso, is still ongoing. "The court sentenced Germany for the murder of 128 people in the Abruzzo village . . . to pay 1.6 million euros to the community and 5 million euros to the bereaved."[26]

> [L]ocals tell of a German who used to return to Pietransiere every year on the anniversary of the massacre. That he would stand alone in the field where the families had been slaughtered in silence for a long period of time, then quietly return to wherever he came from. No one ever spoke to him on these visits. No one ever asked him why he came or what he had done. It was so typical of those villagers to keep their distance and their silence.[27]

Same with the Montenerese. They keep a distance. They keep silent. If all the stories were told, what would change? If the younger generation knew the stories, would they have a different view of those who were in Montenero during the German occupation? Would they see them with more care and tenderness? Would knowing the stories affect the lives of the postwar generations? As is, many who were born after the war do not know the stories. Although the above narratives represent a small chapter of a much greater tome, they contribute to an essential part of the history of Montenero.

WAR'S END

Before the end of April 1944, Allied powers had succeeded in pushing the Axis military units off the Gustav Line. Montenero and the

SOLDATI DI TER

S. CLEMENTE ROTEGG

E FATE CHE RITORNINO

MONTENERO V

Soldiers of earth, sky, and sea. St. Clement, protect our soldiers and let them return victorious to their homes.
▲ Honoring Montenero's soldiers. *Courtesy of Riccardo Collella.*

surrounding area were now secure. Although relative peace had returned to the village, repercussions remained of the previous months of scorched earth.

The military and political situation in Italy was rapidly changing. On 2 June, General Kesselring made the decision to move German troops out of Rome. Allies moved into Rome on 4 June as the German army retreated to its next major line of defense. They dug their heels in at the Gothic Line with the help of more than fifteen thousand slave-laborers. Like the Gustav Line, this line was defended with a couple of thousand machine gun emplacements, bunkers, and strategic artillery placements. The line went from the Ligurian Sea west of Pisa through Florence to Pesero on the Adriatic Sea. Basically, German defenses followed the mountain wall naturally provided by the Apennines. It took two months for the Allies to move north, fighting their way past Florence and closing in on the Gothic Line.

Allied soldiers fought their way north city by city, with much help from Italian partisans. Because there were still two Italian governments in

Courtesy of Jane Caserta.

ERNESTO G. CASERTA (1937–2010)
Some of his publications:

- 2001 *Saggi Critici su Croce.*
  Naples: Loffredo Editore.
- 2001 *Trent'anni di critica italiana.*
  Recensioni (1971–1995).
  Florence: Franco Cesati Editore.
- 1988 *Studi crociani negli Stati Uniti:*
  bibliografia critica (1964–1984).
  Naples: Loffredo.
- 1988 *Venti'anni di Studi Crociani negli Stati Uniti.* Naples: Loffredo Editore.
- 1987 *Croce and Marxism: From the Years of Revisionism*
  to the Last Postwar Period. Naples: Morano Editore.
- 1980 *L'ultimo Leopardi: Pensiero e Poesia.* Rome: Bonacci Editore.
- 1977 *Manzoni's Christian Realism.* Florence: Leo S. Olschki Casa Editrice.
- 1976 *The War of the Mice and the Crabs* (North Carolina Studies
  in the Romance Languages and Literatures),
  by Giacomo Leopardi (Author), Ernesto G. Caserta (Editor).
  Chappel Hill, NC: The University of North Carolina Press.
- 1972 *Croce Critico Letterario (1881–1921).* Naples: Giannini.

▲ Much of Montenero in October 1952 was still in rubble since World War II.
Courtesy of Montenero V. Municipal Office.

opposition, the Italian resistance was drawn into fighting a civil war against the Nazi-backed puppet regime. Winter weather brought a much quieter time, as troop movement was nearly impossible. Renewed offenses went into effect in April with the support of aerial and artillery bombardments. The Gothic Line started to collapse, and Allied troops reached the Po River before month's end. By this time, the German army was exhausted and retreating on all fronts, backed up against the Alps. On 28 April, Fascist dictator Benito Mussolini was shot dead by partisans and hung by his heels in Milan. The Italians now had one government, and Allied forces moved into cities along their northern border. The Germans had no alternative but to give up. General Heinrich von Vietinghoff signed an agreement of surrender at the Royal Palace of Caserta on 29 April 1945. This signaled the end of the conflict in Italy. The surrender of Germany on 2 May formally ended World War II in Europe.

ITALIAN CASUALTIES STATISTICS
Population in 1939	44,394,000
Military Deaths in WWII	319,207
Military Wounded	225,000 to 320,000
Civilian Deaths in WWII	153,147
Civilian Deaths from Holocaust	8,000

chapter 14

Postwar
Pleasures and Pains

At war's end, Italy was a country in ruins. The economy was destroyed, and the populace was divided on many social and political issues. Hundreds of thousands were homeless and unemployed. Food was being rationed.

With hopes to return the country to normal as soon as possible, the government's immediate concerns revolved around reconstruction in addition to social and economic reforms. The Kingdom of Italy, tainted by its association with Fascism, forced the king to bend to the winds of change by holding a general vote. On 2 June 1946, a direct vote was made to choose a new type of government. Programmed by their unique historical experiences, northerners voted for a republic while southerners favored a monarchy. This was the first time in Italian history that women were allowed to vote. As a result of the elections, the monarchy was abolished, and the Republic of Italy was founded. A series of prime ministers would come into office, emerging from a slew of political parties. The major parties were the Christian Democratic Party, the Italian Socialist Party, and the Italian Communist Party. After the war, the Christian Democratic Party dominated with ever-present opposition from other parties, particularly the Italian Communist Party.

Severely damaged industries, the lack of natural resources, crippled railroads and harbors, a paralyzed agricultural sector, and a collapsed currency that doubled the cost of goods . . . how would the Republic of Italy ever recover? Money was the key, and it arrived in 1948 as part of the United States' European Recovery Program, usually referred to as the Marshall Plan. It provided $13.3 billion, divided among sixteen European countries, including Italy. Adjusted for modern inflation, $13.3 billion would be like giving about $145 billion today. Despite this large sum, it took about five years to see the effects from the funds.

The early decades of the Italian Republic reflect the developing Cold War struggle between the United States and Russia. The United States' investment would hinge on Italy's pursuit of democratic ideals versus those of communism. Because the United States fought on Italian soil and was the political and cultural leader on the world stage, most Italians leaned toward democracy.

After visiting the State Department in Washington, DC, Prime Minister Alcide De Garsperi returned in the limelight with an export-import loan of $100 million. Aid also came in goods. Hundreds of ships loaded with food and medicine arrived to Italian ports. "American intervention was breath-taking in its size, its ingenuity and its flagrant contempt for any principle of non-interference in the internal affairs of another country."[1] Italy was brought closer to the United States through economic, political, and military ties. As part of the Cold War strategy, the North Atlantic Treaty (NATO) was established on 4 April 1949. Italy, equipped by the United States, also joined this alliance.

If Italy could become prosperous, it wouldn't happen overnight. "In 1951 the elementary combination of electricity, drinking water and an inside lavatory could be found in only 7.4 percent of Italian households."[2] Bleak living conditions and poor prospects for employment drove many to emigrate. In 1951, the population of the south was about seventeen million, from which about four million left during the 1950s and 1960s. Another option for southerners was to move to more promising areas within Italy. Roughly nine million people did this between 1955 and 1971. By the end of the 1960s, "Turin became the third largest 'southern' city in Italy, after Naples and Palermo."[3] Women found work in the north too, as seamstresses and factory workers, or they fell into petty crime and prostitution.

The millions living in Italy were anxious to see action that would lead to an improvement in their standard of living. As patience wore thin, the late 1940s saw an increase in incidents of social unrest. A huge general strike took place in Turin, followed by a strike in Rome and other cities. Authorities utilized the Carabinieri (a military branch) and public security units to control protests. The combined forces became the largest police force in Europe, gaining a reputation for the harshness brought against protestors, both working class and peasant.

"Marshall Aid, with its influx of American machinery and know-how, had also opened up new horizons for many Italian firms."[4] Like receiving manna from heaven, Italian capitalists schemed on investing. According to the law of supply and demand, practical products were tailor-made for the Italian market from 1951 to 1958. Later, between 1958 and 1963, newer businesses looked beyond Italy and showed a growing interest in exporting products. During these years, industrial production more than doubled. As a result, Italians were finally seeing an improvement in their standards of living.

Fiat cars. Olivetti typewriters. A booming petrochemical industry. Beautiful textiles and nourishing food products could be found on tables at home and abroad. Mass production was providing for the consumers. Also, state-owned RAI television made its first broadcast in 1954. In Mary Melfi's memoir, she quotes her mother: "Television changed the world more than Mussolini, or Jesus Christ. . . . Their stars are our saints."[5]

In 1958, about 12 percent of Italian families owned a television; that number jumped to 49 percent by 1965. In the same years, the ownership of refrigerators went from 13 to 49 percent and washing machines from 3 to 23 percent. The use of private cars went from 342,000 in 1950 to 4.67 million by 1964. Motorcycles went from 700,000 to 4.3 million during the same period. By 1962, all could afford to wear real shoes. The above statistics provided in Ginsborg's fine book, *The History of Contemporary Italy*, hint at stunning development in the standard of living. Homes that once had no indoor plumbing or electricity were now being fitted with washing machines and dishwashers—and Italy became Europe's largest producer of these luxury products. "In less than two decades Italy ceased to be a peasant country and became one of the major industrial nations of the World."[6] This phenomenon became known as Italy's "economic miracle."

Money from the Marshall Plan and other funding sources was invested primarily in the north to foster industrial projects. New lucrative businesses were developed and attracted educated people from the private sector. While the north was set on a road to prosperity, the south was destined to take a different path. In conjunction with the investment from the United States, the Italian government established the Fund for the South (Cassa per il Mezzogiorno) with money earmarked mainly for public-works programs in rural areas. The south did not have the infrastructure to facilitate industrial development, and its basic needs were still a priority needing attention.

Agriculture was life in the south, even if it only provided bare sustenance. In 1951, 57 percent of the population worked in agriculture, the primary work in villages like Montenero. Although it was the largest single sector of employment, nearly half the workforce was underemployed. Increased mechanization in farming made work easier but required fewer employees. Especially stunting for the hill and mountain peasantry were restrictions from credit facilities. A benefit did come from the introduction of the pesticide DDT, which made some malaria-prone lands habitable.

Southern farmers inherited a major problem from medieval times: absentee landownership. This was land under a lord's demesne, or domain. It took until the 1948 Republican Constitution to reform the old laws by stating that the large estates should be redistributed to the peasantry. The law sat stagnant until a number of bloody protests took place in the south, with the Abruzzo-Molise area showing a particularly strong force. Nearly seven hundred thousand hectares of land (1,729,000 acres), albeit of poor quality, were seized and redistributed to about 120,000 peasant families. However, great problems remained for the hill and mountain areas of the south because the land quality was not very productive. A number of villages were being abandoned as people migrated elsewhere. "Between 1961 and 1970 the total cultivated land surface in Italy declined by 1.5 million hectares."[7] There were improvements in the south's standard of living during the 1960s brought about by land redistribution, cheaper energy, control of malaria, and, in large part, because of emigration.

If rural life in the south was difficult after the war, it wasn't much better in any of the overcrowded, destitute cities. In 1952 the active work-force was just 37.5 percent of the total population, and this figure only continued to drop: 34.2 percent in 1961 and 31.2 ten years later. Between 1951 and 1961, retail stores increased, mainly by the efforts of small family enterprises. They created many of the small bars and food shops that still add a dimension to Italian streets. Another prosperous area: the black market!

The Fund for the South invested heavily with an embarrassing show of results. There were a number of attempts to build industries in the south, construct new housing, create a better road system, and provide other services. The "wish list" that was to make the south economically sound and more productive was impressive. From the 1950s on, building speculation brought unplanned sprawls. Construction projects went up quickly, without aesthetic concern, and without much regard for the safety of future inhabitants. The factories that were built, or half-built, are often referred to as "cathedrals in the desert." Many cities expanded without any regulation.

Industry and prosperity grew in the north, while the agricultural south stagnated. The disequilibrium continues to increase. Most immediately point to the illegal crime syndicates as the cause of thwarting southern advancement by sabotaging the economy, draining money from the intended legitimate uses. The Neapolitan Camorra, Sicilian Mafia, and the Calabrian 'Ndrangheta always controlled much of the government work within their own territories. Incompetence and corruption were present before Italy was unified. When an economy is based on favoritism to family and friends (the traditional economic networks) rather than experience and skills, there becomes an inherent inefficiency.

The economic failures of the south should not be blamed solely on criminal organizations. The government itself has a colorful history of interparty squabbling and a famously lethargic mode of working. The legal system has too many laws and loopholes. It is a Rubik's Cube with which lawyers and government officials play endlessly. The civil service functions the best it can within the government and legal systems. Many of the positions have been filled based on clientelism—giving and receiving secure positions through favor. For example, the number of employees greatly increased in the autonomous state agencies that "administered the railways, telephone, postal service, and state monopolies of salt and tobacco."[8] The government and its branch agencies are not held in high esteem, but rather condemned for their dysfunctional characteristics.

It must be noted that, while many in the north pursued work in the private sector and became entrepreneurs, many in the south went into civil service and took offices throughout Italy. Thus, an influence came into government giving it a southern character with the traditional mode of doing business based on the bonds of favoritism.

The national government and its special agencies have held power over elected local governments. Their ineptitude often stunts the regional prospects for economic growth. As a result, Italy suffers under its own hand, earning "the reputation of being a nation both incapable of protecting its heritage, natural and man-made, and unable to govern its future."[9] There seem to be some common weaknesses in the Italian political and economic systems that penetrate throughout the national and local levels. "There were, and are, frequent transfers, betrayals and desertions, splits within factions, and realignments of forces. Infighting becomes the order of the day."[10] The inner workings are certainly opaque, but not beyond understanding.

The fragile 1950s led to another perilous decade that did manage to produce some positive developments. The new government formed in 1962 succeeded in some areas—for example, making electrical power a state monopoly. In the Montenero locality, the railroad track extending north and south from Castel di Sangro was rebuilt, improving the quality of life for those living near this line of transport. The government also made secondary schooling compulsory for children to age fourteen. Within the decade, the number of students doubled. Although small villages usually had their own local grade schools, children often had to commute to nearby larger towns in order to attend secondary schools. Those in Montenero, for example, could attend middle school in Castel di Sangro.

▲ Students in Montenero's elementary school with their teachers and Father Don Pasquale Di Filippo. *Courtesy of Montenero Municpial Office*.

After middle school, many went on to study at universities, causing that student population to nearly double. Unfortunately, the university system was as dysfunctional as the political system. Many eventually graduated but afterwards could not find work in their fields of study. By the late 1970s, many young people were now literate and became more aware of the social and political problems in their country.

Since the 1950s, construction work continued without restraint through the next decades. The one million building permits granted in 1968 alone indicate the fervor of building speculation. Although construction companies made profits, their lack of vision and planning had unpleasant consequences. Their haphazard work resulted in making the landscape more unsightly, providing substandard buildings that were often dangerous to live in for owners and squatters.

Other programs and reforms, such as transferring more power to regional governments, inched forward only to be bogged down in bureaucratic suspension. The government could aptly be described as constipated. "From 1968 onwards paralysis from above gave way to movement from below. There followed a most extraordinary social ferment."[11] Students protested. Workers protested. Fanatics expressed their frustrations through acts of terrorism.

Students protested at universities in Trento, Milan, Torino, and elsewhere. In 1968, at the University of Rome, protests turned violent, with students and police being injured. The movements in Italy reflected the turbulent social currents found elsewhere, as headlined by the Vietnam War and China's Cultural Revolution.

Protests were directed at the dysfunctional government and against poor living and working conditions. It was only natural for workers to raise their voices for better safety regulations and wages. The protests by factory workers inspired laborers in other sectors to likewise protest, be it in small shops or hotels, or in the railroad and construction industries. From the early 1960s, an increasing number of strikes resulted in millions of lost workdays. Work in the north was further complicated by the great influx of southern Italians and the resulting social conflicts.

Many revolutionary groups emerged. They also had a major fault: like the Italian government, they lacked a unified, planned program with clear objectives. The 1969 explosion at the Milan railroad station was terrifying. Some thought Neo-Fascism would provide a solution to Italy's problems. The protests of the 1960s not only halted political progress but set it back a decade.

Even the family and church—longstanding elements of Italian social stability—came under attack as being too oppressive. It was a time of birth control, sexual liberation, and consumerism. The influence of the church was in decline. For better or worse, values were changing. Family size was declining while divorce was on the rise. Dialects and old traditions were slowly being discarded. Perhaps the revolutionists were discarding gems they supposed were plain gravel? "There had been no fiscal reform, no reform of the state bureaucracy, no introduction of a national health system, no reform of agrarian contracts of the Federconsorzi [Federation of Agrarian Consortia]. Even the establishment of regional government . . . had not come into effect."[12]

Enter the 1970s. Under an unstable government, an economic crisis hit, and militancy continued. Reforms were needed across the board, but it was the state itself that needed them most. The formation and elections of regional governments in 1970 only proved to offer new areas of manipulation and exploitation. The inefficient bureaucracy left giant loopholes that allowed many to evade paying their fair share of taxes. This unacceptable political-economic situation added fuel to the fires of protest.

No doubt reflecting the growing frustration with government inefficiency and the economic instability and inequality, militant movements became stronger. The use of hard drugs such as heroin gave a temporary sense of calm to some of the disillusioned, but the problems remained. For the first time, eighteen- to twenty-one-year-olds were allowed to vote. Their voices were as if lost in the wind as the Communist (PCI) and Christian Democrats parties remained in deadlock. Kidnappings and killings became the norm since 1976, the "Year of the Bullet." Aldo Moro, one of Italy's longest-serving postwar prime ministers, was kidnapped and murdered by the Red Brigade militant group in 1978. Thereafter, terrorism increased toward the end of the decade.

Social protests did succeed in making possible some reforms that changed the lives of individuals and families. Family law underwent reforms in 1975 that steered Italian culture away from many traditional values. In the same year, feminism was a national topic that changed the Italian worldview. Divorce became legal at the start of the decade, and in 1978 abortion became legal. Laws were also passed to avoid legal discrimination against children born out of wedlock and to bring a more humane attitude toward mental health. Also in 1978, a national health system was instituted. This major change looked good on paper, but there were flaws. Patients in the south were clearly aware that they were receiving inferior care when compared with care in the north. For example, the north had over twice as many hospital beds per one thousand than the south.

The judiciary system also managed to formulate laws to improve housing. These laws covered aspects such as planning, construction, and fair rent. Again, the laws looked fine in print but could not be enforced. In brief, the legal system did little to help Italians. Weaknesses in the legal and political systems hampered the economy and, in the 1970s, led to recession. Corruption was king, ruling over a divided society that was barely held together by kickbacks and paybacks.

Many capitalist countries experienced an economic crisis in the early 1970s. An oil crisis in 1974 was only one contributing factor. Mass unemployment affected all Italian regions. Inflation reached peak levels in Italy, higher than in any other country in the Western world. Many factories were forced to close. This was the darkest time in Italian history since World War II.

Many big investments in the south were disastrous. For example, agricultural areas in Calabria were destroyed to provide space for mega-steel plants, which were never built due to a collapse in the world steel market. Another area where heavy investments were made in the south

▲ Decades of protests have become a common mode of expressing frustrations.
ID 29825978 | © Raluca Tudor, Dreamstime.com

was in petrochemicals. This too showed little success. Basic utilities, such as water, were still lacking. Just over half of the residences in Naples, for instance, had a bath or a shower. About 18 percent of dwellings still utilized outside lavatories.

There were areas that shone brightly, as exemplified by the increase in household appliances over the decade from 1965 to 1975. The prime examples are in televisions (from 49 percent to 92 percent), refrigerators (from 55 percent to 94 percent) and washing machines (from 23 percent to 76 percent). Ginsborg found a great imbalance between the sale of such goods and the foundation of the nation: "Needs were being met (if not for everyone, everywhere), but institutions and structures were not being modernized, and nor were the worst excesses of unplanned development being checked or curbed."[13]

TVs, refrigerators, and washing machines became common in Montenero. Many ladies continued to wash clothes outside near the spring-fed water fountain built in 1821. They did so well into the 1970s. It took some time to adapt to the new benefits, including more welfare payments received, even though they put the government in great debt. Pensions certainly helped the elderly, and by 1977, regional governments "took over full responsibility in such areas as health care and environmental planning."[14]

Small villages were moving further and further away from the agriculture-based lifestyle, and other occupations developed. The theory of supply and demand gave opportunities for some to establish businesses to meet new needs. "The class structure became more stratified: no longer was the population of the village divided into the small elite of landowners and the mass of the rural poor. Small proprietors, traders, public officials and the professional class all became more numerous. Rigid family hierarchies broke down; a collective code of conduct was replaced by a variety of different behaviour patterns."[15]

By the end of the 1970s, the family remained strong as a social unit. However, values were changing. Dazzled by the growing array of consumer items, the success of the family was becoming judged by the possession of material things. Even in small villages, people were becoming more self-centered and focusing on individual and familial accomplishments and economic status. The collective consciousness that bonded individuals within a village over centuries was weakening, the full effects of which would unfold over the coming decades. Certainly there was an increase in the standard of living, but as Ginsborg writes: "[I]t must be noted that the Italian model of development . . . lacked the dimension of collective responsibility. The state had played an important role in stimulating rapid economic development, but it then defaulted on governing the social consequences."[16]

At the end of the 1970s, acts of terrorism subsided. It seems the Italians were realizing violence would not force the changes they wanted. There were exceptions. In August of 1980, a bomb exploded at the central railroad station in Bologna. Those who plotted this bombing were inspired by neo-Fascism. Two years later, the Mafia murdered General Carlo Alberto Dalla Chiesa and his wife in Palermo. He was well known for his counter-terrorism work during the 1970s. In 1984, the Sicilian Mafia bombed the express train that runs between Bologna and Florence. Even without resorting to violence, the Mafia and political fanatics would continue to pose problems for government and police. Great steps were taken in 1986 to curtail organized crime. One outstanding example was the convicting of 338 Mafia members of numerous criminal activities. However, the Mafia not only survived, but it rose to new heights in its influence.

The connection linking the Mafia, Italian politics, and business is nothing new. Although inflation reached the highest annual rate in 1980, the economy grew by mid-decade, and Italy attained affluence and a high standard of living in many areas of the country. Italians stopped moving abroad in search of work. Large companies such as Fiat prospered. Italian designers were in demand. Italian clothing and shoes were hot products.

Even products made by small firms were quite successful. By the end of the 1980s, Italy became the fifth-largest industrial nation in the Western world. The economy was looking healthy, but the south still found itself as the most neglected area with the most shortcomings.

Montenero serves as an example of the southern struggle to keep up with changing times. Mountain villages face depopulation, in part because of the lower birth rate in Italy. The number of births in the south dropped from 1,032,000 in 1964 to only 552,000 in 1987. A growing fear was that "families have become ever more concerned with their own well being, and less with the collective problems of society as a whole. This trend has undoubtedly been the dominant one in the 1980s."[17] In such mountain agro-villages and small towns, social relationships were morphing into a less collective way of relating to individuals outside the immediate family. The longstanding bonds of village identity were fracturing under numerous pressures, including an aging population, a decline in agricultural production, and a lack of innovation and direction for the future.

Names of the political players may have changed in the 1990s, but the way of participating continued as in previous generations. Regional elections were held early in 1990 and, for the first time, direct elections of town mayors were held in 1993. The new Northern League (*Lega Nord*) political party was founded in 1991 with its primary aim of gaining greater regional autonomy at minimum, while some of its members favored secession altogether from the nation. Embroiled in this movement was a conflict between north and south.

A barrage of scandals, plus national and international turmoil, forced Italy to reform its electoral system. At the end of 1991, the Soviet Union was splitting apart, with some regions becoming independent. It was not a good model of government for the Italians to emulate. In the following year, an infestation of high-level corruption started to be revealed. Tangentopoli—translated as "Bribesville" or "Kickback City"—was exposed as the working mechanism of Italian politics. Judicial investigations were undertaken to clean up the mess. Thousands of public figures came under scrutiny. Some politicians and industrial leaders committed suicide when their names and crimes came to light. The investigations were known as "clean hands" (*mani pulite*). Within a few years, the four main political parties were dissolved, including the Italian Christian Democratic Party and the Communist Party.

Early in 1992, two magistrates known for their anti-Mafia hardline were assassinated. Giovanni Falcone was the top anti-Mafia prosecutor at the time. He, his wife, and his bodyguards were all murdered via car bomb. Soon after this, ex-Prime Minister Giulio Andreotti was placed under investigation for illegal dealings with the Mafia. While Mafiosi from Sicily planned attacks in the major cities of Rome, Florence, and Milan, ex-Prime Minister Bettino Craxi, head of the Socialist Party in 1994, simply ran away to Tunisia to avoid trial.

The political collapse led to the worst financial crisis in Italy since the end of World War II. Throughout the 1990s, Italians with an entrepreneurial inclination shied away from the industrial sector and moved into the service sector. "Which is why it matters that in Italy service industries are the most restricted, conservative and often backward parts of the economy, where competition is weakest."[18] Again we find that those working in services are often hired on the basis of personal connections rather than on their abilities and merit.

Corruption. Trials. The collapse of political parties. All led to a national crisis that seemed to reach a point of no return. Who could possibly lead the nation out of the chaos? Someone without any previous experience whatsoever in government? Perhaps a multibillionaire media mogul who schemed his way to power with "dirty hands"? If you guessed the next prime minister elected in 1994 would be Donald Trump, you'd be close. It was Silvio Berlusconi (b. 1936), supported by a coalition of political groups willing to take a gamble.

The austerity budget that was implemented in 1995 indicates just how much the common Italian was victim to politics. However, the financial situation is not the only indicator of the quality of life. Many reforms were still needed for Italians to attain basic human rights. For example, it wasn't until 1996 that rape was made a proper felony. How does one face such a dire situation? It seems that actor and film director Roberto Benigni offered the only natural escape in his Academy Award–winning movie, *Life is Beautiful* (1997). In the movie, the only way Guido Orefice (his character) can protect the youthful innocence of his son from the horrors of the Holocaust is through fantasy. Pretend it is a game. Remain positive that you can win. You will survive. In real life, Benigni has been highly critical of Berlusconi. One way to escape the troubling Italian politics is to ignore it by diving into the pleasures of dressing and eating well, watching movies, attending concerts, and buying the newest products such as cars, motorcycles, shoes, or Ray-Ban sunglasses.

In the twilight of the 1990s, the most promising source for helping Italy resolve its problems did not come from within Italy. It was the Eurozone. Italy joined ten member countries making up the Eurozone to share a common currency in the euro, and to corroborate on formalizing political policies. Eight more countries would join in the following month. This gave the Italians a sense of hope for the decade to come.

It would take some years to see how joining the Eurozone would affect Italian life. The savings rate per household was only 6.0 percent in 2001, compared with 17.9 percent fifteen years earlier. In 2002 the euro started to circulate as the official currency throughout Italy. It didn't seem to make much difference. The economy and political situation continued, much as in the previous decade.

Despite a lengthy list of allegations and trials, Berlusconi was voted in for his second term as prime minister in 2001. He was the focus of numerous trials and allegations that included extortion, sexual abuse of children, perjury, collusion with the Mafia, tax evasion, and bribery of leading figures. Berlusconi was working within the norm of Italian culture. Of course others did too, as illustrated by the 2003 multibillion-euro fraud involving Parmalat, a food-manufacturing giant. The resulting guilty charge led to the company's collapse.

Forces for good continued to fight against the odds and made headway. The most-wanted man in Italy, Bernardo Provenzano, was captured by police in 2006. He was the suspected head of the Sicilian Mafia. In the same year, Robert Saviano published *Gomorra*—a book detailing and denouncing the Cammora, the Mafia organization in and around Naples.

After Berlusconi won a third term as prime minister in 2008, he faced a recession that was greatly crippling the economy. The Italian public debt would soon be the second largest among European countries. In order to counter the financial drain, a number of austerity measures were put into effect. Although highly unpopular, these actions did help reduce public debt. Somehow, despite the politics and economic handicaps, Italy managed to rank the fifth-largest manufacturer in the world in 2009.

Some natural disasters are predictable. The Molise mountain area from Isernia to Boiano is "one of the most seismically active regions of Italy . . . being characterized by rich historical sources for the last eight centuries."[19] In this area, hundreds of earthquakes have been recorded over the past two thousand years. The 1456 earthquake, with its epicenter in Boiano, "is the most intense seismic event of the Italian peninsula of which there is historical memory.[20] Whole villages were destroyed with thousands of deaths. Another occurred in 1805 with similar results. In Isernia, for example, one-fifth of the population died, and only one-tenth of the houses remained standing.

Montenero was hit twice in 1984 with much damage to buildings, but luckily no deaths. One on 7 May 1984 registered 5.2 with its epicenter near San Donato Val di Comino, about forty miles from Montenero. Four months later, on 6 September, another 5.0 magnitude was centered between Castel di Sangro and Isernia. A quake on a smaller scale at 4.0 occurred on 20 January 1994, with its epicenter in Castel di Sangro. Montenero was the epicenter (along with Alfedena, Barrea, Pizzone, and Rionero) of a 5.0 shock that occurred on 5 May 1996.

More recent is the April 2009 earthquake with its epicenter near L'Aquila, less than sixty miles from Montenero. It killed 308 people and left sixty-five thousand homeless. Structural damage included many centuries-old medieval buildings such as the sixteenth-century castle housing the National Museum of Abruzzo. To get a better idea of how often rumblings can test the nerves of those living in Montenero, we might refer to one article titled "More than 50 earthquakes rock Italy's Molise in five days."[21] All measured over 2.0 on the Richter scale with the largest at 4.3.

When earthquakes damaged homes in Montenero, the state provided assistance. State aid is provided to families suffering from deprivation, not just in the case of disaster. "A constant flow of money payments reaches the villages of the internal regions of the South: invalidity pensions, family benefits, pensions reserved for peasant proprietors, subsidies for artisans, regional assistance, etc."[22] How the money is used and abused is always in question, but there is a definite attempt by the government to include the south in its nation-building programs.

Branches of the European Union are making a difference with their eye on Italy. As part of the union's funding projects, the European Regional Development Fund "aims to strengthen economic and social cohesion in the European Union by reducing imbalances between its regions."[23] For example, in the years between 2007 and 2013, €194 million were earmarked for the Molise region. This amount is the total of funds provided by the European Regional Development Fund, the European Social Fund, and the European Agricultural Fund for Rural Development. "This represents an average of €605 per inhabitant over the seven-year period."[24]

From 2014 to 2020, Italy was to receive €32.2 billion as part of what is called the Cohesion Policy fund. This is an attempt to create new businesses and thus new jobs, complete wastewater projects, and improve internet coverage and railroad services, plus provide aid following any natural disasters such as earthquakes. Molise benefited by a Regional Operational Programme that provided €76.7 million, plus €153 million in funding from the combined financial input of the European Social Fund and national financing. "The programme puts a special emphasis on the fight against unemployment, on social inclusion and on the competitiveness of the regional economy through financial support to local businesses. Promoting research and innovation and offering better access to digital technologies and services are also among the priorities of the programme."[25] A recent plan provides €10 million for road safety in Molise and € 267,868 specifically for energy projects in Montenero.[26]

Government programs must work through the kinship networks, especially strong in the south. "Yet these . . . are networks without collective projects, without a consciousness that transcends family interests. Neither from civil society nor from the state has there emerged a new and less destructive formulation of the relationship between family and collectivity."[27] As a result, of all the potential benefits that could develop from government efforts, only part of them come to be realized. The political alliances, filtered through kinship networks, are "riven by suspicion, by personal rivalry, by an eternal jockeying for position. It makes any strategic planning next to impossible, wastes an extraordinary amount of time and energy and leads inexorably to weak rather than strong government."[28]

In the early years of this century, Italy would continue to wrestle with its dysfunctional political apparatus and evolving economy. Money was being made but, because of corruption, rarely got to the people and places where it was needed most. Major sites of historical importance were being neglected, as with the collapse of the 2010 House of the Gladiators in Pompeii. Buildings are less important than peoples' lives, but we find that south Italians still lacked important services, including transportation, health care, and quality education. Areas like the High Molise continued to suffer from neglect. "Over the last fifteen years the hill and mountain areas have shown further signs of decline. The rural exodus has been so great and property has remained so divided that there has been an increasing abandonment of agriculture and what has been called 'a disintegration of production structures.'"[29]

Not counting immigrants, Italy's population is in decline, further depopulating areas such as the High Molise. In 2010, Italy had the lowest average numbers of babies born per woman in the world. At the same time, elderly retirees made up nearly one-fifth of the population. On the other hand, young people spent much time entertaining themselves with music, television, and going to movies, while hours for reading books lessened. The new pastimes were even subtracting from sporting activities. The vitality of youth was directed toward entertainment and leisure. "Young Italians meet friends on a daily basis, often in the cities' piazzas in the evenings, making frequent trips to bars, cinemas, pizzerias, and discos. . . . [T]he leisurely two-hour-long lunch break is disappearing. Bars and trattorie cater cheaply and quickly to the casual dine."[30]

Toward the end of 2011, the Parliament had no recourse but to approve austerity packages, one in September for $74 billion (€ 54 billion), and a few months later for another $43 billion (€ 33 billion). Taxes rose while attention was finally given to eliminate tax evasion. Some of the blame for the abysmal debt fell on the shoulders of Prime Minister Berlusconi. If this weren't enough for the billionaire to handle, he was charged for abuse of power and sexual scandals. In November 2011, he resigned. Two years later he was finally convicted of tax fraud.

By 2013, Italy was in turmoil again. Its government and economy were failing. High unemployment brought a social drift, especially to the young. As if to throw fuel on the fire, another crisis came to the Italian shores in the form of migrants. In October 2013, 360 migrants departing from Libya died at sea while trying to reach Italy by boat. The governor of Sicily declared a state of emergency. People had been arriving in Italy by legal and illegal means during previous years.

In 2008, for example, 30,140 people applied for asylum. By 2017, the number swelled when 128,850 applied for asylum, coming from countries including Nigeria, Pakistan, Bangladesh, Syria, Afghanistan, and Iraq. Today the illegal entries into Italy and the European Union are the lowest since 2015. The results of a decade of migrant crisis have yet to be seen. It is beyond doubt that crime increased because of the migrations. Considering the high unemployment rate in Italy, it is predictable that many migrants turned to the basic modes of illegal income: drug trafficking and prostitution. Although the number of migrants has lessened, the decade of 2010 to 2019 will be one in which Italy is associated with simultaneously facing a number of crises.

Serving as the president of Italy in 2013, Giorgio Napolitano pronounced: "[T]his is a moment when Italy needs to, and must, both tell the truth to itself and face up to the truth about what needs to be done."[31] How to resolve the migration crisis? How to modernize the state services? Italian leaders in business and politics were famed for their mastery of corrupt methods. Could their highly evolved *modus operandi* ever transform into a transparent, moral mode of operating . . . at least with a much lesser degree of underhandedness? This implies that fiscal administration be honest and more equitable, including the long-neglected areas of south Italy. All the above seems to rest on an ability to enforce laws. With the advice of President Napolitano, hopefully Italy will find solutions to resolve each problem facing the country. He resigned in January 2015.

When Matteo Renzi became prime minister in 2014, a wave of optimism swept the nation. At thirty-nine years of age, he was the youngest in Italy's republican history to be elected to the office. His youth, enthusiasm, and praiseworthy goals for the nation—so contrasting to those of Berlusconi—brought progress. Then the walls of resistance came into view, and Renzi's inroads hit a dead end. All slowed, and the populace turned against him. It's said that in three years of his premiership he aged thirty years. His photo always seems to bring a smile though, not because of his political accomplishments, but because of his uncanny resemblance to Mr. Bean, the British comedian Rowan Atkinson.

When Paolo Gentiloni became prime minister in 2016, he was faced with the migration crisis. He implemented stricter rules and criteria regarding immigration and helped better control the assimilation. In general, he made it more difficult for immigrants to settle in Italy and easier for officials to send them out, such as refusing immigrant boats access to ports, and facilitating the eviction of squatters. Under Gentiloni, the government also made progress in health care. In June 2018, despite having no political experience, Giuseppe Conte officially succeeded Gentiloni as new prime minister. His coalition government became known as the "Government of Change." Conte says he will deal with the obvious problems, including illegal immigration, smuggling, and political corruption. He also pushed for new regulatory laws and tax cuts.

Many details on Conte's official curriculum vitae regarding his education have been proven false. As with so many other dishonest politicians, how can he be trusted with the future of Italy? Conte is a Roman Catholic and devoted follower of the stigmatist and saint Padre Pio of Pietrelcina. Perhaps some divine intervention is necessary to get the Italian government to function? Is there any other way for the inner workings of Italian politics and business to become fair and functional? The future of Italy and villages like Montenero depend on finding the answer. After analyzing the past few centuries of southern Italian history and taking to heart what leading politicians and philosophers have concluded, some answers become obvious.

One after another, foreign powers have controlled the south, including the Normans, Lombards, Swabians, Spanish, and French. Many also consider north Italy as a conqueror. It seems the history of the south was forged on the land in violent clashes, as "in ancient times between the Romans and the Carthaginians and in the Middle Ages among Islam, Byzantium and the Holy Roman Empire."[32] What was the psychological effect upon the peasant masses during these periods? A parallel could be found in the repetitive abuse of a child over decades since birth. We would never expect the child to become a normal adult, and we can't expect south Italy to function normally. In the south, of course there is distrust of outsiders. Of course there is fear and insecurity, stemming from long-standing economic and political weakness. It is logical for the society to find reliance on family and close contacts. Unfortunately, the southern mindset has been one of limited vision. It sees close but not far. The result is centuries of stagnation.

As far back as the sixteenth century, Niccolò Machiavelli (1469–1527) noticed a missing base in the south upon which a government could build. He wrote that in the Neapolitan provinces "there was never any republic or any political system."[33] As far back as Machiavelli's time there was little faith that the south would make much progress politically or socially.

The centuries record numerous efforts to make bureaucracy efficient, formulate and enforce laws, curb corruption, and make the south prosperous. Benedetto Croce wrote: "The moving forces of a people's true history are its so-called ruling class and its statesmen and politicians."[34] But those who ruled the south over the centuries were usually outsiders bent on abusing their subjects to benefit foreign countries or themselves. Medieval barons fought for their own holdings and were unconscious about building a nation. The granting of 160 fiefs by Charles I of Anjou (1226–1285) serves to illustrate the early exploitation of the south. Following centuries likewise allowed the south to be preyed upon. "The barons never even attempted to build up a policy, foreign or domestic, for the good of the Kingdom . . . Their concerns were strictly materialistic, or else capricious . . . self-interest."[35] And in modern times, we see that even under the guidance of intelligent leaders backed by billions of euros, the end results are definitely not as fruitful as could be.

Croce bluntly states that the ethical life (*vita morale*) "was the guiding thread of history."[36] Many hold the same belief that there is something in the human moral core responsible for attaining a high degree of social and political harmony. Above all, there is a key to social cooperation that is imperative for any society, bureaucracy, or business to thrive. It is simply developing an awareness to live and act as an individual within the larger community. This holds true for those living in communities large and small, even for the tiniest village. Sociologist Edward Banfield wrote that, in part, a society's dysfunction could be explained by "the inability of the villagers to act together for their common good or, indeed, for any end transcending the immediate, material interest of the nuclear family."[37] In the book *The New History of the Italian South: The Mezzogiorno Revisited*, the authors concur, writing that there is "an endemic inability to act in the common good—what is popularly called a lack of civic consciousness."[38] Professor Astarita also concludes: "Social scientists critiqued southern peasant culture as backward, amoral, and unable to effect improvement or to act for the common good."[39]

Against these odds, there are many Italian success stories, as illustrated in a number of businesses that produce quality products. The economic boom of the 1950s and 1960s came out of a desperate need to survive and recover. However, it "emphasized individual and familial roads to prosperity while ignoring collective and public responses to everyday needs. As such, the economic 'miracle' served once again to emphasize the importance of the individual family unit within Italian civil society."[40]

However, as successful as the big businesses might be, they are but participants in a system that chokes a great potential lying dormant in Italy. As a personal relative in Montenero said: "Put these Italians in another country, and they would prosper." There are many Italians who possess ambition, great skill, and intelligence. They are like hibernating seeds waiting for their chance to bloom if only the conditions were more conducive.

Post–World War II economic growth increased the standard of living in Italy, but a major flaw shows up in the social side of the Italian arena in which the "crucial sectors of the upper classes turned their faces firmly against a strategy of progress, and against more equitable cooperation with the classes below them."[41] There are many today who enjoy playing the arrogant role of "noble" among the "peasantry," perpetuating the play to satisfy their egos.

Most are aware of the handicaps in Italy that thwart social and economic progress, such as the power of the Mafia, the web of favoritism, and the inequities between the north and south. As pointed out by Barnfield, Astarita, Ginsborg, and others, these are but manifestations of a deeper problem that center on character faults allowing individuals to choose unethical behaviors in pursuit of self-centered goals while neglecting the common good. Altogether, the weight of these problems can be crippling to the human spirit. Benedetto Croce—the philosopher, historian, and politician who was born in Pescasseroli (about twenty-six miles from Montenero)—wrote: "There are both peoples and individuals that have found the strength to achieve renewal out of sheer disgust with themselves, that is, with their past."[42] The call today is for all in Italy, north and south, to seek the inner strength to make the adjustments necessary to create a more harmonious, more prosperous, and happier society.

Destiny

A horse galloping in Montenero's marsh — a symbol of a free spirit.
Photograph by M. DiMarco.

chapter 15

Molise's Future
and Montenero Hereafter

In addition to the new problems that emerged since World War II, Italy also continues to wrestle with other problems it inherited long before the war. In recent years the government has been working to improve living conditions in Molise. Utilities and other services such as internet are improving. In 2001, the Italian regions took over the legislative powers for energy production. Molise established laws governing the installation of wind and solar power plants. In accord with the goals of geotourism, the aesthetics of the land are considered while planning for power plants, which includes establishing buffer zones and identifying areas unsuitable for construction.

Construction projects are being planned with greater concern for aesthetics and safety. Homes, hotels, hospitals, and business buildings are being designed with features that consider the seismic activity in the region. Although medical care has not been up to par with services in the north, new facilities and upgrades in the south are designed to be earthquake proof and ready for emergencies. Because more than 20 percent of residents in Molise are over sixty-five years old, there is a particular need to provide proper care for this aging population.

In step with the modern emphasis on human rights, a new model of justice is changing the methods and practices regarding criminals. This represents a "crucial challenge to traditional ways of resolving conflicts and preventing crime."[1] Meting out justice involves more than just assigning punishments for crimes. It includes reconciliation and rehabilitation. Training courses for criminal mediators are being designed to bring a more humane approach to the justice system with the goal of successfully integrating any offender back into society.

The major change in south Italy during recent decades has certainly been its transition from a deep-rooted agricultural way of life to a totally new way of living. Under the guidance of a government in a political stupor, the fragmented society is struggling to adjust to its present reality. Molise, particularly the High Molise, seems to be most susceptible to the winds of change. The threat is that many of the small villages in the region will eventually meet a fate of total abandonment—a phenomenon spreading across Italy. The question of population is critical in determining the longevity of any particular village.

Molise was hit hard by emigration and migration to the north, losing half its population between 1861 and 2001. From 407,000 inhabitants in 1951, the population dropped to 308,493 by 2017, with Isernia Province representing 85,237 of this total and Campobasso Province the balance. In recent years, females have slightly outnumbered males. Out of the total population, almost thirteen thousand are foreigners, with a fourth of them in Isernia Province. Regardless, the population density for the province of Isernia is only 22.74 inhabitants per square mile compared to the national figure of 76.75. Comparing with other regions, Molise has attracted the least number of immigrants. They are being integrated with 48.8 percent in service sectors, 31.4 percent in industries, and 15.9 percent in agriculture (3.9 percent not attributed).[2]

An important result of the declining population is that it has dispersed those of the younger generation who graduated from institutes of higher education or have professional experience. As clearly stated by Professor Rossano Pazzagli, the loss of this vital segment of population "determines a poor entrepreneurial culture and a low propensity for innovation" for Molise.[3] When compared with other southern regions, the percentage of graduates at age twenty-five is the highest at 24 percent, "but the possession of a degree gives less and less guarantee of securing a job."[4] In an area so highly affected by unemployment and the lack of job opportunities, this youthful group is necessary to revitalize the region. However, it is easier for these young people to pack a suitcase, leave, and find work elsewhere. As a result, their absence "causes a weakening of the social fabric, making it difficult to implement any organizational and operational measures to relaunch the region."[5]

Along with Molise's changing demographics came a decline in agricultural work. Additionally, mechanization required fewer workers. The service industries increased in cities with larger populations, but what potential was there to develop other work in the region? The cost of utilities is high, plus the infrastructure is in dire need of repair and upscaling to meet standards befitting the time. As noted, the attempts have been hindered by the additional burdens of dysfunctional politics, organized crime, taxation, and banking restrictions.

It is possible that adaptations could be made in Molise so production of agricultural products would be profitable. Studies are being made to find areas for investment, such as the cultivation of tomatoes and truffles. Because of the unique Molise vegetation, raising goats for milk production is another area being investigated as a potentially successful area of work. In addition to the economic aspect, there is interest in keeping certain farm animals "in the native lands and traditionally reared . . . to conserve the productive peculiarity of populations at risk of extinction" and to give validity to marginal areas with meager productivity.[6] Scientists are concerned with the preservation of plants and animals as a genetic safeguard for the future.

More studies are needed to see how working with traditional products could become profitable as specialized small-business ventures. Rare plants and animals in the High Molise, for example, could provide the bioactive ingredients for ethnomedicines. One study provides "data on 70 taxa belonging to 39 families; 64 used for human therapy."[7] These ancient concoctions have been used as insect repellants, salves for bruises and wounds, food preservatives, a tonic to regulate menstruation, and ingredients for veterinary medicine, and they have also been utilized in magic rituals.

If Molise food products are mentioned, we should think of the praise-worthy slow-food movement. It started in Italy in 1986, going on to become a worldwide phenomenon. As an antithesis to fast food, the goal of the slow-food movement is to study and preserve traditional cuisines of the regions and utilize ingredients produced locally. The movement is well organized, with a clearly articulated philosophy. This area of specialization could be adapted to the distinctive Molise culinary tradition.

The major hurdles facing Molisan agriculture have been discussed. The prime barrier is the general inability of individuals to work together in order to be competitive on a national or international scale. In Molise there is "a lack of collaboration among producers and a resulting low level of supply; limited vertical supply chain plans, which are necessary to ensure the feed-back of food-farming investments to the agricultural producers; a marketing system which is unfavourable to the producers, and poor dissemination of knowledge and information."[8]

Another area considered for economic development is Molise crafts. There are some famous regional products, such as the Marinelli Bell Factory in Agnone and the knives and scissors made in Frosolone by small family-run businesses. Although known for their high-quality products, such small businesses are limited by production methods and resulting low presence in the market. Except for a Fiat plant near Termoli, large industry has not de-veloped in Molise.

Rodeo Pentro

● Rodeo Pentro, summer 1975. *Courtesy of the Montenero Municipal Office.*

As fully discussed in Christian Pesaresi's excellent book, *The "Numbers" of Molise Mountain Municipalities: New Data, Old Problems, Development Opportunities* (2014), any plan to develop work in the agricultural, craft, or industrial sectors faces many obstacles. After surveying the natural and human resources of the region, Pesaresi evaluated the economic and environmental conditions in order to identify the ventures most likely to flourish by investing time and money. The logical conclusion presented in this book is that Molise should focus on tourism as the most suitable industry for the region. There's much work to do in order to build Molise as a tourist destination, as it is the least visited region in Italy.

Many political and economic experts concur with Pesaresi's optimism. There is a strong belief that tourism "can provide enthusiasm, above all if it is organized creatively in a participative and collaborative way, in order to transform the different forms of spontaneous tourism and returning-emigrant tourism into a coordinated activity and a quality product, by promoting a gentle, long-lasting and multi-target tourism."[9] Of vital importance here is to spice up Molise tourism with the history and culture native to the region. "The past must not be put aside, rather it should be well-known [and appropriately used]."[10] This would make touring Molise a unique experience for all visitors. Local inhabitants and government administrators need to work together to discuss the appropriate elements of the region that would draw tourists. It is hoped that discussions will foster "consciousness of both past and present that can break the spell over those who think that they can survive" solely on their own income.[11]

Molise tourism has slowly increased over the past few decades. Without major investment, it will continue to struggle. When compared with the other Italian regions, it rests at the bottom of the list for the number of visiting tourists in a given year—but there has been growth. The total number of arrivals in 1998 was 163,895, with the average stay of 3.38 days. Five years later, in 2003, the total number of arrivals rose to 178,845, and the average number of nights stayed rose to 3.89. In 2010, there were 209,051 visitors to the region: about 90 percent were Italian, and almost 10 percent were foreigners. The average nights stayed dropped to 2.1 by 2011.[12]

Between the two Molise provinces, most visitors pick the province of Campobasso as their destination, especially the costal area in and around Termoli. While 82.9 percent stay on the coast, only 17.1 percent go for vacations in the mountains. Tourists going to the mountain municipalities numbered 14,340 in the year 2000 and increased to 25,854 by 2011.[13] Peak season is July and August, while January is the lowest month. Cycles of tourism follow the seasons, such as warm months for days at the beach or the winter snows to keep skiers happy on the slopes. The climatic conditions must be considered for the appropriate activities.

Arrivals in Molise staying in hotel accommodations are on the increase. Greater demand has brought growth in the number of rooms, beds, and bathrooms available for tourists. In order to guarantee that tourism increases and that visitors stay for longer periods of time, attractive marketing programs are necessary. Information for tourists needs to be readily available in travel information centers, including books, brochures, maps, and calendars. The overarching question is this: what does Molise uniquely possess that would attract tourists to visit the region? The answer is summarized by the word geotourism, a concept that came into use in 2010.

Geotourism is more than the simple combination of geography with tourism. It is true that the foundation is on the geographic setting. A highly detailed study shows how Molise's land was formed by a process "by which structures within fold-belt mountainous areas were formed, including thrusting, folding, and faulting in the outer and higher layers, and plastic folding, metamorphism, and plutonism in the inner and deeper layers."[14] The Molise topography has been well documented, illustrating how ancient land formations evolved over millennia into the landscape we see today.

From mountains to the sea, the region's land is the stage on which the drama of Molise history enfolded. It includes the evolution of its geodiversity as well as biodiversity, and the human activities that took place over centuries. Like pages in a manuscript, the diverse landscapes have recorded history of tremendous value for our exploration. Tour itineraries have already been designed that focus on varied aspects of geotourism.

The ancient drover roads (tratturi) crossing Molise have been given special attention. Tours have been organized annually, and their itineraries provide details such as the number of participants, distances covered, and places visited. Minotti et al. (2018) have discussed utilizing the drover road that runs south from Castel di Sangro to Lecera as a tourist trail. More research and planning need to be done for other itineraries to develop, such as one through the Matese Massif, a natural draw for tourists.

There are many types of tourism to consider implementing in the Molise countryside, including: "agritourism, farm-tourism, rural tourism, green tourism, eco-tourism, soft tourism, [and] alternative tourism."[15] Much of Molise's economy may rest in developing these areas. Opportunities are as diverse as the region. Creative entrepreneurs will certainly establish businesses and highlight destinations to draw in tourists according to their wide range of interests. For example, these could be (a) schools to study cooking, art, or language; (b) outdoor activities including hunting, fishing, horseback riding, hiking, skiing, or farming; (c) visiting museums, archeological sites, and famous landmarks; (d) intensive programs to nurture the mind, body, and spirit.

Archaeological work is bringing attention to many places worth visiting. In addition to the already famous sites—such as the Paleolithic site at Isernia-La Pineta, the Samnite theatre-temple complex at Pietrabbondante, and the Roman ruins of Saepinum—new discoveries are adding to the rich historic heritage. Some discoveries are accidental. After the Fortore River flooded its banks in 2003, the "Roman bridge of Tufara" became visible. The discovery indicates that "the Tufara bridge and the associated road network in Roman and medieval times are part of a rather complex environmental dynamic."[16]

Photo by Vincenzo Corona.

Another important site is in Campochiaro, Molise, which contains over three hundred skeletal remains of Alvari warriors. They came from what is today Bulgaria, most likely to help fight against Byzantine armies. Many of their weapons, garment decorations, and horse accoutrements are well preserved. The females' burials are rich in items including combs, earrings, and necklaces. The Tufara bridge and Alvari warriors are examples of Molise's rich history. When the known historical sites and those yet to be discovered are connected to other aspects of tourism, they add a special sentiment to each area of Molise for those who have empathy for the past.

The number of tourists in Molise will increase when they become aware of the attractions and know that the facilities are accommodating and hospitable. In large part, the requirements for building tourism are the same for the needs of the resident population.

The possibility that Molise will fail in creating employment opportunities and thus lose population is of grave concern. Predictions have been made that many of the small villages will be abandoned. Where

The Pantano

does Montenero stand in this scenario? One study predicts it will be a ghost town by 2093. In order to prove this forecast wrong, Montenero's politicians and business leaders need to realistically look at its strengths and weaknesses—and prepare for the future.

MONTENERO HEREAFTER

The average human lifespan is about seventy-nine years. For a horse it is thirty-five. A rabbit? Only ten. Even a sun has a limited lifespan of about five billion years. A village also has its own destiny. Much has transpired since the birth of Montenero on the lands of the Abby of San Vincenzo al Volturno. Built on a hill for its protective position and evolving during medieval times for over a thousand years, Montenero is now a relic taking its last wheezing breaths. As one cycle comes to completion, another will be generated, like the mythological phoenix arising from the ashes of its predecessor. Montenero's human history should inspire a transformation. The destiny of the village—if it will experience a rebirth—depends on the will and cooperation of the people who value it.

Photo by Antonio Greco.

Many think that Montenero and other villages in the High Molise are doomed. There is nothing there! The phrase *Il Molise non esiste* (Molise does not exist) became popular because it indicates the insignificance of the region. Perhaps there is reason to value the emptiness? A cup is useful because of the empty space that can be filled with wine. A room is functional for its openness. A vase is valued because the emptiness inside makes it useful. The fact that Molise does not have great industries is a plus! As the world population approaches eight billion, there is tremendous value in isolation and tranquility. Molise offers this. While the High Molise seems to have the least to offer, it may actually have the best to offer.

There are dozens of Molise villages on the verge of abandonment. Which will survive by recreating themselves? Considering the potential of geotourism, Montenero does not possess the best cultural attractions in the region. Its piazza is not extraordinary in its charming beauty. Its churches do not draw the faithful for pilgrimages. Tourists will not arrive to hear a concert, view artworks, or dine on fine cuisine. Montenero does possess its own unique history and a stunning geographic setting that is nationally praised, especially for the valley—the pantano with its rare indigenous breed of Pentro horses and wide variety of rare flowers, birds, and other plants and animals. The pantano and the Zittola River are "placed amongst the Corine Biotopes, the most important sites for the conservation of nature amongst the EU countries."[17] It seems apparent that this is what makes Montenero unique and holds the key to its future.

According to the Regional Agency for Environmental Protection of Molise, and the Environmental Protection and Technical Services Agency, Montenero's pantano

> has numerous archaeological sites and outstanding flora and fauna, as well as unparalleled scenery; there are broad meadows with herds of cattle and horses that are reared in the wild. . . . The wide flood-plain, to the south east of the village of Montenero Val Cocchiara, is one of the most extensive Apennine-bogs in Italy . . . the low-lying area is ringed by a range of hills in such a way as to make it a 'natural amphitheatre'. . . . possesses a wide variety of habitats: meadowland, marsh, peat-bog, woodland with karstic areas, torrents . . . are all features of a zone with notable natural beauty. The water habitats favour the presence and settlement of species of birds that are at risk of extinction, and also rare examples of plants and flora which are important for the preservation of biodiversity. The huge size of the area and its environmental and scenic importance make it a marshland habitat of particular rarity and excellence.[18]

When the first rodeo was organized in 1974, it brought fame to the village. Many Italian and foreign tourists attended the events held every summer in the pantano. Galloping horses thrilled the crowds. Spectators felt the danger when a local cowboy attempted to ride a wild horse and were elated when he was successful. People could mingle while eating grilled sandwiches and quench their thirst on cool drinks under the sun. Other activities kept everyone busy throughout the days of the rodeo. It is only logical that this special annual event would continue forever! However, after thirty-two years, it has not been organized since 2006. After a thirteen-year hiatus, efforts were made to have a rodeo this year, 2019. . . . It didn't materialize.

The Pentro horses have been raised in the same area for over 2,500 years. They have been used for transportation as well as a source of meat. The horses also have a nostalgic value, as well as an altruistic value that others benefit by the breed's very existence. In 2000, there were only 150 registered Pentro horses. A study by Cicia et al. shows that a minimum of a thousand more Pentro horses are needed to guarantee the breed will not become extinct.[19] If achieved, it is possible to market five hundred colts per year and maintain the herd. This may never happen because of lack of interest among the locals.

If the magic of the pantano is the key to Montenero's future, it has been sadly neglected. The fate of the village rests in the hands of those who seem to be unwilling to cooperate. South Italy, the Molise region, Isernia Province, and Montenero village are stunted by a poor attitude. No matter how wonderful an idea may be to improve life in Molise, nothing will work without a change of attitude.

Photo of by M. DiMarco.

There is hope. As Pesaresi writes: "[W]e can say that the static, hesitant and isolationary processes, which often characterise the municipalities of the study area and the Molise Region, are not irreversible and, to begin to invert it, they need to awake from the numbness which leads to ruin. Culture and agriculture, environment and tourism can contribute to development, to create an image that is fresh and alive, to connect the ancient to the modern; preservation and enhancement only if they go together, in a synergic process that aims at general improvement."[20]

Many who have studied the potential of south Italy have underlined common problems that need to be overcome before substantial progress can be made. Planning, financial investing, and changing laws and ordinances are not enough. "Finally, for real change, not only must the local community be able to leave behind the negative legacy of past choices, logically rethinking the network of social, economic and institutional relations (both formal and informal) in order to be more inclusive compared to what has been done so far, plus it is also necessary to overcome the resistance to change—often due to the desire to maintain the existing power structure—of the ruling classes at various levels (national, regional and local)."[21]

On the local village level, there is "a culture in which everyone seeks to gain at each other's expense" and "has proven the detriment of the community as a whole."[22] Can we expect individuals within a longstanding culture of ingrained thought patterns to change? The prospect seems naïve; however, perhaps the "task inspires a new sense of common purpose, analogous, even, to the post-war feeling of the need to reconstruct the nation after the fall of Mussolini and the devastation of war."[23]

In *Good Italy, Bad Italy*, the author concludes that "a sense of crisis helps enormously"[24] when asking for such social change. It is always frightening to face change, but there is excitement and optimism when the road is chosen. If local leaders and residents patiently review data regarding the potential for Molise and practical plans to implement ways to develop the region, "a consciousness of both past and present" would emerge that would inspire a cooperative spirit and forward thinking.[25]

As with Montenero, there is an opportunity to "rediscover old values and social relations . . . recover and restore the rural houses and buildings to their full functionality which today would acquire major economic value and reveal the souls of places and structures that were formerly abandoned or neglected some decades ago."[26] Montenero is blessed to have its rich history unfold in a beautiful geographic location. Those who live in the village or have roots there should feel proud of the land, its resources, and the heritage provided by the labors of ancestors.

Flashbacks

chapter 16

A Three-Day Fictional Tour of Montenero

DAY 1: Early morning. Just outside the bustling Leonardo da Vinci International Airport near Rome, we are soon on the highway in a hired van. Three hours later we reach Castel di Sangro's bus station. The greens and blues of sky and mountains seem more vibrant here than elsewhere, no doubt due to the pure air that lets true colors meet the eye. While waiting for the minibus that will take us to Montenero, we can't help but notice the large two-story building next to the station parking lot. Its walls of alternating horizontal lines of pink and white stone make it look like a layered cake . . . a torte semicovered in black mold. It's said that construction came to a stop some years ago when the builder couldn't fulfill the gratuity the Mafia bosses expected for allowing a new business to open its doors. The minibus finally arrives and we get in to start the fifteen-minute drive to the village. It's just six miles away.

State road 17 is arrow straight from Castel di Sangro to the junction where it meets state road 83 just after passing Orsini Market. Looking back toward Castel, one's eyes are immediately drawn to the magnificent facade of Santa Maria Assunta Basilica, which dominates the city. Just behind it is Point 1009, the peak where the West Nova Scotia Regiment drove off German troops in fierce battles during World War II. Numerous Allied and German troops traveled this section of road. Before we visit the main sites in Montenero, we will see numerous points of interest along the way that have contributed to village history.

At the junction of 17 and 83, we envision the earlier encounter between Austrian and Neapolitan troops in the 1815 Battle of Castel di Sangro. From a far earlier period, we can almost smell the sheep that crossed this intersection since Samnite times. Here the Castel di Sangro–Lecera and Pescasseroli–Candela Drover Roads intersect, and herders could rest at the Zittola Tavern. Sixteen herders from Montenero took the road south but never returned alive: they died during the 1879 earthquake in Bovino.

At the intersection we turn onto the meandering road for Montenero. Immediately on the right side we see the aging, nonfunctional Montenero railroad station and the dilapidated Abruzzo Beer brewery (Birra d' Abruzzo). Thoughts of a cold beer on a hot summer day enter the mind as well as images of the 1917 Peat Revolt, with over one hundred people from Montenero arrested.

▲ Saint Ilario Chapel.

A short distance from the brewery, a road sign tells us we have left Abruzzo and entered Molise. The next small road on the right leads to the restored eighteenth-century chapel dedicated to Saint Ilario. It is surrounded by thick woods. In front of it is a long stone trough in which refreshing spring water runs constantly. Inside are a tabernacle, altar, and statue of the saint. Every year there is a celebration and picnic on the first Tuesday after Pentecost, held here under the trees by the people of Montenero. In former times, "The women rinsed their breasts with Saint Ilario water to get a lot of milk."[1] A short walk down the road there is a much smaller chapel dedicated to St. Anthony.

The chapels around Montenero stand like holy guards protecting all those living in the village. Perhaps they protect those who have passed into the afterlife too? Down the road from St. Anthony's chapel is Montenero's main cemetery. It is surrounded by a stone wall. We enter through a gate flanked by two small buildings. In the past, the bones of the departed would be unearthed years after death and placed in an ossuary, a common area below the cemetery chapel. Many are now entombed above ground, some in family mausoleums, while others find eternal peace in individual plots. The names carved in marble are usually recognizable as Montenerese whose ancestors lived in the village at least during the past two centuries, if not longer.

▶ Cemetery entrance and an inside view.
Photographs above and right by M. DiMarco.

◄ Montenero's relatively new "holy field" (*camposanto*) with a variety of tombs and mausoleums. *Photographs by M. DiMarco.* ▼

There is a little stone statue that is often unnoticed. Worn by age, it shows an anonymous young lady cradling a baby in her arms. There's no engraving to indicate why the statue is here. Oral tradition sadly recounts that she was a woman from the village who was often beaten by her husband. He was especially brutal after she gave birth to a female. He wanted a son. About a year later, he beat her so badly that she appeared lifeless as a result of the trauma she received. Her body was put in the cemetery chapel for the night. In the morning when pallbearers went to bury her, they found her with a newborn in her arms. A male. Seemingly close to death, she found the strength to give birth, then died. It's believed that her father, in order to mark this tragedy in our collective memory, made this statue for all to ponder.

Chances are, even before visiting the cemetery, all would notice the vast expanse of the pantano on the left side of the road. Hundreds of horses and cows graze while rare birds flutter among the flowers

► Statue of an unnamed lady holding her baby boy.

Photograph by Sandra Di Fiore.

growing along the Zittola River banks. In some sections of the valley, fresh hay has been cut, left to dry under the sun's warm rays. A group on horseback enters the valley with their guide from Ranch Brionna. Among the wild horses, the pros who know all things equestrian can spot which are of the ancient Pentro breed.

The pantano—the bog, quagmire, swamp, marshland—is often flooded by rains and overflow from the Zittola River. It makes Montenero famous, particularly for the flora and fauna. However, in ancient times it also gave name to Mala Cocchiara, the pantano site known for breeding mosquitos responsible for malaria. The early settlers to the area wisely chose to build a village on higher ground.

At the corner of the cemetery is a fork in the road with one route leading directly to the upper area of Montenero while the other leads to the base of the village. We follow the latter and reach the Chapel of San Sebastian on the left side where the road bends, marking the traditional entrance to the village. A life-size iron cross standing on its cement foundation has been here since before World War II. It appears on a photograph dated 2 March 1944, near an Allied Universal Carrier with machine gun guarding the approach to Montenero.

Abutting the chapel is a small park facing the valley. It offers shade under the large trees and a wonderful view toward the pantano and surrounding mountains. There is a small playground for children here too. Many visit the park

▲ Military monument.
Photograph by M. DiMarco.

to see the war memorial, which lists those who lost their lives in World Wars I and II.

We pass some homes on Via Nostra Signora Lourdes, and then on the right side we see the post office at the corner of Via Maria Regina. It's next to the Maria Immacolata and Saint Clemente Martyr Kindergarten. The upcoming building is the F. Iovine Primary School. Both schools closed this year (2019) due to lack of enrollment, an ill omen for the village. Across the street is what is referred to as the "Monumentino Mariano," made in 1950 by Marcuccio Di Filippo and Arduino Narducci. It's a focal point for many social gatherings organized by the village for holidays and holy days.

▲ The elementary school on Via Nostra Signora Lourdes. *Courtesy of M. DiMarco.*

After we cross Via Roma, we see a brick-surfaced bus stop on the corner. An assortment of bushes and flowering plants surrounds the area with a tree near the center that provides shade. Locals know when buses arrive and depart, but chances are you won't find a posted schedule here. A few benches and a typical bus shelter are provided for waiting passengers, or to anyone wishing to relax and enjoy the view looking up to the village and eye the passersby.

As we step out of the minibus to grab our luggage, we are met by Michele Fabrizio, owner of Il Corniolo, a bed and breakfast with the ideal location in walking distance from the bus stop. Across the street from the B&B is the remnant of a building bombed during World War II. The stonework of the remaining wall can be clearly seen and represents much of the hand labor used to build all the structures in Montenero.

Once settled in our rooms, we refresh ourselves and decide to go to the MOMU (Molino Museum) on Via Fronte, a two-minute walk from Il Corniolo. The museum is housed in a beautifully restored ancient water mill. This allows us to not only see how a mill works, but to actually touch a large variety of peasant farm tools, see what the work and living areas in the building look like, and to ask questions about many more items on display. The MOMU is a window into how most people in Montenero made a living during the past centuries.

▲ Church of San Nicola di Bari. *Left, courtesy of M. DiMarco; right, Lina Del Sangro Stea.*

With great anticipation of going to the Piazza Risorgimento, we walk along Via Fronte to Via Roma, which will take us directly to our destination. This square is named after the ideological movement for Italy, a plea to all for "rising again" (Risorgimento) with a new national consciousness of a unified Italy. Roughly halfway to the square on Via Roma #5 is Bonaminio's Grocery, the only grocery store in Montenero. With this well-stocked one-room store, run by Sergio Bonaminio and his wife Alexandra (Sandra), there's no great need to drive to a supermarket in Castel di Sangro.

As we continue to walk uphill from the intersection where Via Roma meets Via S. Nicola, we see the Church of San Nicola di Bari. It was built in the area that was formerly the village market. Before 1535, it was the parish of the village. According to a text in the archive of the Diocese of Trivento, the church was founded by a man named Fausto, whose wife's name was Trophina. Built in Romanesque style, a bell hangs from the middle of three arches atop its simple front. A sole rose window is located above the entry door. The church suffered great damage by fire in 1501, and some of the interior space was reduced in 1688 under direction of Monsignor Tortorelli. The small interior has a simple altar that was donated by G. Mannarelli in 1765 with four columns, now rarely seen, as the doors are usually locked.

Today, the facade is of historical importance. Plaster had covered it for nearly two hundred years, but restoration work in 2009 shed the covering to show its beautiful original stonework. The result is largely due to the efforts of the present pastor in Montenero, Don Elio Fiore. High up on the facade near the bell is a stone panel with images of a lion and lizard, medieval symbols of strength and rebirth. More noticeable is a Latin inscription on a stone column to the right of the doorframe. It is a dedication by Fausto and Trophina for their son Faustino, who had died. Because they didn't have an heir, they willed that their property go to the church upon their deaths. Near the epitaph is a "simple but tender engraving depicting a man driving two oxen with clear reference to family activity."[2] The best time to see the church is during the yearly celebration for Saint Nicola on 6 December. The devotees enjoy a traditional meal of fettuccine made with olive oil and garlic.

▲ Welcome to Roxy Bar!
Courtesy of M. Di Fiore.

We walk from the church, and Via S. Nicola leads up a fairly steep incline of steps to the piazza. As we reach the top of the steps, we see the long one-floor municipal hall. Its big room, entered by the door on the left, is used for special meetings and functions organized by the village. The right side of the building is the site of Roxy Bar! It is the heartbeat of Montenero. Why? It is the prime spot for its people to eat, drink, socialize, and soak in the magnificent views over the pantano valley and surrounding mountains. The owner is Marylise Di Fiori, a dynamic young lady whose love of the village and its people is apparent in all she does. Although she was born in France, she decided to start the business in Montenero, where her parents were born and where she has many friends and relatives. After we order some refreshing drinks and some snacks, Marylise responds to some questions about her work:

It is a joy to run the bar and pizzeria where the villagers come to meet us and pass the time. We open at 7:00 in the morning, so we begin the day offering breakfast, including various kinds of coffees, hot chocolate, and other drinks, plus croissants and delicious pastries made by Cupiello—the number 1 Italian pastry company in Italy.

When I lived in France, I longed to return to the simpler lifestyle in this beautiful village. Along with my partner, we decided to leave France, come to Montenero, and create the Roxy Bar to give more service to the place, the villagers, and the tourists. In fact, every summer many immigrants return from France, Canada, Belgium, and elsewhere. And yearlong, many visit from Naples and Rome. We've focused on enlarging the Roxy to fulfill the needs of all our customers.

Since this is a small town, we certainly don't expect to become rich, but the work offers a peaceful, fulfilling life. What I find wonderful is that everyone knows us, and we come to know each customer very well. There is a close human relationship with customers, and we have discussions on every topic. . . . It's a wonderful way to learn the stories of the village, the people, and how life was in Montenero in the past. The summer work is very physically tiring: the village doubles its population with many visitors. Having a bar means being there all day. It's a physical and mental commitment.

I feel my job is important for Montenero because it brings energy to village life, gets people together, and stimulates the social relations and activities. When the bar is open, there is more movement in the square. The Roxy Bar is a place of reference for the villagers where they can learn what is happening here and in the lives of friends and relatives—a meeting place for all ages.

Sitting on our patio with a cold beer or soft drink is the most common way customers pass an afternoon viewing our beautiful vistas. Evenings are very relaxing for the customers. They relax and enjoy the variety of pizzas and specialty drinks, especially when there is music.

I think every moment we live together remains an indelible memory. Offering my clients a moment of relaxation, laughter, and joy becomes for me a gift of life. On one wall in the bar there are hundreds of photographs of the villagers—the people who meet at the Roxy are always in our hearts. They will form habits and traditions that will influence future generations.

Coming here from France, I had a fear that I would not be accepted, even though my roots are here in Montenero. It's a great satisfaction to have met so many people, to learn the past of this place, and to be able to provide a service, a collaboration with the whole village, to live and work in Montenero.

In a place with many elders, Roxy Bar provides a shot of youthful freshness to the village while always respecting its simplicity, tranquility, and its unique heritage.

▲ Marylise Di Fiore with Saverio Bucsicchio. Right, Sandra (Di Fiore) Caserta. *Courtesy of M. Di Fiore and S. Di Fiore.*

After enjoying the tasty food, drink, and hospitality, we decide to continue our walk from where the steps of Via S. Nicola ended. Right at the corner, across from the municipal building, there is an area covered with grass and some shrubs. This is the site where local theatre productions were organized by the musician and composer Nicola Martino in his home just before World War II. It provided entertainment through a mix of singing, dancing, and stage plays. It seems that after television became available, there wasn't much activity at the theatre. Now it is empty space.

On level with the top of the municipal building is the central Piazza Risorgimento. In the early 1970s, a number of houses were torn down in order to expand the piazza. The space usually serves as a parking area, especially for tourists who can easily come to view the main surrounding attractions. On occasions it provides a gathering space for numerous types of entertainment, such as professional concerts and projects designed to get locals to participate and show off their talents. The piazza has long been the gathering arena for holidays and holy days, such as the Feast of San Andun'.

THE FEAST OF SAN ANDUN' (SAINT ANTONIO ABATE)

San Andun' (251–356 CE) was a Christian monk who lived eighty of his 105 years as a hermit. He was often tormented by hellish supernatural visits and temptations. Because he could defeat any disease that burned like hellfire, San Andun' is called upon to prevent or cure any infectious disease, particularly skin diseases. Owing to his association with these diseases, a number of painful ailments were known as St. Anthony's fire.

Followers of San Andun' living in a monastery were said to have kept domesticated pigs, which wore a collar and a bell around their necks. Symbolically, the wild pig is evil, which followers of San Andun' control by the "collar" of their good deeds. The saint has been honored as the patron associated with animals and those involved in related work as breeders and butchers. Montenero—with its history of raising animals for meat, milk, eggs, and other products—shows special appreciation to the saint every 17 January by holding the Feast of San Andun'. Sandra Di Fiore, sister of Marylise of Roxy Bar, tells us of the tradition, which continues today:

In ancient times, a piglet was specially selected in Montenero in honor of the saint. It was identified according to the ritual of tying a red ribbon around its neck to which a bell was hung. Also a cross was drawn on its back. "Ùr purch de San Andun'" [a pig for St. Anthony was nourished by the community during the entire year].

On the day before the actual feast, children passed through the streets of Montenero, ringing bells and singing:

Andun', Andun', Andun'	Anthony, Anthony, Anthony
E ppr legna a San Andun'	Fetch wood for Saint Anthony
E chi n' g vo dà	Whoever doesn't want to give it
Che c' possen' schatta	We wish they die.

Hearing the singing and bells, all Montenerese came out of their homes to offer a wooden log. The kids then tied two or three logs together and dragged them to the square, where the adults stacked the wood to form a large pyre. A little boy would stand like a sentry beside it.

Also on that day, the Montenerese prepared a small bread called chiachiarel' [blessed flat oven-baked bread]. These were distributed on the feast day to the poor, who came from the surrounding towns to Montenero to beg.

On the night between 16 and 17 of January, a small fire was built. That's called ur fucarigl'. Youngsters showed off by jumping over the fire. The next morning, with the help of ur fucarigl', a huge bonfire was lit during mass.

After the solemn Holy Mass, a statue of San Andun' was transported on a platform to the fires, where the parish priest blessed it. Then all walked in a procession to bless the animals—cows, sheep, horses, pigs, dogs—around the village.

After an afternoon mass, youngsters gathered in a house to dress up in costumes [*pulciunnel*: mascara, or disguise] and then went noisily parading around the village streets. When people heard their noisy approach, bread and wine were given out to celebrate the evening.

Among the youngsters [traditionally, as well as today], there is always a person dressed as a devil who repeatedly passes by the bonfire with an entourage behind him that pretends to attack the bystanders. In a euphoric atmosphere enhanced by drink, a lottery is made, and a lucky winner gets the well-fattened pig. Whoever wins must provide a piglet designated for the festival the following year.

This tradition is carried on in much the same way under the supervision of today's parish priest. The statue of San Andun' is always carried to the bonfire, where the priest recites a prayer. San Andun' is invoked so that the animals are saved from all evils. The priest blesses the fire, all the people, and the domestic animals. The blessings are even sent from the square to the animals located in the pantano.

In 2014, the Caserta brothers played the roles of the devil (Gino) and the priest (Norméo). In the evening, all gather around the warmth of the bonfire to cook sausages (*chiutc* and *fasciul*), and sing and dance in the company of good wine.

San Andun' Ce magn' e ce vev'!

Saint Anthony's Day, eat and drink!

▲ The finale of the San Antun' celebrations.
Courtesy of Emma Iacobucci.

What could we see next on the piazza? There are a number of interesting sites in any direction. We choose to go to the closest point of interest, which is a residential area noted for its beautiful architecture. As we walk past the empty field where Martino's theatre was located, we look left to see a two-story archway attaching some huge Renaissance-style buildings dating to 1751. The main structure was in the prosperous Mannarelli family. They had a flourishing business transporting sheep along the drover trail to Foggia and back. It also served as a hospital.

Built into the second floor is a passageway with three arches that visitors can walk under to get to residences. Unfortunately, the 1984 earthquake did some damage to the archway and attached buildings, and the repair

▲ Mannarelli building. *Courtesy of M. DeMarco.*

work is easily spotted. If you enter any of the homes on the right, there are excellent window views west toward the Monti della Meta peaks, exceptionally majestic when covered in snow. Below the windows is Via Roma, where, as some remember, young boys died from a German bomb during World War II.

Next we come to the Church of the Blessed Virgin of Carmel. Consecrated on 28 October 1701, the church was funded by Archpriest Angelo Mannarelli for tending the spiritual and health needs of the locals. A wonderful golden mosaic on the church's high facade overlooks the entire piazza. The mosaic was created in 1962, and it represents the Madonna of the Assumption. A commemorative plaque on the wall states that Father Don Pasquale Di Filippo dedicated this fine artwork to the Virgin Mary on 8 September 1968, the twenty-fifth anniversary of his priesthood.

▲ Church of the Blessed Virgin of Carmel. *Courtesy of Federico de Vincenzi.*

▲ Piazza Risorgimento on Saint Clemente's Feast Day, 2005.
Courtesy of Vincent Caserta.

We enter the main door and see a wooden vestibule that was originally in the Church of S. Maria di Loreto. Because the central nave is usually closed, one can go either left or right to enter the interior. It is small but cozy, with warm-colored walls and a low ceiling. There are three naves demarcated by massive arches. Natural light from side windows offers a calm, peaceful atmosphere. The Baroque altars were originally in the Church of S. Maria di Loreto.

Author Benito dello Siesto aptly describes the interior:[3]

> In the vault of the central nave there is a large oval medallion with the Madonna enthroned between cherubim and the Carmelite saints Simone Stock and Teresa, who receive the Scapular of the Order from the Virgin and Child. The high cone of the high altar, in polychrome marble, houses the statue of the Madonna.

In the right aisle is placed the altar of St. Rocco made of marble inlay that also decorates the rungs of the semi-columns on which rests the entablature decorated with cherubs. In the other aisle is the simple altar of St. Antonio Abate. The saint is very revered in the culture of breeding.

Along the side aisles are the statues of S. Emmio, patron of earthquakes, of S. Maria del Carmine and of the Sacred Heart of Mary.

Just around the corner of the Church of the Madonna del Carmine on Via Pio XII is a home built in 1853 that belonged to the Evangelista Mannarelli family. It's natural stone walls, drainage channels, and covered terrace illustrate some common architectural designs in the village. The wooden roof was damaged during World War II, but it was later restored. There are finely carved images above the two entranceways. One shows a single ox with a plow; above the other door are two oxen. Some say the stonecutters competed to see whose image would be selected for the front door. Others think the owner was deliberately expressing his decision on how to split the inheritance among his children.

Near the Mannarelli home is a low wall that separates the land from Via Pio XII. On top of it someone roughly etched a cross into the cement. Local legend has it that one man from the town was so horrible that many villagers got together to decide how to keep all safe from this dangerous person. They concluded that the only way was just to kill him. They threw his dead body over this small wall. When the police came to question the locals about the apparent murder, all answered: "We know nothing of the incident."

We move on toward the quaint municipal square (*piazza municipio*). The short street between the Risorgimento and the municipal square has witnessed much over the centuries, such as religious processions, baptisms, funerals, weddings, and revolts. As we look up the street, all attention is immediately drawn to the S. Maria di Loreto Church. Even before reaching the six steps to the church's front courtyard, visitors are engulfed by all the surrounding beauty in and around this area: arches, gates, bells, clock and bell towers, flowers, two-hundred-year-old linden trees, stained glass, and stone and woodwork. Thunderstruck by being in the center of this spectacle, we decide to take in the area little by little.

▲ Musicians approach the S. Maria di Loreto Church on San Clemente's Feast Day. Built-in seating made of stone is on both sides of the courtyard.

▶ The former municipal building (light yellow) now houses the library and medical center. Locals relax and chat in the municipal square. *Photos courtesy of M. DiMarco.*

We walk up a few steps to reach the municipal square, where we see the former municipal office building. This is the same spot where the Peat Revolt started when villagers attacked members of the municipal council in 1917. A newer municipal building was constructed at the foot of Montenero, not far from our bed-and-breakfast. Today the old structure houses a library and a pharmacy. There are two arched doorways with the one on the left used to enter the marvelous little library staffed by Guido Martino. The great collection here has something of interest for everyone, including items related to the village. Of course Guido can guide you through the special collections on the shelves, but he is a quiet treasure himself. It was his talented father Nicola who ran the theatre next to the main piazza. Artistic talent runs through the family. Last year seventeen of Guido's oil paintings were exhibited in the Palazzo de Petra, in Castel di Sangro's Civic Gallery of Modern Art. It seems Guido's formal training in biology helped his artistic eye in painting objects of nature, faces, and figures.

The pharmacy in Montenero provides a number of services with the help of Dr. Ubaldo Manzelli and Dr. Vittoria Milò. They have numerous products for both health and beauty, such as cosmetics with particular attention to dermatology, phytotherapy, and homeopathy. In addition, there is a modern examination room and medical tools on hand for the doctors to handle many of the common patient needs for their health care.

The municipal square could have been walled off from the higher, older part of Montenero. In medieval times, many villages were built on hills to take advantage of the defensive position. Stone walls and buildings were arranged as fortifications, with specific gates that could be locked closed if necessary. Under the Abby of San Vincenzo al Volturno, Montenero was required to build as a fortified town. Here we see the Portanuova, or "New Gate," which guards the entry to Via Portanuova and to the upper area known as the court (corte or trabucco in the Montenero dialect). It was near this portal that the German firing squad attempted to shoot a group of local men during World War II.

Facing Portanuova, we look to the right and see an archway leading to a narrow alley that runs along the side of the church. Referred to as the Connuottolo, the alley is a shortcut to the eastern part of the village. We walk a few steps from Portanuova and are again in the front courtyard of S. Maria di Loreto Church. The stone seating that blends in with the walls on the left and right side of the courtyard is ideal for Sunday "people watching" of those going to mass. More women actually go into the church than men. How some of the younger ladies dress for mass today would not have been tolerated twenty years ago—the greater exposure of skin and fashionably tight jeans leave little to the imagination. From this front courtyard, visitors usually go through the gated archway on the right side to enter the Renaissance-style loggia that dates to the original sixteenth-century structure of the church. The vista affords a spectacular view over much of the village and extends to the pantano and the mountains beyond.

Set high on the hill above most of the village homes, the seventeen arches and bell tower form the most important architectural elements in Montenero. These structures create a visual hub that holds the village and its territory together. Dello Siesto writes that the seventeen arches were spaced according to religious symbolic use of numbers.[4]

◀ Arches of the S. Maria di Loreto Church.

▼ Church courtyard viewed from the archway.
Photos by M. DiMarco.

▼ Portanuova.
Courtesy of Lisa Freda.

BELL TOWER

Suddenly we hear the resonating sound of bronze bells and return to the courtyard to see them swinging in the bell tower. According to a record in the Diocese of Trivento archive, dated 1706, "The bell tower has four bells, one called the clock, the other of the Rosary, the other of the Doctrine and the other of the Holy Oil and Communion."[5] Siesto adds that one of the bells, decorated with a stork and a lizard, was made in the famous Marinelli Pontifical Foundry in Agnone.

Another set of bells is atop the large clock tower that is just beyond Portanuova. Before watches and iPhones, the tolling bell indicated the time of day and when a funeral or mass would take place, among other messages the residents understood. Today, I'd rather check my iPhone—the cacophony of bells, chimes, and whistles just gets on my nerves.

Writing chiseled into a stone rectangle on the bell tower is not readable, except for the date of 1570 and the Italian-Savoy coat of arms. The tower underwent some repairs and reconstruction. What we

Photos by M. DiMarco.

see today is the result of work done in 1863, including the octagonal pyramid. An inscription on the tower states that master stonemason Luigi Ziroli was the director of the repairs, and Giulio Gigliotti was mayor in 1863. Another inscription records the commemorative dedication, which I freely translate:

QUESTA TORRE
REDIMITA DI SACRI BRONZI
PIÙ SOLIDA ED ELEGANTE
SU LE ROVINE DI VECCHIA E ROZZA MOLE
IL MUNICIPIO EDIFICAVA
QUANDO
SU I ROTTAMI DI TRONI INFRANTI
S'INNALZAVA IMPERITURE
LA SUA LIBERTÀ UNITA ED INDIPENDENZA
LA GRAN PATRIA ITALIANA
MDCCCLXIII

This tower
A redemption for sacred bronze bells
Made more solid and elegant
On the ruins of an old and rough pile.
The Town Hall was built
when
From the wreckage of broken thrones [the Bourbons]
rose up enduringly
The Great Italian Homeland
1863

During Saturday evening prayers on 1 January 1946, a lightning strike damaged the top of the tower. There are a few photos of its repair work being done. One photo shows Nicola Scalzitti, husband of Rovenza Calvano and father of Michele, working precariously to fit the stonework accurately in place. Here in the courtyard—actually anywhere in Montenero—images emerge of the stoneworkers' callused hands and sweat rolling off their dusty foreheads. It is more difficult to approximate the thousands of exhausting hours they labored to build and regularly repair the village's buildings and streets.

▶ Part of the courtyard in front of the bell tower.
Photos by M. DiMarco.

271

CHURCH OF
S. MARIA DI LORETO

It seems there was a small religious structure present on this location in the fifteenth century, replaced by a formidable structure in 1530 and inaugurated in 1535. The Church of S. Maria di Loreto was later enlarged when Montenero came under the hand of noble Cesare Greco in 1591. Perhaps he ordered the expansion because of a growing village population? Or perhaps because he was getting older and his mind was drawn to the spiritual realm? He died in 1615. According to an epigraph on the altar of the crucifix, further changes came in 1620, apparently under Cesare's son Francesco. After these major enhancements were made, the main church included three naves. The central nave measures 108.27 x 26.25 feet and 26.25 feet in height, while the side naves are 65.5 x 13 feet and 13 feet in height. This gives the interior its standard Latin cross design. In 1880, iron beams were added in the vaults as part of a renovation.

Dedicated to the Madonna of Loreto—the protector of travelers including the transhumant shepherds—the church is the main place of worship in the village, and so is usually referred to as the Mother Church (Chiese Madre). Dating 1780, the gray stone door frame with Baroque embellishments contrasts nicely with the wooden entrance door and surrounding stone walls. Set just above the door is a modern glasswork of the Sacred Heart of Jesus, which looks best at night from the outside. Higher up, between this window and the roof, is a small, eye-shaped window.

Through the entranceway we find ourselves in a modern foyer. Most enter the interior through the middle double door, which is flanked by single doors on both sides. The original three-door partition of carved wood is now in the Church of the Madonna del Carmine. An earthquake in 1805 may have caused damage to the church. It's certain that in the late nineteenth century a new wooden ceiling had to be installed. In a 1706 report by Montenero's parish priest to the bishop of Trivento, Don Angelo Mannarelli writes that, "[T]he white washed stone floor was founded in 1530 as carved in stone lintel and consecrated by the bishop Matteo Grifonius [Griffin] on September 8, 1559."[6] However, the flooring was replaced not long ago with white and rust-colored marble. Other restructuring and repairs occurred regularly over the centuries, as with the restructuring of S. Maria di Loreto, implemented in 1774.

▲ The main altar behind the marble balustrade. *Photo by M. DiMarco.*

ALTARS

Entering the central nave, one's eyes are immediately drawn to the main altar and then to side altars. All embody designs of polychrome marble created in the eighteenth century, reflecting a fancy Baroque style. The altars and their superb works of marble inlay are both aesthetically beautiful as well as economically valuable. The artists who did this work were most likely from Naples, but there may have been contributions from marble workers in Pescocostanzo.

- **Altar of S. Domenico Soriano (Seventeenth Century):** Saint Dominic (1170–1221), a vegetarian and ascetic, founded the Dominican Order and is the patron saint of astronomers. He appears in an icon here with a lily and the book of the rule of his order. An altarpiece depicts the Blessed Virgin wearing a jeweled tiara, and portraits of St. Mary Magdalene and St. Catherine of Alexandria are displayed.
- **Altar of Our Lady of the Rosary (Sixteenth Century):** Dedicated to the Virgin Mary, this is the oldest altar in the church. It is a relatively plain shrine carved in stone. Although it has some decorative elements, its simplicity indicates it was probably the work of a local artisan. Seen here are a fine Greek cross and a statue of Christ.

- **Altar of the Crucifix (1620):** This altar also shows fine artistry in the use of colored marble and inlays of mother of pearl. Behind this altar is the choir stall from the sixteenth century.
- **Presbytery Altar (1754):** This is the main altar, which many believe represents the highest quality of workmanship among all other altars in Molise. The inlays of decorative florals, vegetables, and sacred symbols are alive with vibrant colors. Angels keep their eyes on the ornamented tabernacle housing the sacred chalice. The golden doors of the tabernacle were made by an artist named Scipione in his Naples workshop.
- **Altar of St. Clemente (1777):** On this polychrome marble altar is a casket made of metal and glass displaying the body of the martyr St. Clemente. The patron saint of Montenero has been here since 6 June 1776. Plants and sacred symbols can be seen in the decorative marble rails and supports. A statue of the martyr remains here, except when ported through the village on special occasions, such as the annual Festa of San Clemente, which takes place in early August.
- **Altar of the Immaculate (1680):** View an eighteenth-century statue of the Immaculate and a representation of St. Margaret of Antiochia that is within a small shrine.
- **Altar of Our Lady of Sorrows (1758):** Although damaged, this altar is the only one in the church with an altarpiece that is signed and dated (1758). It has a walnut canopy supported by carved columns. At the sides of the canopy are figures of St. John the Evangelist and the less-known St. Francis Caracciolo.
- **Altar of St. Nicholas (1664):** The altar of St. Nicholas dates to the seventeenth century. Busts of the Dominican missionary St. Vincent Ferrer (associated with wings of an angel) and St. Roch (a protector from the plague) share the marble table.
- **Altar of the Madonna of the Graces:** The Madonna shown here is symbolically giving her good grace by offering her breast milk, a source of physical and spiritual nourishment. Saint Joseph, John the Baptist, and Saint Donatus are by her side.
- **Altar of Our Lady of Loreto:** This altar was created by a local artist about two hundred years ago. It includes images of Saints Joseph, Bernardine of Siena, Carlo, and Camillo.

In the sacristy—the room where the priest prepares for services and where vestments and other items are kept—is the shiny silver overlaid wooden bust of Saint Margaret. She is a patron saint for the village. The work was made in the eighteenth century by a Neapolitan silversmith. Other religious furnishings are in the sacristy as well as ancient writings on three tables preserving special formulas, known as carteglories, from which a priest can recite. The sacristy door is flanked on one side by an elegant holy-water basin, which is supported by the palm of a carved hand.

▲ Mass in celebration of Saint Clemente.
Photo by M. DiMarco.

ARTWORKS

There are many paintings in the Mother Church, both contemporary and from past centuries. As we enter the central nave, six large paintings stand out, three on the left wall and three on the right. These oil paintings, commissioned by Montenero priest Don Pasquale Di Filippo, were all created by a well-known Molise artist, Giovanni Leo Paglione (1917–2004). He was born in Capracotta and worked mainly in Campobasso. His religious paintings and frescoes can be found in many Molise convents, chapels, and churches throughout the province. Also in the church is Paglione's *The Lost Sheep* (*La Pecorella Smarrita*) dated 1967. His six large oil paintings (all measuring 98.43" height by 137.8" width) on canvas are as follows:

1) *Proclamation of the Immaculate to the Patron of Montenero Val Cocchiara* (dated 8 December 1955).
2) *Madonna between Pope John XIII and Paul VI.* Gift of Nicola Ricchiuto in honor of parents Domenico and Giuseppina Narducci.

3) *Mary receives the Announcement of the Angel* (Annunciation)
   Gift of Di Fiore Teresa in honor of her husband.
4) *Proclamation of the Dogma of the Immaculate Conception*
   (dated 8 December 1854).
5) *Consecration of Montenero to the Sacred Heart of Mary*
   (dated 8 September 1967). Commemoration of the twenty-fifth
   year of Don Pasquale Di Filippo priesthood in Montenero.
6) Proclamation of the Dogma of the Madonna (dated 1 November
   1950). Gift of Fabrizio Carmelina, daughter of Biase.

There are other paintings by Paglione in the church. In the four corners of the rooms that support domes, for example, are the Evangelists, and saints Gregory and Ambrose. But there is more. A gem in the Mother Church is an eighteenth-century painting called *Dinner* (*Cena*). Although unsigned, the style points to a Naples influence, and more precisely to a painter named Francesco De Mura.

Another painting comes from the seventeenth century with a detailed scene from the Passion of Christ. Before Jesus and the cross are Mary, Saint John, and an unknown reverent woman. The fine details include items we associate with the event, including the spear, ladder, vinegar and sponge, nails, and even the bag containing thirty coins.

Here in the Santa Maria di Loreto Church is a silver processional cross of great importance in art history. Giovanni di Onofrio, a master goldsmith from Sulmona, made the cross in 1414. It bears di Onofrio's signature, verifying the influence Abruzzo artists have had in Molise. There is much more to see in the church. It is worth taking a casual walk through the main nave and side isles to study the statues, baptismal font, stations of the cross, vaulting, and more. Before moving into the foyer to depart, we observe each detail of the choir.

From the ground level we can see the front railing of the choir, designed to beautifully set off the space of the gallery for singers and musicians, while providing a margin of safety to prevent any fall from the balcony. The painted woodcarvings on the front of the balcony, strongest in rich blues and gold, are highlighted by the warm natural walnut wood tones and latticework. Matching colors and design encase a towering cane harmonium, looking somewhat like an armoire housing the musical pipes. The organ has nine registers and stops, adjusted in order to produce the desired sound. On the organ is an inscription that clearly presents the maker and date of the instrument, translated as follows: "Giuseppe de Marino and the Catholic Majesty's Royal Chapel of the City of Naples made this instrument in the year 1721."

▲ View of the church interior toward the choir. *Courtesy of Lisa Freda.*

It's been a long day with our energy fueled by the exciting sites of Montenero. We don't realize how tired we actually feel until we return to Il Corniolo at 6:00 p.m. A splash of cool water and a short rest invigorates us. At 7:30 we head out on foot for dinner, since we have reservations at the Casa Nuova Restaurant and Pizzeria, operated by Giani Pede. He is the brother of Pasquale Pede, who was the first person I met when I hitch-hiked to the village about forty years ago. Pasquale had a degree in political science from Sapienza University of Rome, and worked in Italian foreign-affairs offices in Spain, Ethiopia, Luxemburg, and Switzerland. He then worked as Italian consul in Argentina from 2011 until his passing in 2016. He was known for his competence in prestigious international diplomatic duties: head and later secretariat of the General Directorate for Italians Abroad and Migration Policies and then for being the executive secretariat of the General Council of Italians Abroad.

▲ Entrance to the Casa Nuova Restaurant. *Photo by M. DiMarco.*

It's a pleasant evening walk along Via Nostra Signora Lourdes, passing the school and then turning the corner onto Via Maria Regina, where the post office is located. We soon reach Corso Vittorio Emanuele III, the street named after the man who was the king of Italy from 1900 until his abdication in 1946. The old residential buildings and the stonework in their walls, windows, and doorframes are delightfully medieval, transporting our imaginations back in time. The Casa Nuova stands out for its fine renovation and transformation from a rustic building into a cozy restaurant. A beautiful, wide stone archway invites us into a warm atmosphere, very pleasant for food, drink, and long conversations. The varied menu goes from mouthwatering pizza to pasta dishes with exquisite sauces. Gianni worked in the restaurant business in New York, but gamblers would bet his wonderful dishes were mainly inspired by his mother's recipes. Montenero is very lucky to have Casa Nuova, a high-quality restaurant you think you'd find in a big city, but Gianni built here to be in the village that's been home to the Pede line for centuries. Pede, or *Pedis* in Latin, is one of the forty-six surnames listed in Faraglia's 1447 census record for Montenero.

After a marvelous evening with friends and mixing with the locals at the restaurant, we return to Il Corniolo. We sleep so well that we're not sure if we dreamed of counting sheep or actually saw them.

▶ Entrance to the Palazzo.

DAY 2
Palazzo De Arcangelis del Forno

We hear a rooster crow as we arise to the morning sunshine and the fragrance of fresh-ground coffee enlivening the air. All is prepared for us at the table, where we discuss the day's itinerary. The route will allow us to traverse a good portion of the village to see many of the homes, old and new. First on the list is one of the noble homes known as the Palazzo De Arcangelis del Forno, which is located on Via Alessandro Marracino, near the Church of S. Maria di Loreto. We know the way to Piazza Risorgimento, and it doesn't take long to get there.

Courtesy of Davide De Archangelis.

As we near the Palazzo De Arcangelis, we all stop in our tracks. The size and design of the building are overwhelming. It emits a noble presence. The building surely evolved over the past centuries, but we know that ancestors of the De Arcangelis and Del Forno families built it in 1691. They had moved to Montenero from another mountaintop village named Opi. The present occupants are Andrea De Arcangelis and his wife Teresa Satelli, living on the second floor. We ring the doorbell, and they warmly greet us and invite us inside to chat and to enjoy the views of the village from the windows on the upper level.

Andrea conveys the story of how the two families were associated. Seven Del Forno relatives arrived in Montenero. Five were chaplains, one a priest, and another a physicist. Symbols of the family's occupation were included in the family coat of arms. During this period, a Del Forno married a De Arcangelis woman. Because they couldn't bear children, they arranged to adopt a De Arcangelis boy. Since then, the double surname of De Arcangelis Del Forno has been thought of as one.

The palazzo had long been the location of an apothecary. Gaetano De Arcangelis was the most recent to provide this service, after inheriting it from his father, Eusebio De Arcangelis. Symbols of the family's occupation were included in the family coat of arms. As World War II came

◀ A view of the Palazzo from the municipal library window. *Courtesy of Lina Del Sangro Stea.*

▶ The Palazzo foyer. *Courtesy of Davide De Archangelis.*

to an end, the Germans burned the pharmacy and a rare garden of medicinal herbs as well.

From the outside, the building retains its medieval aspects. The palazzo is a historical treasure of eighteenth-century architecture. Built for security and defense, it was constructed of strong wood and stone: heavy doors with a beam to lock it and a rifle portal to guard the door. The floor of the elegant foyer is decorated with black and white pebbles in circular patterns. Delicate pillars give a sophisticated air to the entrance. The living quarters are all modernized and barely hint of the age of the palazzo. Andrea's cousin of the same name and his wife Isa Di Marco live on the first floor, Claira Di Marco on the second, and Nicolina De Arcangelis with her sons Silvio and Guido Tavolieri have their separate quarters too.

A narrow ground-level passageway links the palazzo to a smaller building. Some say this semisecret passage allowed locals to slip away from bandits or others in times past. There are similar passageways in the village

. . . if you know where they are located. They certainly provide shortcuts to get around. At ground level there is also a large, extra-high archway, indicating that it once was the entrance to a stall where a horse-drawn coach could be stored. Similar stalls can be seen elsewhere in the village. They usually have short stone pillars to protect the left and right sides of the doorframe from being hit by the carriage axels.

▲ View of Piazza Risorgimento from the Palazzo De Archangelis. *Photo by M. DiMarco.*

Andrea De Arcangelis is a model gentleman. It's a pleasure that he joins us on our walk to another landmark usually referred to as the Mannarelli House, which was a little pasta factory in the past. By 1753, according to the *Catasto Onciario* land registry, the building was in the hands of Vincenzo Mannarelli, a "fabricator and tailor." He was certainly a highly skilled stonemason, as testified by his work on the building's facade to advertise his business. This includes inscriptions that praise his own achievements, decorative designs, religious symbolism, and expressions of the artist's wit. As a mark of his profession, Vincenzo carved an elongated pair of tailor's scissors on the side of the entrance. Most locals would say the scissors have another meaning: that they are a phallic symbol to entertain the passersby. Perhaps Mr. Mannarelli's humor represents the typical mind-set of the Montenerese over the centuries?

Mannerelli
House

Above right door:
"1735, Vincenzo Mannarelli."
Photo by M. DiMarco.

It's a short walk to Piazza Risorgimento, and we pass through Portanuova, then turn right on Il Vicolo Corte up a long series of steps to get to the top of Montenero. We pass under the stone clock tower and see a mix of older ruins embodied into newer buildings. An ancient circular structure emerges in one area and hints that it was the base of a tower in earlier centuries. We continue walking upward until the ground levels out. "In the highest and perched part of the town—far from the mists of the pantano and in the most convenient position for the control of the valley—rises the oldest core of housing. . . . The whole presents a vaguely ellipsoidal plan and narrow and intricate streets of the medieval hill settlement, which guarantees security, defense and control of the valley."[7]

▲ Looking up past the former municipal building courtyard to the clock tower. *Photo by Lina Del Sangro Stea.*

▼ Coat of arms on a home in The Court, dated 1613. *Photo by M. DiMarco.*

Close to the top, facing south toward the pantano, we see some stone walls that indicate the parameter of the village core. The view is spectacular from the few homes here. One home has "a large arch with a coat of arms of 1613, a lovely balcony with two arches overlooking the valley and a narrow 'secret' passage, which opens in a hidden slit and crosses the entire length of the building, to emerge in a small terraced garden."[8] In this area lives Alan Frenkiel. Born in France to a Polish mother and Lithuanian father, Frenkiel lived in many cities, including New York, London, and Milan. He's adopted Montenero for his residence, studied the village in depth, and is sometimes called upon to give tours to visitors. Like other foreigners now living in the village, Mr. Frenkiel brings a vital cosmopolitan perspective to the relatively insular town.

▲ Homes on Via Corte. The tallest is Palazzo Ducale. *Photo by M. DiMarco.*

We are almost to the top of the village. The scholar Franco Valente writes that, "The upper part of Montenero Val Cocchiara seems to know how to resist the urban violence that characterizes many of the surrounding villages. Indeed . . . one gets the impression that a lot of people, including foreigners, have decided to make Montenero a kind of tranquil haven retaining and enhancing its environmental characteristics."[9] Beautiful homes, some surrounded by greenery and flowers, offer great views in all directions. But it was not always Time continuously morphed the ancient center, including what may have been constructed as part of the village fortifications. Dello Siesto wisely concludes that it is not possible to state with certainty how the village evolved "for the repetition over time of rebuilding, collapses, demolitions and transformations."[10] Great damage was done during World War II and from an earthquake that occurred in 1984. Without intensive archeological studies, we can only guess how the village summit looked in earlier times.

▼ Passageway between buildings in the Court. *Photo by M. DiMarco.*

▶ The Duke's Palace has worn the wear of earthquakes and World War II
Photos by Sandra Di Fiore.

Continuing to ascend Via Corte, we finally settle on a level, open space, 4,111 feet above sea level—the highest point of Montenero. We've just emerged from a cluster of homes that were remodeled after World War II and the 1984 earthquake. High grass and weeds outline the vacant space of a former home. But ahead of us is a massive three-level structure. It's a hodgepodge of four different styles of doorways on the ground level, and a dozen windows and balconies of varied shapes and sizes. This is called the Palazzo Ducale: the Duke's Palace. It is one of the oldest dwellings in Montenero. The incongruity of the building shows clear signs of alterations, which may be due to hereditary partitioning. Carved in stone is the date 4 November 1743. Two nearby buildings, dated 1566 and 1590, are among the oldest known in Montenero.

It is apparent that nobility lived in this area. The stone used in this palazzo was of better quality than elsewhere in the village. The palace was originally constructed under the House of Anjou, when they controlled south Italy. In the fifteenth century, after the House of Aragon invaded and took over as rulers, the palace came under their administration. We see the noble Carafa, Sangro, and Caracciolo families living there until the eighteenth century. Although the palace has undergone numerous architectural changes, there remain some medieval elements as small loggias and arches. Because of its presence at the summit of Montenero, the surrounding area has been known as the Court, which can refer to a courtyard, or simply to the area where people of authority lived.

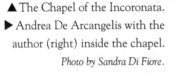

▲ The Chapel of the Incoronata.
▶ Andrea De Arcangelis with the
author (right) inside the chapel.
Photo by Sandra Di Fiore.

Our next destination is the Chapel of the Incoronata (Our Crowned Lady), which was recorded in the Trivento archdiocese to have been here at least since 1685. This is another rural chapel on the north side

of Montenero, greeting anyone entering on Via Belvedere. This beautiful chapel is in pristine condition due largely to its caretakers, the De Arcangelis Family. The natural stone foundation contrasts nicely with the faint yellow plastered walls. A dainty bronze bell is suspended in a stone arch atop of the roof. Andrea De Arcangelis has brought the key to open the solid wood door and invites us inside. In the altar facing us is a statue of the Madonna sitting on a tree with branches flanking her. Above her on clouds are two angels holding a triple crown. It's a bright room, well illuminated by the daylight and by fresh colors and carpeting.

▲ Walking past one of the stations of the cross on a path that leads to the Chapel of Calvary. *Photo by M. DiMarco.*

287

We exit this chapel to stroll up to another: the Chapel of Calvary. Usually associated with the hill were Jesus was crucified, in Latin *calvary* actually means "place of the skull." In Montenero, this is the area where the fourteen Stations of the Cross follow along Via Crucis. This pathway leads to the cemetery that served Montenero before the twentieth century. At each station is a bronze work of art by Ettore Marinelli (1963), cast at the famous Marinelli Pontifical Foundry.

A bronze tablet records the following:

> In memory of Don Pasquale Maria Di Filippo (1911–1995) who was pastor of Montenero Val Cocchiara (1942–1992) and for the monuments of Via Crucis, with 14 bronze stations by Ettore Marinelli di Agnone (1963), which was inaugurated by the Bishop Mons. Achille Palmerini (1906–2000) in the ceremony that took place on 8 September 1973 on the occasion of the 30th anniversary of the consecration of the Immaculate Conception of Mary.

▲ The last station of the cross in front of the Chapel of Cavary. At right, one of the small tombstones that are scattered on the grounds, most pre-1900. *Photo by M. DiMarco.*

The chapel is situated at the top of a hill. Before we reach the chapel, we see small tombstones, difficult to notice because the grasses and fallen pine needles nearly hide them. Many of the graves here were for people who died from cholera epidemics. One that occurred in 1854 took seventy-two souls. In 1911 a hundred locals died of the disease. The cemetery area here had reached maximum capacity even earlier. On 6 June 1895, the municipal council had already selected a location for the new cemetery.[11] After World War II, the chapel was in drastic need of repair. By 1946 the repairs were completed. There was an inaugural celebration on 8 September 1947, and a commemoration on 2 November. The chapel design is a basic square with a peaked roof. One enters through a high archway set off by an iron gate leading into an anteroom. The door is usually locked, but a window offers a peek into the church space.

In the past, an annual celebration was held during Holy Week that concurred with the ascension of Jesus on Easter morning. Locals would walk in procession along Via Crucis to the Chapel of Calvary and then wait for sunrise. Although this ritual has not taken place since the early 1970s, the hilltop setting around Chapel of Calvary is a pleasant and unique place to visit.

The sound of an SUV approaches with Eugenio Simioli at the wheel. He is the owner of the Valcocchiara Retreat, described as a "country house and hiking base" that we'll visit soon. For now, we get in his vehicle and drive down Via Belvedere to make a few stops.

First is the Capotosto Nadia bakery. This is the only bakery in Montenero. It was established years ago by Pino Ziroli and his wife, Nadia. The aroma from the wood oven makes your mouth water. Eugenio gets a few loaves for this evening's dinner. From here, we drive to Corse Vittorio Emanuele III to the only cheese shop in town. It is owned by Albino Scalzitti. Some caciocavallo and scamorze from here with the bread from Pino's is a heavenly combination. While we watch cheese being made and hung on racks to dry, Eugenio picks up his order, and we are ready to go.

About twenty steps from Albino's cheese shop is Bar Madison. This is a modern style establishment popular for its variety of drinks available and TV to watch sporting events. You can usually find card players at the tables, enjoying friendly rounds of scopa. Owner Guido Scalzitti has his hands full with the regulars as well as with special events such as evenings with live music. We have time for a cool drink to refresh ourselves. Dinner is scheduled at the Valcocchiara Retreat at 8:00, but we want to get there early to tour the premises.

Marma Massel © 123RF.com

Brent Hofacker © 123RF.com

Valcocchiara Retreat

From Bar Madison we backtrack to the Chapel of the Incoronata, then take an unpaved road for a few minutes to arrive at the retreat's front gate. A pack of Abruzzo sheepdogs, known as *maremma*, meets and greets us. The animals are justly famous for their friendly bonding with humans as for their strengths as alert guardians. Before

▲ The Retreat's main building.
Courtesy of The Valcocchiara Retreat.

our eyes is much more than a refurbished farmhouse. Everything here—doorways, signs, lighting, sinks, fireplace . . . has an artist's touch, which results in a natural, calming atmosphere that caresses visitors. We learn that this is the main building for the retreat. It contains the kitchen, dining and living rooms, bathroom, a traditional food-storage room, a large hot tub, and a sauna room. That's the first floor. The second floor and attic are mainly employee quarters.

Outside there are two organic gardens and a chicken coop that provide much for the dinner table. A large wood deck on the east side of the house is perfect for exercising or relaxing. The south-side lawn is an even better place to relax, converse, or absorb the vista that extends to the distant Mainarde Mountains. Even if you're not religious, the vision from here may bring on what can be described as a spiritual experience.

It's literally downhill from here. A dozen or so steps take us to another level on the hill. There is a roofed area where all can gather around a long table for lunches. Another set of stairs leads us to an outdoor pool. Its blue water matches the color of the sky. Chaise lounge chairs line a wooden deck. The sun lingers with you here into the evening.

On down to the next level, we see a building that blends with the landscape. It has an apartment for guests and also a large room, usually used for yoga practice. In front of this room is a stone patio. A stairway in this building goes down another floor to what can be called a playroom. We find games, a billiard table, a bar, exercise equipment, and more. The next level down is a large parking space, built into the hill. Its wide stone driveway leads to Vicolo Secondo Incoronata and to the village. From here, at leisurely walking pace, it takes fifteen to twenty minutes to get to the main piazza.

The Valcocchiara Retreat. Wow! This is an amazing place! We walk back up the hill to the top only to learn there is more. More? We start down another path to two more beautiful buildings that are also for guests. These have the same fine construction and aesthetic touch as the other buildings. Walk far enough, and the path turns into Via Papa Pio XII, which leads directly to the central piazza.

Wonderful buildings, scenery, meals, and guest apartments. What do guests actually do here? Eugenio and his wife Chiara work with many different types of groups, but most certainly enjoy hiking around the mountains and through the wooded lands. All activities are adjusted to the level of individual skill: swim in the pool; walk to the village; learn the Asian arts of tai chi, yoga, or qigong; bike; or go horseback riding in the pantano. In winter, there is skiing. See the sites in Montenero or nearby towns. Of course, it is a great place to just relax.

The Valcocchiara Retreat is secluded within the embrace of nature but still within walking distance to the village center. During our evening homemade dinner, we discuss the future of the retreat and Montenero. How can a new business like this, started in 2017, flourish in harmony with the ancient medieval village? Most guests at the retreat come for more than a visit to the village. It certainly offers much to visiting Italians as well as foreigners who arrive with different expectations.

It's late and our last night in Montenero. Eugenio drives us back to Il Corniolo. He has arranged for us to go horseback riding in the morning. We wish all a good night's sleep. Within minutes it's quiet. There's no doubt each of us is visualizing what we did that day and what we'll do tomorrow.

▲ The Retreat's swimming pool. *Courtesy of The Valcocchiara Retreat.*

DAY 3

▲ Denis Buongiorno of Ranch Brionna with a group of riders crossing the pantano. *Courtesy Ranch Brionna.*

Ranch Brionna

Following breakfast, we are ready to go horseback riding in the pantano . . . an activity most of us have never tried. Eugenio pulls up and opens his vehicle's doors. We jump in his SUV to drive twenty minutes to Ranch Brionna, located in the National Park of Abruzzo, Lazio and Molise. Our guide is Denis Buongiorno, an expert who grew up in a family steeped in all things equestrian. The ranch has special activities and itineraries for beginners all the way to very advanced riders. He helps us pick out appropriate horses, saddle up, and we're off to traverse the Pantano!

Saddled on a nine-hundred pound horse whose weight is largely solid muscle is thrilling by itself. Yet riding is a thrilling, practical way to experience the rich habitat of Montenero's famous spoon-shaped valley, which exceeds 988 acres (four hundred hectares). As we cross the Zittola River, we leisurely ride through herds of wild horses and cows that are grazing. It's endearing to watch how the young foals and calves stick close to their mothers as the horses and cows make their way across the field. In the far distance, high mountaintops appear behind the closer mountain range. Along the river, rare birds drink as butterflies are drawn to colorful flowers. We absorb much in the hour's ride from one end of the pantano to the other. We dismount near a picnic area. Denis Buongiorno gathers our horses, and we thank him for all he's done. We notice Mr. Simioli

292

practicing tai chi next to his vehicle while waiting for us.

Val Cocchiara—a valley shaped like a spoon—is the flat plain where the Pentro horses roam free. Montenero faces the pantano. It seems the village is the only inhabited place in this bowl surrounded by hills, mountains, and sky. The rest of the world is concealed from view, freeing one's spirit from contamination. Even without a cowboy hat and spurs, experiencing the pantano on horseback is unforgettable.

The one-lane road from the valley to the village is Via Immacolata. We pass some green fields and small vegetable gardens and come to an intersection where there are a couple of tennis courts and a soccer field. Two- and three-floor apartment buildings with their TV satellite dishes are near the sports area. We reach a fork in the road, and on the left side is Cafe Lunik. After horseback riding, we're ready for a cool beer here (Peroni, not Abruzzo Beer). It is near the Monumentino Mariano, at the foot of the village. Relaxing on the front patio, we get a slightly different view of the village and daily life here.

We have a few more hours before departure and decide to go see the fountain that was built in 1821 to provide fresh spring water to the village. To get there, we drive past Il Corniolo to Via Fonte and follow this short road to its end. The old fountain is in disrepair and vandalized. We see the newer water system, which looks like squares of plain cement. Not very aesthetic. Some horses are nearby drinking from a trough. Women have not washed clothes here for the past few decades.

After a two-minute drive from the fountain, we find another rural chapel dedicated to the Madonna of the Assumption. This chapel sits on the south side of the village. It is a beautiful and well-maintained rectangular stone building, roughly thirty-two by sixteen feet. A three-rail wooden fence sets off a front yard that has some benches for visitors to enjoy the pleasant surrounding greenery. The entrance door is flanked

◀ Chapel of the Madonna of the Assumption.

by a window on both sides, and an eye-shaped window above it. Another eye-shaped window is on one side wall too. Inside are twenty-three wooden chairs positioned along the walls, except for the altar area. There is also ample standing space on the plain Saltillo-tiled floor. The terra-cotta color of the floor blends well with the white walls and rich deep browns of the ceiling and its beams.

The altar is very simple. It has an image of the Last Supper on the lower front, and a statue of Mary and baby Jesus in an alcove above. A white marble tabernacle with a golden door sits atop in the middle. Two small angels are perched at the sides of the statue and two others at the sides of the tabernacle. The clean elegance of the interior and the tranquil setting offer an atmosphere conducive for individual meditation or small religious services.

As noon approaches, we drive a few minutes to the town hall, located close to our bed-and-breakfast. Here we are greeted at the door by Guard Tonino Luongo, who serves as the village arm of law enforcement. Among his responsibilities are all aspects related to village life as well as on village lands—including hunting, fishing, and forest and pastoral land use. He relaxes by playing guitar and listening to the blues.

We go to the offices of Mayor Filippo Zuchegna and Vice Mayor Carmen Marotta, who graciously give us a tour of the premises. On 31 May 2015, village residents elected Zuchegna mayor when he was only twenty-four years old. Filippo was not a total rookie, as he benefited greatly from his father, Dr. Alessio Zuchegna, who was mayor ten years prior.

The modern offices are designed to meet the needs of the adminis-tration: individual offices, a large meeting room, copy machine, computers. . . . The basement houses the village archives, where Vice Mayor Marotta helps me locate documents to copy that are very useful for my research on Montenero. We meet others in the building:

- *Assessor:* Elisabetta Fabrizio
- *Council Members:* Lorenzo Caiazza, Normeo Caserta, Mauro Centracchio, Alessandro Corsi, William Di Giovanni, Andrea Esposito, Elisabetta Fabrizio, Marco Gonnella, Carmen Marotta, Liberato Pezzetta, Francesca Sanzo.
- *Secretary:* Mario Barone
- *Financial Manager:* Anna Maria Pragliola
- *Technical Manager:* Eng. Irene Barilone
- *Registrar:* Maria Rosaria Caserta
- *Protocol:* Silvio Tavolieri

All in the municipal building are busy bees, handling the daily matters and a variety of major and minor emergencies. We thank all for their time and for letting us visit. They return to their work as we depart. We have little time left in Montenero. A minibus will soon take us to Castel di Sangro, where members in our group will continue to other destinations in Italy.

We take a few minutes to see the last of the rural chapels, the tiny Chapel of San Teresa. Located near the town hall, the unassuming church is attached to a home. Restored in 1991 by Michele Miraldi, there is room to hold about a dozen people inside. There are four chairs next to each sidewall, facing the altar, and a large window on the left. Between two small windows flanking the altar is a statue of Saint Teresa. The cream-colored walls and natural light through the windows keep the interior bright and bring out the golden-brown wood ceiling. We offer a prayer of thanks for the fulfilling stay we had in Montenero.

We stroll back to Il Corniolo. The view from Via Santa Teresa offers a special perspective toward the village center. From here we easily recognize the Church of San Nicola di Bari, the bell tower, and the cluster of buildings surrounding the village center to its fringe. Thoughts of the history and people of Montenero flood our minds. Before we know it, our bags are packed, the minibus arrives, and we're already zipping past familiar landmarks. And we're wondering: Will we ever visit again?

The Face of Montenero

When people talk about Montenero, they usually talk about the beauty of the land, the Pentro horses, and specific architectural gems of historical significance. It is unfortunate that the native people are rarely mentioned and do not hold the highest position of interest. A long line of Montenerese farmed the land, tended the horses, and made the buildings. Without people, Montenero would not exist.

afterword

Montenero's Grand Relationship

Did you find this book about a little ol' Italian mountain village of five hundred inhabitants worth reading? Some born in Montenero may find it special. Others with similar backgrounds, especially those who have ties to small villages in Abruzzo and Molise, may relate. But you don't need to have Italian roots to appreciate the story of the High Molise. Anyone who takes the time to digest the story of Montenero should benefit because it could represent any village in any country. Look back far enough in time, and everyone has such an ancestral home. The village story is one about being human, in a specific location. Under similar circumstances, how would others fair?

Many who have long since moved from Montenero write that the old village is the best place in the world. Their warm and fuzzy sentiments are certainly fostered by heavy doses of nostalgia. However, things are not always the way they seem. There are good reasons why millions left south Italy and why Montenero's population today is one-fourth of what it was in 1900. A harsh truth requires heavy editing in order for us to keep happily optimistic. History bears witness to the rough reality of Montenero, Molise, and southern Italy.

Life has always been extra difficult in the south. It seems to have hardened the inhabitants, especially those who live in the interior, generally making them distrust outsiders. Southern Italians have a reputation of being highly emotionally driven and often uncooperative. Brilliant Italian scholars and politicians have clearly expounded on the mind-set of southern Italy. Reading their foreboding assessments provides some insight and understanding. Experiencing it firsthand offers another vantage point.

When I started to conduct research for this book, I contacted hundreds of Montenero residents, asking for a personal story and any photographs that could contribute to this book. Vice Mayor Carmen Marotta was considerate, sending me copies of old documents and photographs from the municipal and church archives. Together we organized and preserved much that benefited everyone associated with Montenero.

I offered to all others a free service to scan their photographs, improve them with Photoshop, and return the originals with new prints and digital files. None took the offer. Chances are their decaying photographs will eventually turn into dust. None shared even a single story. Chances are their memories will fade into oblivion.

I also contacted leading scholars in Italy, experts of Molise history and culture, in addition to librarians in Abruzzo and Molise. Their knowledge could have greatly enriched and facilitated the book project, even by suggesting a single reference on a specific topic. They never shared anything from their personal hoard of books, articles, and photographs.

A pleasant surprise was when Dr. Sergio Raimondo offered to drive to Montenero from Rome to help with research. Employed at the Library of Modern and Contemporary History, the professor had the interest and skills to locate pertinant information for my book project. He treated me as a fellow scholar and friend.

When I contacted scholars in Belgium, Scotland, England, Germany, and Poland for their help, all responded graciously. They provided documents, references, maps, and photographs, and they offered suggestions. They were helpful, considerate, and friendly.

Others who showed an interest in the book project were people with roots in Montenero but who live outside Italy. Rachel Bonaminio shared hundereds of photographs and thoughtsful insights. Vivian Jacabozzi sent family histories. A few mailed photographs for me to scan and share on the Montenero Val Cocchiara Facebook page. These are Montis living free from the invisible restraints woven into south Italian culture. They proved to be much more open and cooperative.

A number of times during visits to Montenero in 2014 and 2017, I witnessed confrontations between individuals and groups. For example, if somebody stole firewood, anger over the incident would mount, tempers would flair, and accusations would fly. Most interestingly, in such situations it was evident that those blaming others would do so before gathering all the pertinent facts. They would jump to conclusions through impatience and anger. Unbridled feelings got in the way of clearly seeing problems, making matters worse between the people involved, leaving negativity to affect their relationships. In one instance when this happened to me, I had to explain myself, and the one making the accusation later apologized. Time and time again, allegations like these occurred, frazzling the already fragile bonds between people. Many problems remain unsolved. Italian philosophers and others place the blame on the lack of reason and virtue, character flaws especially evident in southern Italians.

If individuals in a small village find difficulty living together peacefully, we certainly can't expect regions or countries to maintain friendly relationships. In the past, a common religion was a bonding force that helped guide human relationships and provided social stability. Legal systems developed to help maintain harmony among the governed. However, the threat of everlasting suffering in hell or years of imprisonment does not guarantee that individuals will behave ethically or that societies will be peaceful.

Don't the problems of today's Montenero and elsewhere stem from the same source? Modern media seem to be pushing individuals to become more and more self-centered and to compete for greater self-fulfillment and pleasure at the expense of others. To act this way, it is necessary to desensitize oneself and to view others as being of less worth. Too often we get attracted to superficial glitter, be it expensive homes, cars, or dress— and then throw temper tantrums when our desires are not satisfied. Shortsightedness prevents seeing a fuller picture and, because of it, we suffer in the long run. Some elder Montenerese knew through experience what was important: family, friends, work, and cooperation to put food on the table and maintain peace among people. People have been successful in doing this to varying degrees in different times and places.

As the two-time Pulitzer Prize winner and "the father of sociobiology," Edwin O. Wilson writes: "How well a group performs depends on how well its members work together, regardless of the degree by which each is individually favored or disfavored within the group."[1] Improving a relationship between couples or countries calls for patiently cultivating empathy, compassion, and caring. Such qualities forge strong bonds between people and build a sense of community. It is far too easy to become withdrawn and bitter whenever those around us are mean spirited. Doing that only contributes to the existing social strains. The special person who knows how to maintain a friendly, optimistic character while being considerate for others is a *rara avis*, a rare bird indeed. Such people of high integrity have forged their spirits through the work of self-cultivation. It's a process easier to do when the social environment is conducive.

In my youth, while living close to my grandparents, I was fortunate to be surrounded by many fine people. Decades later it became apparent that this nurturing environment was only possible because my grandparents chose to associate only with people of good character. I also learned of others, others who were *pazzo* (crazy) or *cattivo* (evil). There were relatives and others who, for good reason, I never saw in my grandparents' home.

In any location—Erie, Montenero, or elsewhere—there is always a mix of personalities. In plain terms, in any setting involving people, there is always a blend of good and evil. Depending on the ratio, the results of the combination differ in expression, much like mixing two different colors of paint.

Of course the mix of people and personalities occurs in an ever-changing cultural setting. Culture is a sacred vessel. A very fragile one. It bears heavily on whether a society progresses or digresses. What actually determines whether or not that setting provides a pleasant living environment and functional working condition? Every country, city, and family deals with the same factors that create culture. Strong influences on culture are the nearly invisible attitudes and values held by individuals. We live with choices that are often made on a whim rather than logic, driven by personal desires rather than any concern for others. Usually the results then are not so pleasant. It's like pairing red wine with seafood.

Since the Paleolithic periods as we've seen in Isernia, humans have learned to work together in small groups to hunt animals and gather plants for sustenance. They were driven by an innate survival instinct. When they encountered other small groups, they competed violently. When humans began to settle into a stationary agricultural lifestyle, it became necessary to organize more complex social systems and to work with other groups in order to survive. The Samnites, for example, organized into a large confederation. By modern times, greater alliances were necessary. During World War II, for example, many countries formed an alliance in order to resolve major issues of the time.

With the eventual growth of populations, cities, and countries, even greater methods of organization evolved to fit the social changes. In each step of the sociopolitical development—from Paleolithic to today—we see that humans had to learn how to live together in order to survive. It's not that they wanted to do so, or even intelligently decided that they should: they simply had to. Today we are still learning how to live together and adapt to our ever-changing world. We must do so because it is the only way to solve the massive world problems we face, such as pollution, violence, and international rivalry.

Many Montenerese should be held in the highest esteem for adapting and overcoming the limitations present in small-village life. They have worked hard to raise themselves out of poverty. Many now have college degrees when, not long ago, those considered fortunate had only a few years of elementary-school education. Some Montis have gone on to become lawyers, doctors, politicians, and scholars. Others have served in embassies or become military officers. Many have earned great respect for their hard work in agriculture and in areas requiring skilled labor. Above all are those who have cultivated the best of human values in themselves, manifested in their friendly character and altruistic action.

Montenero functioned as an agricultural medieval village for over one thousand years. Today it is in the process of redefining itself. Like a seasoned actor given a new script, it is impossible to give a good performance without first learning what the new play is about. Montenero residents are now reading the script in preparation and actively moving toward the future.

New homes are being constructed, and wonderful medieval buildings are being refurbished. People with foresight have created new businesses in the village. Foreigners from Romania, India, the United States, Belgium, and elsewhere have taken up residence in Montenero and become Italian citizens. They bring fresh energy and stimulating views. Their influx is nothing new. The millennia of migrations provided Italy with a good mix of DNA, reflecting every century of history. My own DNA story shows a direct genetic link to Abruzzo-Molise with a tinge of Greek and French. Other Montenerese may show traces of Spanish, Arabic, Germanic, and Nordic in their genetic makeup. As the newest members of the village, babies of varied genetic inheritance are learning to walk on the paths formerly used only by farmers and their donkeys.

The exemplary work ethic from previous generations is reflected today by those working with horses, cattle, and in dairy. All the locals have come to expect the regular delivery of top-quality milk, cheeses, and bread provided by attentive hands. There is also no shortage of social activities in the bars and eateries. Behind the scenes, talented Montenero artists have been producing exquisite artworks, particularly in such fields as painting and sculpture.

What makes Montenero a great place to live and work rests greatly in the hands of those in the municipal office. They bear the responsibility for all aspects relating to the village, such as meticulous accounting, maintenance, utilities, and regulation enforcement. They also arrange and schedule a variety of entertainment throughout the year. Overseeing the sports facilities is important to help keep the youth active and healthy. All are proud of the Montenero soccer team for keeping a head above the rest in their play category.

Like birds in seasonal migration, expatriates return every summer to Montenero, mostly from the United States, Canada, and a number of European countries. Many maintain ancestral homes there, so it is convenient for them to stay a month or two. Their presence doubles the population, bringing an international flair to every inch of the village. Over many decades, these foreigners have certainly enhanced and supported the village financially, culturally, and emotionally. More so, being infused by blood ties to the village, they have transferred cultural traits from Montenero to many parts of the world.

People who have intimate knowledge of village history are often inspired by the lives of their ancestors. By knowing the hardships of their parents, grandparents, and great-grandparents, they become energized with a strong work ethic and a desire to not waste time with superficial distractions. In addition to the hard labor required to live in an agricultural village in the High Molise, our ancestors experienced the horrors of war, poverty, famine, and earthquakes. Shouldn't we show appreciation for their suffering and sacrifices by living each day the best way we can? Those of the younger generation, without awareness of their roots, have no clear vision for the future. Perhaps if families and friends talked more about ancestors and the past, they would understand the present better—and be inspired for creating the future.

Hopefully this book will bring topics to the table for many stimulating discussions so more can appreciate our heritage. Doing so may motivate us to regularly nourish the qualities in our characters that make us better human beings and a vital part of family and community.

NOTES

CHAPTER 3
1 Britannica, 30 October 2013

CHAPTER 4
1 Salmon, 2010: 59
2 Salmon, 2010: 67
3 www.vieverdi.org
4 Salmon, 2010: 140
5 Salmon, 2010: 180 note 2
6 Salamon, 2010: 133
7 Salmon, 2010: 216
8 Dench, 2002: 210
9 Salmon, 2010: 331
10 Salmon, 2010: 360

CHAPTER 5
1 Astarita, 2006: 20
2 Astarita, 2006: 17
3 Bury, 1913: 198
4 Bury, 1913: 201
5 Gattei, et al., 1980: 8
6 Kreutz, 1996: 14
7 Kreutz, 1996: 33-34
8 Kreutz, 1996: 203, note 2
9 Kreutz, 1996: 112
10 Wickham, 1985: 165
11 Wickham, 1985: 166
12 Wickham, 1985: 166
13 Kreutz, 1996: loc 2708
14 Brown, 2003: loc 295
15 Astarita, 2006: 25
16 Kreutz, 1991: loc 3031; Wickham, 1985
17 Rivera, 1926: 31
18 Bonaminio et al., 2017: 4
19 Brown, 2003: 59
20 Brown, 2003: 67
21 Brown, 2003: 10
22 Brown, 2003: loc 2007
23 Brown, 2003: 160
24 Brown, 2003: 191
25 Brown, 2003: loc 2790
26 Brown, 2003: 198
27 Astarita, 2006: 31
28 Astarita, 2006: 36
29 Astarita, 2006: 36
30 Astarita, 2006: 39
31 Astarita, 2006: 48
32 Astarita, 2006: 49
33 Bonaminio, et al., 2107: 4
34 Giannone, 1729: 736
35 Molise2000 Blog, 2013
36 Pierce, J., n.d.
37 Astarita, 2006: 53
38 Astarita, 2006: 84

CHAPTER 6
1 Astarita, 2006: 70
2 Croce, 1970: 62
3 Astarita, 2006: 71
4 Faraglia, 1898: 208-45
5 Astarita, 2006: 70
6 Croce, 1970: 67
7 Astarita, 2006: 71
8 Black, 2001: 53
9 Astarita, 2006: 93
10 Croce, 1970: 79
11 Croce, 1970: 73
12 Astarita, 2006: 84
13 Taylor, 2003: 1
14 Astarita, 2006: 95
15 Croce, 1970: 166 note 46
16 Astarita, 2006: 100
17 Astarita, 2006: 102
18 Astarita, 2006: 127
19 Croce, 1970: 113
20 Astarita, 2006: 164
21 Mariano, 2006: 420
22 Taylor, 2003
23 Neapolitan Nobles, 2001
24 Bonaminio et al., 2017: 5-6
25 Senatore and Storti, 2011: 112-113
26 Bonaminio, et al., 2017: 6
27 Bonaminio, et al., 2017: 5
28 Bonaminio, et al., 2017: 5
29 Biblioteca Michel Eromano
30 Valente, 2015
31 Black, 2001: 109
32 Muto, 2006: 280
33 Muto, 2006: 266
34 Musi, 2006: 74
35 Black, 2001: 50-51
36 Muto, 2006: 280
37 Muto, 2006: 263
38 Marino, 2006: 417

CHAPTER 7
1 Dandelet and Marino, 2007: 7
2 Musi, 2006: 96
3 Marino, 2007: 405-429
4 Dandelet and Marino, 2007: 14
5 Astarita, 2006: 98
6 Marino, 2006: 409-410
7 Croce, 1970: 119
8 Dandelet and Marino, 2007: 5
9 Malanima, 2006: 389
10 Musi, 2006: 95
11 Marino, 2006: 414
12 Astarita, 2006: 107
13 Astarita, 2006: 175
14 Astarita, 2006: 177
15 Astarita, 2006: 188

16 Astarita, 2006: 115
17 Astarita, 2006: 117
18 Astarita, 2006: 117
19 Croce, 1970: 137
20 Mariano, 2006: 417
21 Chavarria and Cocozza, 2015: 202-211
22 Chavarria and Cocozza: 53
23 Astarita, 2006: 190
24 Astarita, 2006: 190
25 Astarita, 2006: 141
26 Astarita, 2006: 141
27 Astarita, 2006: 140
28 Astarita, 2006: 139
29 Colletta, 1858: 16

CHAPTER 8
1 Bonaminio, et al., 2017: 5
2 Colletta, 1858: 21
3 Astarita, 2006: 205
4 Astarita, 2006: 206
5 Astarita, 2006: 209
6 Astarita, 2006: 134
7 Astarita, 2006: 155
8 Astarita, 2006: 133
9 Astarita, 2006: 157
10 Astarita, 2006: 157
11 von Salis-Marschlins, 1795: 429-430
12 Astarita, 2006: 206
13 Catasto Onciario
14 Wiegert, 2004: 183
15 Astarita, 2006: 99
16 Astarita, 2006: 214
17 Astarita, 2006: 210
18 Payne, 1973: 371
19 Filangieri, in Croce, 1970: 186
20 Astarita, 2006: 250
21 Astarita, 206: 253
22 Astarita, 2006: 245
23 Astarita, 2006: 218
24 Astarita, 2006: 218
25 Astarita, 2006: 253
26 Astarita, 2006: 256
27 Astarita, 2006: 255
28 Astride, 2006: 254
29 Croce, 1970: 205

CHAPTER 9
1 Colletta, 1858: 441
2 Astarita, 2006: 257
3 Astarita, 2006: 259
4 Ross, 1977: 127
5 Ross, 1977: 127
6 Di Fiori, et al., 2018: 138
7 Di Fiori, et al., 2018: 138
8 Teti, 2015: 71

9 Teti, 2015: 62
10 Artz, 1934
11 Astarita, 2006: 216
12 Croce, 1970: 30
13 quoted in Croce, 1970: 162
14 Croce, 1970: 233
15 Colletta, 1858: 126

CHAPTER 10
1 Colletta, 1858: 52-53
2 Astarita, 2006: 286
3 www.lamontagnadelcilento.it
4 Maffei, 1865: 308
5 Maffei, 1865: 35
6 Di Fiore, et al., 2018: 13
7 Di Fiore, et al., 2018: 13
8 A free translation from an original report in Montenero's Municipal Office.
9 Di Fiore, et al., 2018: 15
10 Maffei, 1865: 186
11 Di Fiori et al., 2018: 47
12 Di Fiori et al., 2018: 47
13 Di Fiori et al., 2018: 47

CHAPTER 11
1 Baravelli, 2015
2 Keegan, 2000: 226
3 Thompson, 2010: 5
4 Keegan, 2000: 344
5 Tucker and Roberts, 2005: 431
6 Mockenhaupt, June 2016
7 Thompson, 2010: 2
8 Keegan, 2000: 227
9 Thompson, 2010: 267
10 Mougel, 2011: 9
11 *New York Times*, 1917: 146-147
12 Schindler, 2001: 206

CHAPTER 12
1 Stamperia Reale, 1832: 42
2 Municipal Library, s.d., s.l., 6
3 Caserta and Standen, 2007
4 State Archive of Isernia
5 Parish Archive, Registry of the Deceased
6 Santucci, 2014: 12

CHAPTER 13
1 Hibbert, 2008: 52
2 Blinkhorn, 2006: 4
3 Astarita, 2006: 304
4 Kemp, 1963
5 Nicholson, 1956: 278
6 Nicholson, 1956: 276
7 Kemp, 1963
8 Cole, 1983: 122

9 Cole, 1983: 122-123
10 Nicholson, 1958: 281
11 Nicholson, 1958: 281
12 Cole, 1983: 123
13 Cole, 1983: 123
14 Kemp, 1963
15 Cutler, 2015
16 Cutler, 2015
17 Cutler, 2015
18 Cutler, 2015
19 Van der Bijl, 2006: 15
20 Williams, 2017: 151
21 Bielatowicza, 1966: 154
22 O'Sullivan, February 2, 2017
23 O'Sullivan, 2017
24 O'Sullivan, 2017
25 Kirby, 2015
26 Mattern, 2017
27 Paolicelli, 2004

CHAPTER 14
1 Ginsborg, 2003: 115
2 Ginsborg, 2003: 210
3 Ginsborg, 2003: 220
4 Ginsborg, 2003: 213
5 Melfi, 2009: 145
6 Ginsborg, 2003: 212
7 Ginsborg, 2003: 232
8 Ginsborg, 2003: 146
9 Ginsborg, 2003: 246
10 Ginsborg, 2003: 181
11 Ginsborg, 2003: 298
12 Ginsborg, 2003: 281
13 Ginsborg, 2003: 343
14 Ginsborg, 2003: 388; Bond, 2003
15 Ginsborg, 2003: 337-338
16 Ginsborg, 2003: 240
17 Ginsborg, 2003: 413
18 Emmott, 2013: 100
19 Galli and Galadini, 2003: 70-1
20 Diaferia, 2018
21 The Local, 18 January 2016
22 Ginsborg, 2003: 417
23 European Commission Press release, 14 July 2015
24 europa.eu, 2009
25 European Commission Press release, 14 July 2015
26 Regione Molise, archive, 2013 July
27 Ginsborg, 2003: 418
28 Ginsborg, 2003: 419
29 Ginsborg, 2003: 417
30 Murray, 2014: 62
31 Emmott, 2013: 279
32 Croce: 1970: 29

33 Croce, 1970: 60
34 Croce, 1970: 33
35 Croce, 1970: 64
36 Croce, 1970: xvi
37 Lumley and Morris, 1997: 107
38 Astarita, 2006: 310
39 Ginsborg, 2003: 216
40 Ginsborg, 2003: 265
41 Croce, 1970: 55

CHAPTER 15
1 Tramontano, 2010: 81
2 Pasquale, 2015
3 Pesaresi, 2014: 406
4 Crisci, 2015: 21
5 Pesaresi, 2014b: 406
6 Cassamamassi, et al., 2009: 173
7 Guarrera, et al., 2008: 1
8 Fanelli, 2001: 108
9 Petrocelli, 2011: 316-317
10 Massullo, 2012: 48
11 Petrocelli, 2011: 317
12 Di Matteo, 218; Iarocci, 2015
13 Pesaresi, 2014a: 142-143
14 Scorocca and Tozzi, 1999
15 Mastronardi, et al., 2017: 247
16 Rosskopf, 2006: 146
17 Cicia, et al., 2001: 9-10
18 APAT, ARPA Molise, 2005: 15-16
19 Cicia, et al., 2001: 15
20 Pesaresi, 2014a: 162
21 Storti, 2016: 5
22 Ciesluk, 2003: 22
23 Emmott, 2012: 262
24 Emmott, 2012: 261
25 Petrocelli, 2011: 317
26 Pesaresi, 2014a: 98

CHAPTER 16
1 Bonaminio, et al., 2017: 52
2 Visco, 2010
3 dello Siesto, n.d.: 86
4 dello Siesto, n.d.: 76
5 dello Siesto, n.d.: 80
6 dello Siesto, n.d.: 71 note 75
7 dello Siesto, n.d.: 40
8 dello Siesto, n.d.: 45
9 Valente, 14 settembre 2007
10 dello Siesto, n.d.: 42
11 Campobasso State Archive

Postscript
1 Wilson, 2013: 53

APPENDICES

Pallotta, Vincenzo	1809	Gigliotti, Pio (podestà)	1932–1936
Del Forno, Gaetano	1810	Milò, Felice (podestà)	1936–1937
Mannarelli, Matteo	1811	Bonaminio, Pio (podestà)	? 1937–1939
Mannarelli, Vincenzo	1812–1814	Gigliotti, Pio (podestà)	1939–1943
Mannarelli, Remigio	1815–1816	Di Marco, Giacomo	1943
Iacobozzi, Mariano	1817	Mannarelli, Domenico	1944
Ricchiuto, Cipriano	1818	Ricchiuto, Giovanni	? 1946
Gigliotti, Giambattista	1819–1824	Pallotto, Clemente	? 1947
Scalzitti, Felice	1825–1827	Calabrese, Mario	1948
Pallotta, Felice	1828–1830	(Special Prefectural Commissioner)	
Gigliotti, Pio	1831–1833	Gigliotti, Pio	1949
Scalzitti, Nicola	1834–1837	Scalzitti, Eliseo	1950
Gigliotti, Romualdo	1838	Tornincasa, Albino	1951
Orlando, Vincenzo	1839	Procario, Enzo	1953
Iacobozzi, Donato	1840–1841	Gigliotti, Teresa	1957
Gigliotti, Pio	1842–1845	Procario, Enzo	1961
Di Fiore, Marino	1846–1848	Orlando, Emilio	1964
Del Forno, Andrea	1849–1850	Orlando, Emilio	1970
Iacobozzi, Ferdinando	1851–1854	Mannarelli, Giovanni	1975
Gonnella, Basilio	1855–1857	Santucci, Alberino	1980
Gigliotti, Pio	1858–1860	Zuchegna, Alessio	1985
Gigliotti, Giulio	1860–1872	Di Fiore, Domenico	1990
Mannarelli, Francesco Saverio	1873–1877	Di Nicola, Carlo	1995–1999
Di Fiore, Angelo (acting mayor)	1877–1878	Tornincasa, Giuseppe	2000–2005
Danese, Guglielmo	1879	Zuchegna, Alessio	2005–2010
Milò, Felice	1880–1882	Orlando, Roberta	2010–2015
De Archangelis, Eusebio	1883–1885	Zuchegna, Filippo	2015–?
Di Fiore, Angelo	1886–1887		
Alati, Tommaso	1887		
Scalzitti, Nicola	1887–1888		
Mannarelli, Giacomo	1888–1890		
Di Fiore, Angelo	1890–1895		
Gigliotti, Alessandro	1895–1899		
De Archangelis, Andrea	1899–1903		
De Archangelis, Andrea	1903–1907		
De Archangelis, Andrea	1907–1911		
Mannarelli, Clemente	1912–1913		
Gigliotti, Alessandro	? 1914–1917		
Orlando, Giovanni	1918		
Mannarelli, Domenico	1921–1926		
Scalzitti, Adriano	1926		
De Archangelis, Andrea	1927–1932		

NOTE: There were periods when government intervention was necessary to restore functionality to civic offices in which a royal commissioner was appointed:

• Marzari Alceste in 1913
• Pietro Micarelli in 1918
• Michele Capo, who served until 1921.

List List of Archpriests 1600 to 2018

Moricone, Vincenzo	1600–1629
Quaglia, Angelo	1630–1644
De Bellis, Vincenzo	1645–1648
De Marco, Nunzio	1648–1676
Del Forno, Scipione	1677–1690
Mannarelli, Angelo	1691–1712
Donatelli, Nicola	1713–1717
Mannarelli, Giovanni	1718–1758
Mannarelli, Benedetto	1759–1785 / 1785–1787
Mannarelli, Florenzo	1788–1797
Mannarelli, Felice	1798–1808
Danese, Guglielmo	1809–1836 / 1837–1838
De Lugo, Giuseppe	1839–1840
Bonanotte, Agostino	1841–1847
Mannarelli, Pietro	1847–1894 / 1895
Santucci, Federico	1896–1928
Colicchio, Alfredo	1928–1939
Fioritto, Antonio	1940–1942

Population

1447	46	households (*fuochi*)	1971	814	inhabitants
1532	80	households	1981	767	inhabitants
1545	62	households	1991	683	inhabitants
1561	69	households	2001	608	inhabitants
1595	93	households	2002	596	inhabitants
1648	93	households	2003	594	inhabitants
1669	83	households	2004	585	inhabitants
1753	106	households	2005	572	inhabitants
1780	1,285	inhabitants	2006	557	inhabitants
1795	1,523	inhabitants	2007	558	inhabitants
1805	1,413	inhabitants	2008	572	inhabitants
1835	1,535	inhabitants	2009	573	inhabitants
1861	1,379	inhabitants	2010	575	inhabitants
1871	1,784	inhabitants	2011	558	inhabitants
1881	1,769	inhabitants	2012	556	inhabitants
1901	2,089	(*peak population*)	2013	554	inhabitants
1911	2,008	inhabitants	2014	556	inhabitants
1921	1,891	inhabitants	2015	538	inhabitants
1931	1,519	inhabitants	2016	524	inhabitants
1936	1,485	inhabitants	2017	514	inhabitants
1951	1,244	inhabitants	2018	513	inhabitants
1961	988	inhabitants			

BIBLIOGRAPHY

Agostini, S. (2010). Le pietre da construzione e decorative dell'Abruzzo e del Molise [Construction and decorative stones from Abruzzo and Molise]. In M. Somma (Ed.), *Cantieri e maestranze nell'Italia medievale*, (pp. 265–278). Spoleto: Centro Italiano di Studi sull'Alto Medioevo.

Amato, V., Aucelli, P., Bracone, V., Cesarano, M., and Rosskopf, C. (2017). Long-term landscape evolution of the Molise sector of the central-southern Apennines, Italy. *Geologica Carpathica*, 68, 29–43. DOI: 10.1515/geoca-2017-0003.

Angeli, F. (22 May 2018). Devoto di Padre Pio, secchione e di sinistra. Il 'Financial Times' lo stronca: Un novellino [Devotee of Padre Pio, nerd and of the left. The 'Financial Times' beats him: A newbie]. *Il Giornale* [Online]. Available: www.ilgiornale.it

Aprile, P. (2011). *Terroni: All that has been done to ensure that the Italians of the south became "southerners."* NY: Bordighera Press.

APTA-ARPA (2005). Molise. ARPA [Online]. Available: http://www.arpamolise.it

Artz, F. (1934). *Reaction and revolution: 1814–1832.* NY: Harper Brothers.

Ascione, A., Cinque, A., Miccadei, E., Villani, F., and Berti, C. (2008). The Plio-Quaternary uplift of the Apennine chain: New data from the analysis of topography and river valleys in central Italy. *Geomorphology*, 102(1): 105–118. DOI: 10.1016/j.geomorph.2007.07.022

Ascione, A., Miccadei, E., Villani, F., and Berti, C. (2007). Morphostructural setting of the Sangro and Volturno Rivers divide area (Central-southern Apennines, Italy). *Geografia Fisica e Dinamica Quaternaria*, 30: 13–32.

Astarita, T. (2006). *Between salt water and holy water: A history of southern Italy.* NY: W.W. Norton & Co.

Aucelli, P., Izzo, M., Mazzarella, A., and Rosskopf, C. (2007). La classifiazione climatica della regione Molise [The climatic classification of the Molise region]. *Bollettino della Società Geografica Italiano*, Roma, Serie XI, Vol. XII, pp. 615–617.

Badagliacca, P., Gentile, L., Marruchella, G., Latini, R., Di Pirro, V., Carosi, E., Ruberto, A., Scioli, E., and Di Provvido A. (2014). Mass mortality by lightning in Apennine chamois (Rupicapra pyrenaica ornata): A case report from the Abruzzo Lazio e Molise National Park, Italy. Conference paper. *Chamois International Congress*, Maiella National Park, Lama dei Peligni, Abruzzo, Central Italy, 17th–20th June 2014.

Baravelli, A. (07 July 2015). War aims and war aims discussions (Italy). *1914–1918: International Encyclopedia of the First World War* [Online]. Available: https://encyclopedia.1914-1918-online.net

Barone, P., and Ferrara, C. (2015). Geophysics applied to landscape archaeology: Understanding Samnite and Roman relationships in Molise (Italy) using geoarchaeological research methods. *International Journal of Archaeology*, 3(1-1): 26–36.

Ben-Ghiat, R. and Hom, S. (2016). *Italian mobilities.* London: Routledge.

Bieganski, S. (Ed.) (1963). *Działania 2 korpusu we włoszech, Tom I* [Activities of the 2nd corps in Italy. Vol. 1]. London: Historical Commission of the 2nd Corps. Chapter: "Defense Over the Sangro River."

Bielatowicza, J. (1966). *Ułani Karpaccy. Zarys historii pułku* [Upland Carpathian: Outline of the history of the regiment]. Londyn: Zwiazek Ułanów Karpackich.

Biondi, M., G. Osella, G., and Zuppa, A. (1994). Studi zoologici sulla palude della Zittola (Abruzzo-Molise). III. Il popolamento a Coleoptera Chryso-melidae [Zoological studies on the Zittola marsh (Abruzzo-Molise). III. The population of Coleoptera Chryso-melidae.]. *Rivista di Idrobiologia*, 31(1/2/3): 51–93.

Black, C. (2001). *Early modern Italy: A social history.* London: Routledge.

Blasi, C., Fortini, P., Grossi, G., and Presti, G. (2005). Faggete e cerrete mesofile nell'Alto Molise [Beechwood and mesophilous Quercus cerris woodlands in the High Molise]. *Fitosociologia*, 42(2): 67–81.

Blasi, C. et al. (2010). *Le aree importanti per le piante nelle regioni d'Italia: Il presente e il futuro della conservazione del nostro patrimonio botanico* [Important areas for plants in the regions of Italy: The present and the future of conservation of our botanical heritage]. Roma: Progetto Artiser.

Blinkhorn, M. (2006). *Mussolini and Fascist Italy.* London: Taylor & Francis.

Bonaminio, L., Di Fiore, D., Felice, M., Mannarelli, G., Milò, G., and Milò, L. (2017). *Montenero Val Cocchiara festa del ricordo: Opuscolo 2017* [Montenero Val Cocchiara memorial celebration: Booklet 2017]. Montenero Val Cocchiara. n.p.

Bond, A. (2003). Crisis, reform, and achieving financial stability in the Italian pension system. Conference Paper 2. *Contradictions and challenges in 21st century Italy.* Lehigh University.

Brown, G. (2003). *The northern conquest of southern Italy and Sicily.* London: McFarland and Co.

Bury, J. (Ed.) (1936/2012). *The Cambridge medieval history, Vol. 3: Germany and the western empire.* (Classic Reprint). Original published by Cambridge University Press.

Capula, M. (2010). Il progetto atlante degli anfibi e rettili del Molise [The atlas project of the amphibians and reptiles of Molise.]. Conference paper. *Proceedings VIII National Congress Societas Herpetologica Italica,* Chieti, 22-26 September 2010.

Caserta, J. and Standen, A. (March 2007). Pig slaughter, Montenero Val Cocchiara, Italy. *Meatpaper Zero* [Online]. Available: http://meatpaper.com/articles/2007/ 0528_caserta.html

Cassamamassi, D., et al. (2009). Produzione e qualita del latte in capre autoctone allevate estensiva-mente nella regione Molise [Milk yield and quality in autochthonous goats extensively reared in Molise region]. *Large Animal Review,* 15: 165–174.

Chavarria, E. and Cocozza, V. (2015). Montenero 1685, In *Comunità e territorio: Per una storia del Molise moderno attraverso gli apprezzi feudali (1593–1744)* [Community and territory: For a history of modern Molise through fief appraisals (1593–1744)]. Campobasso: Palladino Editore, pp. 202–211.

Choate, M. (2008). *Emigrant nation: The making of Italy abroad.* Cambridge, MA: Harvard University Press.

Cialdea, D., and Mastronardi, L. (2014). Renewable energy resources and their impact on rural landscape. *WSEAS Transactions on Environment and Development, Volume 10,* pp. 423–433.

Cialdea, D., and Maccarone, A. (2014). The energy networks landscapes. Impacts on rural lands in the Molise Region. *TeMa Journal of Land Use Mobility and Environment INPUT.* Eighth International Conference IMPUY, Naples.

Cicia, G., D'Ercole, E., and Marino, C. (2001). Valuing farm animal genetic resources by means of contingent valuation and a bio-economic model: The case of the Pentro horse. Research paper. Milan: The Foundazione Eni Enrico Mattei.

Ciesluk, C. (2003). The southern question. Contradictions and challenges in the 21st century. Conference paper 4. Lehigh University, *Perspectives on Business and Economics.* Available: http://preserve.lehigh.edu /perspectives-v21/4

Cocozza, V. (2017). *Trivento e gli Austrias: Carriere episcopali, spazi sacri e territorio in una diocesi di Regio Patronato* [Trivento and the Austrias: Episcopal careers, sacred spaces and territory in a diocese of royal patronage]. Palermo: Quaderni Mediterranea.

Cirese, E. (2000). *Molisan poems.* Bonaffini, Luigi Trans. Toronto: Guernica.

Cole, D. (1983). *Rough road to Rome: A foot-soldier in Sicily and Italy, 1943–44.* London: William Kimber and Co.

Colletta, P. (1858). *History of the Kingdom of Naples, 1734–1825.* (Horner, S., Trans.). Edinburgh: T. Constable and Co.

Costanzo, S., et al. (2018). Alcohol consumption and hospitalization burden in an adult Italian population: Prospective results from the Molisani study. *Society for the Study of Addiction,* pp. 1–15. DOI: 10.1111/add.14490

Crisci, M. (2015). *Mobilità temporanea per lavoro: Introduzione* [Temporary mobility for work: Intro-duction]. Isernia: Cosmo Iannone.

Croce, B. (1970). *History of the Kingdom of Naples.* Chicago: The University of Chicago Press.

Cutler, I. (9 November 2015). Recollections: Ivor Cutler, 5th Battalion, The Northamptonshire Regiment. Monte Cassino Society [Online]. Available: www.montecassinosociety.co.uk

D'Acunto, S. (1969). *Il Molise attraverso i secoli* [Molise through the centuries]. Roma: La Tribuna del Molise.

Dandelet, T. and Marino, J., (Eds.) (2006). *Spain in Italy: Politics, society, and religion 1500–1700.* Leiden: Brill.

Davies, M. (19 January 1944). Il Calvario: Report by OC, 'E' Company on German Raid at Calvario on 19th January 1944. *Irish Brigade* [Online]. Available: www.irishbrigade.co.uk

Del Sangro, E., and Mannarelli, G. (1996). *Come parlavamo, come parliamo, dove stiamo andando* [How we talked, how we talk, where we're going]. Isernia: N.P.

Dello Siesto, B. (2014). *Un antico paese: Montenero Val Cocchiara e il suo pantano* [An ancient village: Montenero Val Cocchiara and its marshland]. Comunita Montana del Volturno. Isernia: Cicchetti Industrie Grafiche.

Di Bucci, D. and Scrocca, D. (1997). Assetto tettonico dell'Alto Molise (Appennino centrale): Considerazioni stratigrafiche e strutturali sull'unita di Montenero Val Cocchiara [Tectonic asset of Upper Molise (Central Apennines): Stratigraphic and structural considerations on the Montenero Val Cocchiara unit]. *Bollettino della Società Geologica Italiana*, 116, 221–236.

Di Fiori, Felice, M., Mannarelli, G., Milò, L. (2019). *Montenero Val Cocchiara festa del ricordo: Opuscolo 2019* [Montenero Val Cocchiara memorial celebration: Booklet 2019]. Montenero Val Cocchiara. N.P.

Di Fiori, Felice, M., Mannarelli, G., Milò, L. (2018). *Montenero Val Cocchiara festa del ricordo: Opuscolo 2018* [Montenero Val Cocchiara memorial celebration: Booklet 2018]. Montenero Val Cocchiara. N.P.

Di Iorio, E. (2014). *Suoli e Paleosuoli tardo Pleistocenici-Olocenici in sequenze fluvio-lacustri della regione Molise* [Late Pleistocene-Holocene soils in fluvio-lacustrine sequences in the Molise region]. Campobasso: Università degli Studi del Molise.

Di Matteo, A. (13 August 2018). Turismo, ancora un record negativo per il Molise: nel 2017 è all'ultimo posto tra le regioni italiane [Tourism, still a negative record for Molise: In 2017 it ranks last among the Italian regions]. *Il Giornale* [Online]. Available: IlGiornaledelMolise.it.

di Pietro, S. et al. (2000). Pomodori pelati, le cultivar per il Molise [Peeled tomatoes, the cultivars for Molise]. *Terra e Vita*, (16): 91–94.

Diaferia, G. (2018). The 14 August 2018 M=4.6 southern Italy quake: Why prevention is fundamental in areas of moderate seismic risk. Posted on August15, 2018. *Temblot* [Online]. Available: http://temblor.net

Elliott, L. (5 December 2016). How Italy became this century's 'sick man of Europe.' *The Guardian* [Online]. Available: www.theguardian.com

Emmott, B. (2013). *Good Italy, bad Italy: Why Italy must conquer its demons to face the future.* New Haven: Yale University Press.

European Commission Press (14 July 2015). Investing in growth and jobs: Italy to benefit from €2.17 billion of EU Cohesion Policy Funds. *European Commission Press* [Online]. Available: http://europa.eu/rapid/press-release_IP-15-5369_en.htm

European Commission Press (13 May 2009). On a visit to the Molise region of Italy, Danuta Hübner (Commissioner) points out that cohesion policy provides a steady flow of investment during a period of recession. *European Commission Press* [Online]. Available: http://europa.eu/rapid/press-release_IP-09-755_en.htm

Fanelli, R. (2018). Rural small and medium enterprises development in Molise (Italy). *European Countryside*, 10(4): 566-589. DOI: 10.2478/euco-2018-0032

Faraglia, N.F. (1898). Numerazione dei fuochi nelle terre della Valle del Sangro fatta nel 1447 [Numbering of the hearths in the land of the Valle del Sangro made in 1447], *Rassegna Abruzzese di Storia ed Arte*, 2: 208–45.

Faralli, G. (1997). Molise. In L. Bonaffini (Ed.), *Dialect poetry of Southern Italy: Texts and Criticism.* Brooklyn, NY: Legas Publishing.

Filocamo, F., et al. (2015). The integrated exploitation of the geological heritage: A proposal of geotourist itineraries in the Alto Molise area (Italy). *Rendiconti Online Società Geologica Italiana*, Vol. 33: 44–47. DOI: 10.3301/ROL.2015.11

Filocamo, F., et al. (2010). Itinerari geoarcheologici in Molise: Una risorsa turistica da valorizzare [Geoarchaeological itineraries in Molise: A tourism resource to be exploited]. *Geologia e Turismo: Atti del quarto Congresso Nazionale*, Bologna, Ottobre 21, 22, 23. Associazione Italiana di Geologia e Turismo.

Forte, G., et al. (2013). Seismic permanent ground deformations: Earthquake-triggered landslides in Molise Apennines. Conference paper. *Rendiconti Online Società Geologica Italiana*, Vol. 24: 134–136.

Fortini, P. and Di Marzio, P. (2014). Preliminary study of the plants used in the folk medicine in the Molise sector of the Abruzzo, Lazio and Molise National Park. Italy. Conference paper. *109th Congresso della Società Botanica Italina International Plant Science Conference*. Florence, 2–5 September.

Frate, L., Imbriaco, M., and Petrocelli, A. (3 aprile 2018). Comuni a rischio scomparsa nell'isernino [Municipalities at risk of disappearance in the Isernia area]. Rome: Agenzia Nazionale Stampa Associata. Available: www.ansa.it

Galli, P. and Naso, J. (2009). Unmasking the 1349 earthquake source (southern Italy). Paleoseismological and archaeoseismological indications from the Aquae Iuliae fault. *Journal of Structural Geology*, 31: 128–149. DOI:10.1016/j.jsg.208.09.007

Gattei, S., La Regina, A., Mainardi, R., Pace, V., and Pirovano, S. (1980). *Molise*. Milan: Electa International.

Germano, G., Meini, M., and Ruggieri, A. (2014). Tourists walking along, territories moving on. The experience of a small Italian region to sustain community-based tourism. In *The European pilgrimage routes for promoting sustainable and quality tourism in rural areas*, Proceedings of the International Conference, Firenze, Italy, 4–6 December 2014; Bambi, G., Barbari, M., (Eds.); Firenze University Press: Firenze, Italy; pp. 675–687.

Giannone, P. (Ogilvile, J., Trans.) (1729). *The civil history of the Kingdom of Naples, Vol. 1*. London: Self-published.

Ginsborg, P. (2003). *A history of contemporary Italy: Society and politics 1943-1988*. NY: Palgrave McMillian.

Grignoli, D., and Boriati, D. (2018). Immigrants and labor market: A comparative perspective. *European Sociological Association regional research network on "southern European societies," Mid-Term Conference*, Catania, 4–6 October. pp. 42–43.

Guarrera, P., Lucchese, F., and Medori, S. (2008). Ethnophytotherapeutical research in the high Molise region (central-southern Italy). *Journal of Ethnobiology and Ethnomedicine*, 4:7. DOI: 10.1186/1746-4269-4-7

Hay, M. (2013). Genetic history of the Italians. Brussels: Eupedia Genetics Haplogroups, pp. 1–7. *Eupedia* [Online]. Available: www.eupedia.com

Hibbert, C. (2008). *Mussolini: The rise and fall of Il Duce*. NY: Palgrave MacMillan.

Iarocci, G. (2005). Statistiche del turismo nel Molise, anni 1998–2003. Conference paper. Università degli Studi del Molise.

Irish Brigade War Diaries, 1942 to 1945. *Irish Brigade* [Online]. Available www.irishbrigade.co.uk

Jamison, E. (Oct., 1929). The administration of the county of Molise in the twelfth and thirteenth centuries. *The English Historical Review*, 44(176): 529–559.

Keegan, (2000). *The First World War*. NY: Vintage Books.

Kemp, J. (1963). *The history of the Royal Scots Fusiliers 1919–1959*. Glasgow: Robert MacLehose and Co.

Kingdom of Naples, (1743). *Montenero Val Cocchiara Catasto Onciario 1743*. Naples: State Archive.

Kirby, P. (16 July 2015). My SS family: German meets survivors of Italy WW2 massacre BBC News. British Broadcasting Company [Online]. Available: www.bbc.com.

Kreutz, B. (1996). *Before the Normans: Southern Italy in the 9th and 10th centuries*. Philadelphia: University of Pennsylvania Press.

Lamanna, G., and Loprevite, V. (2010). Il contesto demografico del Molise [The demographic context of Molise]. In *Assistenza socio-sanitaria in Molise. Rapporto 2009 bisogni, strutture, servizi a cura di Americo Cicchetti e Angelo Palmieri*. Milano: Franco Angeli, s.r.l. pp. 13–19.

Levoli, C., Basile, R., and Belliggiano, A. (2017). The spatial patterns of dairy farming in Molise. *European Countrysides*, 9(4): 729–745.

Linklater, E. (1951). *The campaign in Italy*. London: H.M. Stationery Office.

Lovari, S., Ferretti, F., Corazza, M., Minder, I., Troiani, N., Ferrari, C., and Saddi, A. (2014). Unexpected consequences of reintroductions: Competition between reintroduced red deer and Apennine chamois. *Animal Conservation*, 17(4): 287–398. DOI: 10.1111/acv.12103

Lumley, R., and Morris, R. (Eds.). (1997). *The new history of the Italian south: The mezzogiorno revisited*. Exeter, UK: University of Exeter Press.

Maffei, A. (1865). *Brigand life in Italy: A history of Bourbonist reaction*. London: Hurst and Blackett.

Malanima, P. (2006). A declining economy: Central and northern Italy in the sixteenth and seventeenth centuries. In T. Dandelet and J. Marino (Eds.), *Spain in Italy: Politics, society, and religion, 1500–1700* (pp. 383–403). Leiden, Brill.

Marazzi, F. (2012). *San Vincenzo al Volturno l'abbazia e il suo territorium fra VIII e XII secolo* [San Vincenzo al Volturno the abbey and its territories between the 8th and 12th century]. Monte Cassino: Pubblicazioni Cassinesi.

Marchetti, M., De Toni, A., and Sallustio, L. (2017). Caratterizzazione dei cambiamenti d'uso del suolo in Molise ed impatti sui servizi ecosistemici [Characterization of changes in land use in Molise and impacts on ecosystem service]. In: *Consumo di suolo, dinamiche territoriali e servizi ecosistemici*. Roma: Istituto Superiore per la Protezione e la Ricerca Ambientale, pp. 180–181.

Marino, J. (2006). The rural world in Italy under Spanish rule. In T. Dandelet and J. Marino (Eds.), *Spain in Italy: Politics, society, and religion, 1500–1700* (pp. 405–429). Leiden, Brill.

Mastronardi, L. (2014). Renewable energy resources and their impact on rural landscape. *WSEAS Transactions on Environment and Development*, Vol. 10.

Mastronardi, L., Giaccio, V., Giannelli, A., and Stanisci, A. (2017). Methodological proposal about the role of landscape in the tourism development process in rural areas: The case of Molise region (Italy). *European Countrysides*, 2, pp. 245–262.; DOI: 10.1515/euco-2017-0015

Mattern, J. (6 November 2017). *Poland: Renewed reparation claims*. *Telepolis*. Heise Medien GmbH & Co., Hannover, Germany. Available: www.heise.de/tp/

McGinniss, J. (1999). *The miracle of Castel di Sangro*. Boston: Little, Brown and Co.

Meini, G., Di Felice, G. and Petrella M. (2018). Geotourism perspectives for transhumance routs: Analysis, requalification and virtual tools for the geoconservation management of the drove roads in southern Italy. *Geosciences*, 8, 368; DOI: 10.3390/geosciences8100368

Menale, B., Amato, G., Di Prisco, C., and Muoio, R. (2006). Traditional uses of plants in north-western Molise (central Italy). *Delpinoa*, 48: 29–36.

Microzonazione Sismica (2009). *Carta della indagini, regione Molise, comune di Montenero Val Cocchiara centro* [Survey maps, Molise region, municipality of Montenero Val Cocchiara center]. Campobasso: Universita degli Studi del Molise.

Microzonazione Sismica (2009). *Carta della microzone omogenee in prospettiva sismica, regione Molise, comune di Montenero Val Cocchiara centro* [Map of the homogeneous micro-zone in a seismic perspective, Molise region, municipality of Montenero Val Cocchiara center]. Campobasso: Universita degli Studi del Molise.

Milanese, G. and Ricci, D. (2010). *Piano D'Assestamento Forestale per il periodo 2009–2023* [Forest settlement plan for the period 2009–2023]. Agnone: Forest Office Municipality of Pietrabbondante.

Minotti, M., Giancola, C., Di Marzio, P. and Di Martino, P. (2018). Land use dynamics of drove roads: The case of trattturo Castel dei Sangro-Lucera (Molise, Italy). *Geosciences*, 7(3): 368. DOI: 10.3390/land7010003.

Mockenhaupt, B. (June 2016). The most treacherous battle of World War I took place in the Italian mountains. Washington, D.C.: *Smithsonian Magazine* [Online]. Available: www.smithsonianmag.com

Molise2000 Blog (23 luglio, 2013). Il Molise medievale: Un 'contado' o una "contea" [Medieval Molise: A "contado" or a "contea"]? *Molise2000* [Online]. Available: https://molise2000.wordpress.com/2013/07/23/contadodi-molise-o-contea-di-molise/

Monticelli, G. (Summer, 1967). Italian emigration: Basic characteristic and trends with special reference to the last twenty years. In *The International Migration Review*, 1(3), Special Issue: The Italian Experience in Emigration, pp. 10–24. Sage Publications, Inc.

Mougel, N. (2011). *World War I casualties. Reperes. Partenariat Educatif Grundtvig 2009–2011*. CVCE, Gratz, Julie, (Trans.). Available: www.centre-robert-schuman.org.

Murray, L. (Ed.). (2014). *The Britannica guide to countries of the European Union: Italy*. NY: Britannica Educational Publishing.

Muscarà, L., and Sarno, E. (2011). Il paesaggio telofonico del Molise. Le utenze fisse come indicatore demografico [The telephone landscape of Molise. Fixed utilities as a demographic indicator]. In *Atti del Quarto Seminario di studi storico-cartografici dalla mappa al GIS* (Roma, 21–22 aprile 2009), by M. Maggioli e C. Masetti (Eds.) (pp. 1–27). Genoa: Brigati.

Muscarà, L. (2008). Capitolo 2: Geo demografia storica del Molise [Chapter 2: Geo historical demography of Molise]. In G. Cannata et al. (Eds.), *Relazione sullo Stato dell'Ambiente della Regione Molise*. Campobasso: Università degli studi del Molise, pp. 34–65.

Musi, A. (2006). The Kingdom of Naples in the Spanish imperial system. In T. Dandelet and J. Marino (Eds.), *Spain in Italy: Politics, society, and religion, 1500–1700* (pp. 72–97). Leiden: Brill.

Muto, G. (2006). Noble presence and stratification in the territories of Spanish Italy. In T. Dandelet and J. Marino (Eds.), *Spain in Italy: Politics, society, and religion, 1500–1700* (pp. 251–297). Leiden: Brill.

Neapolitan Nobles. (2001). Carafa della Spina. *Neapolitan Nobles* [Online]. Available: www.nobilinapoletani.it/Carafa_Spina.htm

New York Times, (October–December 1917). Italian army's spring offensive: Official narrative of the operations of General Cadorna's forces from March to June, 1917. *The European War, 13*. NY: The New York Times Co.

Nicholson, G. (1956). *Official history of the Canadian army in the Second World War, Volume II: The Canadians in Italy 1943–1945*. Ottawa: Minister of National Defence.

Nuti, C., et al.(2004). Seismic assessment of the Molise hospitals and upgrading strategies. *13th World Conference on Earthquake Engineering*, Vancouver, B.C. Canada, August 1–4. pp. 1–14. Paper number 2773.

Opfell, S. (2001). *Royalty who wait: The 21 heads of formerly regnant houses of Europe*. London: McFarland & Co.

O'Sullivan, E. (March 26, 2017). E Company at Montenero: Report of enemy raid on 2 LIR positions on Calvario, 19 January 1944. *Irish Brigade* (War Diaries) [Online]. Available: www.irishbrigade.co.uk

O'Sullivan, E. (Feb. 8, 2017). 2 LIR–December 1943. *Irish Brigade* (War Diaries) [Online]. Available: www.irishbrigade.co.uk

Paolanti, M., Paura, B., Chirici, G., and Rivieccio, R. (2014). *Carta della potenzialità tartuficola in scala 1:100.000 della provincia di Campobasso (Molise)* [Map of the potentiality of truffle in scale 1: 100,000 of the province of Campobasso (Molise)]. Technical Report. Campobasso: Università del Molise, Dipartimento di Scienze e Tecnologie per l'Ambiente e il Territorio.

Paolicelli, P. (16 January, 2004). Paul Paolicelli on WWII massacre of Italian civilians by former German ally. *The ANNOTICO Report* [Online]. Available: http://italiausa. com/ra/ 1323.htm

Paratore, E. (1970). *Abruzzo Molise*. Milian: Touring Club Italiano.

Pasquale, G. (February 2015). Immigration in Molise and some paths towards integration. Conference paper. *7th World Conference on Educational Sciences* (WCES-2015), 05–07, Novotel Athens Convention Center, Athens, Greece. Also: *Procedia: Social and Behavioral Sciences 197* (2015): 1179–1182.

Peretto, C., et al. (2016). The prehistoric settlement of Molise in the light of the latest research. *Incontri Annuali di Preistoria e Protostoria, 1*: 24–26.

Perry, A. (22 January 2018). Blood and justice: The women who brought down a Mafia clan. *The New Yorker*, pp. 36–47.

Pesaresi, C. (2014a). *The "Numbers" of Molise mountain municipalities*. Rome: Edizione Nuova Cultura.

Pesaresi, C. (2014b). La caduta demografica del Molise dal 1861 a 2011 con uno squardo sul futuro [The demographic fall of Molise from 1861 to 2011, with a look at the future]. *Bollettino della Società Geografica Italiana*, Serie XIII, Vol. VII, pp. 391–412.

Petrocelli, E. (2011). I luoghi e i valori universali della società operaie Molisane [The places and the universal values of Molisan workers' societies.] Volturnia Ed. Quoted in: Pesaresi, C. (2014a), *The "Numbers" of Molise mountain municipalities*. Rome: Edizione Nuova Cultura, pp. 74–75.

Pierce, J. (n.d.). Molise in the Norman period: The historical development of fortification architecture. *Morrone del Sannio* [Online]. Available: www.morronedelsannio.com/molise/eng_molise/historical_development.htm

Regione Molise, archive (2013/Luglio). Edifici pubblici a risparmio energetico, via alla rivoluzione verde. [Energy-saving public buildings, way to the green revolution]. *Region Molise* [Online]. Available: www3.regione.molise.it/flex/cm/pages/Serve BLOB.php/L/IT/IDPagina/8989

Rivera, C. (1929). Valva e' i suoi conti. [Valva and its counts.] *Bullettino della r. Deputazione Abruzzese di storia patria*, pp. 1–90. J. de May, (Trans.) (2006). L'Aquila: Regia Deputazione.

Rizzo, S. and Stella, G. (22 settembre 2010). Pontelandolfo: Il rogo delle case e 400 morti che nessuno vuole ricordare [Pontelandolfo: The burning of houses and 400 deaths that nobody wants to remember]. *Corriere della Sera* [Online]. Available: www.corriere.it

Ross, M. (1977). *The reluctant king: Joseph Bonaparte king of the Two Sicilies and Spain*. NY: Mason Charter Publishers.

Rossi, G., et al. (2013). *Natura protetta*. Pescasseroli: Parco Nazionale d'Abruzzo Lazio e Molise, pp. 2–24.

Rosskopf, C. and Scorpio, V. (2013). Geomorphologic map of the Biferno River valley floor system (Molise, Southern Italy). *Journal of Maps*, 9(1): 1–9. DOI: 10.1080/ 17530350.2012.755385

Rosskopf, C., et al. (January 2015). The integrated exploitation of the geological heritage: A proposal of geotourist itineraries in the alto Molise area. *Rendiconti Online Società Geologica Italiana*. DOI: 10:3301/ROI.2015.11

Rosskopf, C., De Benedettis, G., and Mauriello, P. (2006). Indagini geo-archeologiche integrate nel Molise centrale (Italia meridionale): Il ponte Romano di Turara [Geo-archaeological surveys integrated in central Molise (southern Italy): The Roman bridge of Turara]. *Il Quaternario Italian Journal of Quaternary Science, 19*(2): 239–250.

Rosskopf, C., Filocamo, F., Amato, V., and Cesarano, M. (2016). The promotion of geotourism in protected areas: A proposal of itinerary Through the Matese Massif (Campania and Molise Regions, Italy). *Geophysical Research Abstracts, Vol. 18*, EGU2016-6126.

Rubini, M. (2017). Gli Avari in Molise: LaNecropoli di Campochiaro Morrione. (The Avars in Molise). *Archeologia Via*, p. 16–25. Also in: *Journal Archaeological Science*.

Russumanno, D. (n.d.). Brigandage in south Italy. *Made in South Italy* [Online]. Hamilton, Ontario. Available: www. madeinsouthitalytoday.com

Salmon, E. (2010). *Samnium and the Samnites*. NY: Cambridge University Press.

Sakellariou, E. (2012). *Southern Italy in late middle ages: Demograpic, institutional, and economic change in the Kingdom of Naples, c. 1440–1530*. Leiden: Brill.

Santucci, M. (Maggio-Giugno 2014). Birra D'Abruzzo [Abruzzo beer]. *Il Barattolo*, Anno XXXIV. (191): 11–14.

Sardella, B. (sett/dic 2018). Nuove scoperte archeologiche nell'alta valle del Volturno [New archaeological discoveries in the upper valley of the Volturno]. In *Archeomolise*, (32): 6–17.

Schindler, J. (2001). *Isonzo: The forgotten sacrifice of the Great War*. Westport, CT: Praeger Publishers.

Scrocca, D. and Tozzi, M. (1999). Tettogenesi mio-pliocenica dell'Appennino Molisano [Mio-pliocene tectogenesis of the Molise Apennines.]. *Bollettino della Società Geologica Italiana*, 118: 255–286.

Scutellà, M. et al. (2012). Human papillomaviruses and cervico vaginal co-infections in a population of Molise. *Microbiologia Medica, 27*(4): 165–170.

Severgnini, B. (28 July, 2017). Governing Italy turns a young man old. *The New York Times* [Online]. Available: www.nytimes.com.

Siviero, P., et al. (2000). Pomodori pelati, le cultivar per il Molise [Peeled tomatoes, the cultivars for Molise]. *Terra e Vita*, (16): 91–94.

Spartaco, G. and Guacci, C. (ottobre 2014). L'orso marsicano nel Molise, ieri, oggi e . . . domani [The Marsicano bear in Molise, yesterday, today and . . . tomorrow]? *Quaderni di scienza e scienziati molisani*, (17–18): 131–148.

Stamperia Reale, (1832). *Collection of laws and royal decrees of the Kingdom of the Two Sicilies, Year 1832*. Naples: Royal Printing House.

Starratt, K. (9 Oct 2018). Honoring the historic connection with Castel di Sangro: West Novia Scotia Regiment welcomes delegates from Kentville's twin community in Italy. *Valley Journal Advertiser* [Online]. Available: www.pressreader.com

Storti, D. (June 2016). Innovazione e sviluppo nelle aree interne: Il caso delle aree prototipo in Puglia, Campania e Molise [Innovation and development in inland areas: The case of the prototype areas in Puglia, Campania and Molise.] *Agriregionieuropa Anno, 12*(45): 1–6.

Taylor, D. (2003). *The Spanish viceroyalty: The first hundred years*. Naples: Life, Death, and Miracles [Online]. Available: www. naplesldm. com/vicerealm1.php

Teti, A. (2013). *Castel di Sangro 1943–1945. Storia documentata degli avvenimenti bellici dal 1943 al 1945* [Castel di Sangro 1943–1945. Documented history of war events from 1943 to 1945]. Trento: Edizioni del Faro.

Teti, A. (2015). *Castel di Sangro, 13 maggio 1815: Una battaglia dimenticata* [Castel di Sangro, 13 May 1815: A forgotten battle]. Trento: Edizioni del Faro.

The Local (18 January 2016). More than 50 earthquakes rock Italy's Molise in five days. In *The Local*. Stockholm. Available: www.thelocal.it

Thompson, M. (2010). *The white war: Life and death on the Italian front 1915–1919*. New York: Basic Books.

Tramontano, G. (Sept. 2010). Verso un centro di mediazione penale in Molise [Towards a penal mediation center in Molise]. *Minori Giusticia, 1*, 237. DOI: 10.3280/MG2010-001023

Tucker, S. and Roberts, P. (2005). *The encyclopedia of World War I: A political, social, and military history*. Santa Barbara, CA: ABC-CLIO.

Valente, F. (4 febbraio 2015). La statua di S. Gaetano a Napoli e don Alfonso Carafa, duca di Montenero e Rionero e signore di Petrella [The statue of St. Gaetano in Naples and don Alfonso Carafa, duke of Montenero and Rionero and lord of Petrella]. *Franco Valente* [Online]. Available: www.francovalente.it

Van der Bijl, N. (2006). *No. 10 (inter-allied) commando 1942–1945: Britain's secret commando*. Oxford: Osprey Publishing.

Vezzani L., Festa, A., and Ghisetti, F. (2010). *Geology and tectonic Evolution of the Central-southern Apennines, Italy*. Supplementary material (DVD) for special paper 469. Boulder: The Geologicl Society of America.

von Salis-Marschlins, C. (1795). *Travels through various provinces of the Kingdom of Naples in 1789*. Anthony Aufrere, (Trans.). London: T. Cadell, Jun. and W. Davies.

Wiegert, L. (2004). *Weaving sacred stories: French choir tapestries and the performance of clerical identity*. Ithica, NY: Cornell University Press.

Wickham, C. (1985). *Early medieval Italy: Central power and local society 400–1000*. Ann Arbor, MI: University of Michigan Press.

Williams, M. (2017). *From Warsaw to Rome: General Anders' exiled Polish army in the Second World War*. South Yorkshire: Pen and Sword Military.

ARCHIVES:
Biblioteca Apostolica Vaticana
Montenero Val Cocchiara Municipal Archives
Montenero Val Cocchiara, Parish Archives, Register of Deceased.
State Archives of Campobasso
State Archives of Isernia
State Archives of Naples

INDEX

Incoronata

Mundunur

VALLE   CERASITA

St. Sebastiano

S. Sebastiano

strada   provinciale

Mohtenero   Voj Cocchiola

S. Martino

Cappella
S. Martino

CPSIA information can be obtained
at www.ICGtesting.com
Printed in the USA
LVHW030239071220
673520LV00040B/1010